Also by Joan Acocella

Mark Morris

Creating Hysteria: Women and Multiple Personality Disorder

Willa Cather and the Politics of Criticism

Twenty-eight Artists and Two Saints: Essays

As Editor

André Levinson on Dance:
Writings from Paris in the Twenties (with Lynn Garafola)

The Diary of Vaslav Nijinsky

Mission to Siam: The Memoirs of Jessie MacKinnon Hartzell

THE BLOODIED NIGHTGOWN
and Other Essays

THE
BLOODIED
NIGHTGOWN

and Other
Essays

———

Joan Acocella

Farrar, Straus and Giroux
New York

Farrar, Straus and Giroux
120 Broadway, New York 10271

Copyright © 2024 by Joan Acocella
All rights reserved
Printed in the United States of America
First edition, 2024

Library of Congress Cataloging-in-Publication Data
Names: Acocella, Joan Ross, author.
Title: The bloodied nightgown and other essays / Joan Acocella.
Description: First edition. | New York : Farrar, Straus and Giroux, 2024. |
    Includes index.
Identifiers: LCCN 2023038961 | ISBN 9780374608095 (hardcover)
Subjects: LCGFT: Essays. | Literary criticism.
Classification: LCC PS3601.C66 B57 2024 | DDC 814/.6—dc23/eng/20230829
LC record available at https://lccn.loc.gov/2023038961

Designed by Patrice Sheridan

Our books may be purchased in bulk for promotional, educational, or business
use. Please contact your local bookseller or the Macmillan Corporate and
Premium Sales Department at 1-800-221-7945, extension 5442, or by email at
MacmillanSpecialMarkets@macmillan.com.

www.fsgbooks.com
Follow us on social media at @fsgbooks

1 3 5 7 9 10 8 6 4 2

To Noël Carroll

CONTENTS

LIST OF ILLUSTRATIONS

PREFACE

A firmly held principle of twentieth-century modernism was that the evaluation of art should exclude any discussion of the artist's inner life. In an early and famous statement of the rule, T. S. Eliot in 1919 wrote that "poetry is not a turning loose of emotion, but an escape from emotion; it is not an expression of personality, but an escape from personality." It took a while for people to realize that Eliot's exaltation of escape from personality probably had something to do with his miserable marriage, and that any poem, any painting, has deep-dwelling roots in the artist's moral experience.

Do people agree on these matters even now? In the 1980s, the notion of an artwork undefiled by the artist's experience gave birth to an even weirder child, the postmodern idea—or, in any case, Roland Barthes's idea—of the "death of the author." The artist was so deeply influenced by external forces—above all, prior artworks—that we could no longer seek sources in him/her alone, or even primarily. Ten years ago or so, I stood in a gallery at the Museum of Modern Art in New York and listened as a specialist assured a group of patrons that the sharp-toothed, menacing figures in Willem de Kooning's *Woman* series did not, not, refer to de Kooning's mother, with whom he was known to have had a terrible relationship. The magic cloak of art had rendered all of that invisible. Insofar as commentary on the arts did not hew to this principle, it was not criticism but "journalism."

The essays in this book were written mostly for *The New Yorker*, and a few for *The New York Review of Books*, between 2007 and 2021. In most of them I shuttle back and forth between the artist's life and his/her art. I was schooled by teachers who believed in Eliot's rule— forget personality—but I could not do without the life. It was too exciting to watch these people, most of them young, with no money and no prospects, find their way into art. At the same time, I respect the antibiographical folk, with their steady focus and also their anxiety to protect artists' reputations from reductionism, not to speak of Mrs. Grundy. De Kooning's *Woman I* may have been about his mother, sort of, but more than that, it was a painting. Reportedly, it took him two years.

THE BLOODIED NIGHTGOWN
and Other Essays

Bela Lugosi, as Dracula, preparing to bite the neck of Helen Chandler (Mina) in Tod Browning's film *Dracula*, released in 1931

THE BLOODIED NIGHTGOWN

Dracula

"Unclean, unclean!" Mina Harker screams, gathering her bloodied nightgown around her. In chapter 21 of Bram Stoker's *Dracula*, Mina's friend John Seward, a psychiatrist in Purfleet, near London, tells how he and a colleague, warned that Mina might be in danger, broke into her bedroom one night and found her kneeling on the edge of her bed. Bending over her was a tall figure, dressed in black. "His right hand gripped her by the back of the neck, forcing her face down on his bosom. Her white nightdress was smeared with blood, and a thin stream trickled down the man's bare breast which was shown by his torn-open dress. The attitude of the two had a terrible resemblance to a child forcing a kitten's nose into a saucer of milk to compel it to drink." Mina's husband, Jonathan, hypnotized by the intruder, lay on the bed, unconscious, a few inches from the scene of his wife's violation.

Later, between sobs, Mina relates what happened. She was in bed with Jonathan when a strange mist crept into the room. Soon, it congealed into the figure of a man—Count Dracula. "With a mocking smile, he placed one hand upon my shoulder and, holding me tight, bared my throat with the other, saying as he did so: 'First, a little refreshment to reward my exertions. . . .' And oh, my God, my God, pity me! He placed his reeking lips upon my throat!" The Count took a long drink. Then he drew back and spoke sweet words to Mina. "Flesh of my flesh," he called her, "my bountiful wine-press." But now he wanted something else. He wanted her in his power from then on. A person who has had his—or, more often, her—blood repeatedly sucked by a vampire turns into a vampire, too, but the conversion can be accomplished more quickly if the victim also sucks the vampire's blood. And so, Mina says, "he pulled open his shirt, and with his long sharp nails opened a vein in his breast. When the blood began to spurt out, he . . . seized my neck and pressed my mouth to the wound, so that I must either suffocate or swallow some of the—Oh, my God!" The unspeakable happened—she sucked his blood, at his breast—at which point her friends stormed into the room. Dracula vanished, and, Seward relates, Mina uttered "a scream so wild, so ear-piercing, so despairing . . . that it will ring in my ears to my dying day."

That scene, and Stoker's whole novel, is still ringing in our ears. Stoker did not invent vampires. If we define them, broadly, as the undead—spirits who rise, embodied, from their graves to interfere with the living—they have been part of human imagining since ancient times. Eventually, vampire superstition became concentrated in eastern Europe. (It survives there today. In 2007, a Serbian named Miroslav Milosevic—no relation—drove a stake into the grave of Slobodan Milosevic.) It was presumably in eastern Europe that people worked out what became the standard methods for eliminating a vampire: you drive a wooden stake through his heart, or cut off his head, or burn him—or, to be on the safe side, all three. In the late seventeenth and early eighteenth centuries, there were outbreaks of vampire hysteria in western Europe; numerous stakings were reported in Germany. By 1734, the word "vampire" had entered the English language.

In those days, vampires were grotesque creatures. Often, they were pictured as bloated and purple-faced (from drinking blood); they had long talons and smelled terrible—a description probably based on the appearance of corpses whose tombs had been opened by worried villagers. These early undead did not necessarily draw blood. Often, they just did regular mischief—stole firewood, scared horses. (Sometimes, they helped with the housework.) Their origins, too, were often quaint. Matthew Beresford, in his recent book *From Demons to Dracula: The Creation of the Modern Vampire Myth*, records a Serbian Gypsy belief that pumpkins, if kept for more than ten days, may cross over: "The gathered pumpkins stir all by themselves and make a sound like 'brrrl, brrrl, brrrl!' and begin to shake themselves." Then they become vampires.

This was not yet the suave, opera-cloaked fellow of our modern mythology. That figure emerged in the early nineteenth century, a child of the Romantic movement. In the summer of 1816, Lord Byron, fleeing marital difficulties, was holed up in a villa on Lake Geneva. With him was his personal physician, John Polidori, and nearby, in another house, his friend Percy Bysshe Shelley; Shelley's mistress, Mary Godwin; and Mary's stepsister Claire Clairmont, who was angling for Byron's attention (with reason: she was pregnant by him). The weather that summer was cold and rainy. The friends spent hours in Byron's drawing room, talking. One night, they read one another ghost stories, which were very popular at the time, and Byron suggested that they all write ghost stories of their own. Shelley and Clairmont produced nothing. Byron began a story and then laid it aside. But the remaining members of the summer party went to their desks and created the two most enduring figures of the modern horror genre. Mary Godwin, eighteen years old, began her novel *Frankenstein* (1818), and John Polidori, apparently following a sketch that Byron had written for his abandoned story, wrote *The Vampyre: A Tale* (1819). In Polidori's narrative, the undead villain is a proud, handsome aristocrat, fatal to women. (Some say that Polidori based the character on Byron.) He's interested only in virgins. He sucks their necks; they die; he lives. The modern vampire was born.

The public adored him. In England and France, Polidori's tale spawned popular plays, operas, and operettas. Vampire novels appeared, the most widely read being James Malcolm Rymer's *Varney the Vampire*, serialized between 1845 and 1847. *Varney* was a penny dreadful and faithful to the genre. ("Shriek followed shriek. . . . Her beautifully rounded limbs quivered with the agony of her soul. . . . He drags her head to the bed's edge.") After *Varney* came *Carmilla* (1872), by Joseph Thomas Sheridan Le Fanu, an Irish ghost-story writer. *Carmilla* was the mother of vampire bodice rippers. It also gave birth to the lesbian vampire story—in time, a rich subgenre. "Her hot lips traveled along my cheek in kisses," the female narrator writes, "and she would whisper, almost in sobs, 'You are mine, you *shall* be mine.'" *Varney* and *Carmilla* were low-end hits, but vampires penetrated high literature as well. Baudelaire wrote a poem, and Théophile Gautier a prose poem, on the subject.

Then came Bram (Abraham) Stoker. Stoker was a civil servant who fell in love with theater in his native Dublin. In 1878, he moved to London to become the business manager of the Lyceum Theatre, owned by his idol, the actor Henry Irving. On the side, Stoker wrote thrillers, one about a curse-wielding mummy, one about a giant homicidal worm, and so on. Several of these books are in print, but they probably wouldn't be if it were not for the fame of Stoker's midcareer novel *Dracula* (1897). The first English Dracula play, by Hamilton Deane, opened in 1924 and was a sensation. The American production (1927), with a script revised by John L. Balderston and with Bela Lugosi in the title role, was even more popular. Ladies were carried, fainting, from the theater. Meanwhile, the films had begun appearing: notably, F. W. Murnau's silent *Nosferatu* (1922), which many critics still consider the greatest of Dracula movies, and then Tod Browning's *Dracula* (1931), the first vampire talkie, with Lugosi navigating among the spiderwebs and intoning the famous words "I do not drink . . . wine." (That line was not in the book. It was written for Browning's movie.) Lugosi stamped the image of Dracula forever, and it stamped him. Thereafter, this ambitious Hungarian actor had a hard time getting non-monstrous roles. He spent many years as a drug addict. He was buried in his Dracula cloak.

From that point to the present, there have been more than 150 Dracula movies. Roman Polanski, Andy Warhol, Werner Herzog, and Francis Ford Coppola all fathered films about the Count. There are subgenres of Dracula movies: comedy, pornography, blaxploitation, anime. There is also a *Deafula*, for the hearing-impaired: the characters conduct their business in American Sign Language while the lines are spoken in voice-over. After film, television, of course, took on vampires. *Dark Shadows*, in the 1960s, and *Buffy the Vampire Slayer*, in the 1990s, were both big hits. Meanwhile, the undead have had a long life in fiction. Anne Rice's Vampire Chronicles and Stephen King's 'Salem's *Lot* are the best-known recent examples, but one source estimates that the undead have been featured in a thousand novels.

Today, enthusiasm for vampires seems to be at a new peak. Stephenie Meyer's Twilight novels, for young adults (that is, teenage girls), have sold forty-two million copies worldwide since 2005. The first of the film adaptations, released late last year, made $177 million in its initial seven weeks. Charlaine Harris's Sookie Stackhouse novels (*Dead Until Dark*, plus seven more), about a Louisiana barmaid's passion for a handsome revenant named Bill, were bought by six million people, and generated the HBO series *True Blood*, which had its debut last year and will be back in June. Also from last year was the haunting Swedish movie *Let the Right One In*, in which a twelve-year-old boy, Oskar, falls in love with a mysterious girl, Eli, who has moved in next door. She, too, is twelve, she tells Oskar, but she has been twelve for a long time. A new Dracula novel, co-authored by the fragrantly named Dacre Stoker (a great-grandnephew of Bram's), will be published in October by Dutton. The movie rights have already been sold.

The past half century has also seen a rise in vampire scholarship. In the 1950s, Freudian critics, addressing Stoker's novel, did what Freudians did at that time. Today's scholars, intent instead on politics—race, class, and gender—have feasted at the table. Representative essays, reprinted in a recent edition of *Dracula*, include Christopher Craft's "'Kiss Me with Those Red Lips': Gender and Inversion in Bram Stoker's *Dracula*" and Stephen D. Arata's "Occidental Tourist: *Dracula* and the Anxiety of Reverse Colonization."

Other writers have produced fantastically detailed annotated editions of Stoker's *Dracula*. The first of these, *The Annotated "Dracula"* (1975), by Leonard Wolf, a Transylvanian-born horror scholar, dealt, for example, with the scene of Dracula's assault on Mina by giving us the biblical sources of "unclean, unclean" and "flesh of my flesh"; by cross-referencing "my bountiful wine-press" to an earlier passage, about Transylvanian viniculture; by noting, apropos of Dracula's opening a vein in his chest, that this recalls an old myth about the pelican feeding its young with blood from its bosom; by telling us that the vein Dracula slashed must have been the superficial intercostal; by exclaiming over the sexual ambiguity of the scene ("Just what *is* going on here? A vengeful cuckoldry? A *ménage à trois*? Mutual oral sexuality?"); and so on. None of this information is needed by the first- or even second-time reader of *Dracula*. Indeed, it would be a positive hindrance, draining away the suspense that Stoker worked so hard to build.

The fullness of Wolf's commentary did not discourage others. In 1979, a second annotated edition came out, and in 1998 a third. Last October, a fourth—*The New Annotated "Dracula,"* by Leslie Klinger, a Los Angeles tax and estate lawyer who has a sideline editing Victorian literature—was published by Norton. What could Klinger have found to elucidate that his predecessors didn't? Plenty. In the scene of Mina's encounter with Dracula, for example, he honorably cites the earlier editions, and then he goes on to alert us to a punctuation error; to conjecture, revoltingly, about the source of the mist in which Dracula enters Mina's bedroom ("Perhaps this was not a vapor but rather a milky substance expressed from Dracula's body"); to speculate that Jonathan Harker's excitement, upon awakening from his swoon, may be a form of sexual arousal; and to question the medical accuracy of Stoker's claim that Harker's hair turns white as he listens to Mina's story: "In fact, whitening is caused by a progressive decline in the absolute number of melanocytes (pigment-producing cells in the skin, hair, and eye), which normally decrease over time." Even that old sentimental convention does not get past him.

What is all this about? Why do publishers think that readers will care? One could say that *Dracula*, like certain other works—*Alice's Adventures in Wonderland*, the Sherlock Holmes stories (both, like Klinger's *Dracula*, published in the Norton Annotated Series; Klinger was the editor of the Holmes)—is a cult favorite. But why does the book have a cult? Well, cults often gather around powerful works of the second rank. Fans feel that they have to root for them. What, then, is the source of *Dracula*'s power? A simple device, used in many notable works of art: the deployment of great and volatile forces within a very tight structure.

The narrative method of *Dracula* is to assemble a collage of purportedly authentic documents, most of them in the first person. Many of the materials are identified as excerpts from the diaries of the main characters. In addition, there are letters to and from these people— but also from lawyers, carting companies, and Hungarian nuns—plus telegrams, "newspaper" clippings, and a ship's log. This multiplicity of voices gives the book a wonderful liveliness. A long horror story could easily become suffocating. (That is one of the reasons that Poe's tales are tales, not novels.) *Dracula*, in a regular, unannotated edition, runs about four hundred pages, but it is seldom tedious. It opens with four chapters from the diary of Jonathan Harker describing his visit, on legal business—he is a solicitor—to the castle of a certain Count Dracula, in Transylvania, and ending with Harker howling in horror over what he found there. Then we turn the page, and suddenly we are in England, reading a letter from Mina—at that point, Harker's fiancée—bubbling to her friend Lucy Westenra about how she's learning shorthand so that she can be useful to Jonathan in his work. This is a salutary jolt, and also witty. (Little does Mina know how Jonathan's work is going at that juncture.) The alternation of voices also lends texture. It's as if we were turning an interesting object around in our hands, looking at it from this angle, then that. And since the story is reported by so many different witnesses, we are more likely to believe it.

In addition, we are given the pleasure of assembling the pieces of a puzzle. No one narrator knows all that the others have told us, and this allows us to read between the lines. One evening, as Mina is returning to a house she is sharing with Lucy in Whitby, a seaside resort in Yorkshire, she sees her friend at the window, and by her side, on the sill, "something that looked like a good-sized bird." How strange! Mina thinks. Not strange to us. By then we know that the "bird" is a bat—one of the Count's preferred incarnations. (Dracula will destroy Lucy before turning to Mina.) Such counterpoint, of course, increases the suspense. When are these people going to figure out what is going on?

Finally, most of the narration is not just first person but in the moment, and therefore unglazed by memory. "We are to be married in an hour," Mina writes to Lucy as she sits by Jonathan's bed in a Budapest hospital. (That's where he landed, with a brain fever, after escaping from Castle Dracula.) He's sleeping now, Mina says. She'll write while she can. Oops! "Jonathan is waking!" She must break off. This minute-by-minute recording, as Samuel Richardson, its pioneer (in *Pamela*), discovered a century and a half earlier, lends urgency—you are there!—and, again, it seems a warrant of truth.

But the narrative method is not the only thing that provides a tight receptacle for the story. Most of this tale of the irrational is filtered through minds wedded to rationalism. *Dracula* has what Noël Carroll, in *The Philosophy of Horror* (1990), called a "complex discovery plot"—that is, a plot that involves not just the discovery of an evil force let loose in the world but the job of convincing skeptics (which takes a lot of time, allowing the monster to compound his crimes) that such a thing is happening. No people, we are told, were more confident than the citizens of Victorian England. The sun never set on their empire. They were also masters of science and technology. *Dracula* is full of exciting modern machinery—the telegraph, the typewriter, the "Kodak"—and the novel has an obsession with railway trains, probably the nineteenth century's most crucial invention. The new world held no terrors for these people. Nevertheless, they were bewildered by it, because of its challenge to religious faith and to the emotions religion had taught: sweetness, comfort, reverence, resignation.

That crisis is recorded in work after work of late nineteenth-century fiction, but never more forcibly than in *Dracula*. In the opening pages of the novel, Harker, on his way to Castle Dracula, has arrived in Romania. He complains of the lateness of the trains. He describes a strange dish, *paprika hendl*, that he was given for dinner in a restaurant. But he is English; he can handle these things. He does not yet know that the man he is going to visit has little concern for timetables— the Count has lived for hundreds of years—and dines on something more peculiar than *paprika hendl*. Even when the evidence is in front of Harker's face, he cannot credit it. The coachman driving him to Castle Dracula (it is the Count, in disguise) is of a curious appearance. He has pointed teeth and flaming red eyes. This makes Harker, in his words, feel "a little strangely." Days pass, however, before he comes to hold a stronger opinion. The other characters are equally slow to get the point. When Professor Abraham Van Helsing, the venerable Dutch physician who becomes the head of the vampire-hunting posse, suggests to his colleague John Seward that there may be a vampire operating in their midst, Seward thinks Van Helsing must be going mad. "Surely," he protests, "there must be *some* rational explanation of all these mysterious things." Van Helsing counters that not every phenomenon has a rational explanation: "Do you not think that there are things in the world which you cannot understand, and yet which are?" Throughout the novel, these self-assured people have to be convinced, with enormous difficulty, that there is something beyond their ken.

According to Nina Auerbach in *Our Vampires, Ourselves* (1995), Dracula's crimes are merely symbols of the real-life sociopolitical horrors facing the late Victorians. One was immigration. At the end of the century, eastern European Jews, in flight from the pogroms, were pouring into western Europe, thereby threatening to dilute the supposedly pure blood of the English, among others. Dracula, too, is an émigré from the East. Stoker spends a lot of words on the subject of blood, and not just when Dracula extracts it. Fully four of the book's five vampire hunters have their blood transfused into Lucy's veins, and this process is recorded with grisly exactitude. (We see the incisions, the hypodermics.) So Stoker might in fact have been thinking of the racial threat. Like other novels of the period, *Dracula* contains invidious remarks about Jews. They have big noses; they like money—the usual.

At that time, furthermore, people in England were forced, by the scandal of the Oscar Wilde trials (1895), to think about something most of them hadn't worried about before: homosexuality. Many scholars have found suggestions of homoeroticism in *Dracula*. Auerbach, by contrast, finds the book annoyingly heterosexual. Earlier vampire tales, such as Polidori's story and *Carmilla*, made room for the mutability of erotic experience. In those works, sex didn't have to be man to woman. And it didn't have to be outright sex; it might just be fervent friendship. As Auerbach sees it, Stoker, spooked by the Wilde case, backed off from this rich ambiguity, thereby impoverishing vampire literature. After him, she says, vampire art became reactionary. This echoes Stephen King's statement that all horror fiction, by pitting an absolute good against an absolute evil, is "as Republican as a banker in a three-piece suit."

According to some critics, another thing troubling Stoker was the

New Woman, that turn-of-the-century avatar of the feminist. Again, there is support for this. The New Woman is referred to dismissively in the book, and the God-ordained difference between the sexes—basically, that women are weak but good, and men are strong but less good—is reiterated with maddening persistence. On the other hand, Mina, the novel's heroine and a woman of unquestioned virtue, looks, at times, like a feminist. She works for a living, as a schoolmistress, before her marriage, and the new technology, which should have been daunting to a female, does not bewilder her. She's a whiz as a typist—a standard New Woman profession. Also, she is wise and reasonable—male virtues. Nevertheless, her primary characteristic is a female trait: compassion. (At one point, she even pities Dracula.) Stoker, it seems, had mixed feelings about the New Woman.

Whether or not politics was operating in Stoker's novel, it is certainly at work in our contemporary vampire literature. Charlaine Harris's Sookie Stackhouse series openly treats vampires as a persecuted minority. Sometimes they are like Black people (lynch mobs pursue them), sometimes like homosexuals (rednecks beat them up). Meanwhile, they are trying to go mainstream. Sookie's Bill has sworn off human blood, or he's trying; he subsists on a Japanese synthetic. He registers to vote (absentee, because he cannot get around in daylight). He wears pressed chinos. This is funny but also touching. In the Vampire Chronicles, Anne Rice also seems to regard her undead as an oppressed group. Their suffering is probably, at some level, a story about AIDS. All this is a little confusing morally. How can we have sympathy for the devil and still regard him as the devil? That question seems to have occurred to Stephenie Meyer, who is a Mormon. Edward, the featured vampire of Meyer's *Twilight*, is a dashing fellow, and Bella, the heroine, becomes his girlfriend, but (because of the conversion risk) they do not go to bed together until the last volume. Neither should you go to bed with anyone, Meyer seems to be saying to her teenage readers. They are compensated by the romantic fever that the sexual postponement generates. The book fairly heaves with desire.

But in Stoker's time no excitement needed to be added. Sex outside marriage was still taboo, and dangerous. It could destroy a woman's life—a man's, too. (Syphilis was a major killer at that time. One of Stoker's biographers claimed that the writer died of it.) In such a context, we do not need to look for political meaning in Dracula's transactions with women. The meaning is forbidden sex—its menace and its allure. The baring of the woman's flesh, her leaning back, the penetration—reading of these matters, do you find your mind drifting to the socio-politics of immigration?

The novel is sometimes close to pornographic. Consider the scene in which Harker, lying supine in a dark room in Dracula's castle, is approached by the Count's "brides." Describing the one he likes best, Harker says that he could "see in the moonlight the moisture shining on the scarlet lips" and hear "the churning sound of her tongue as it licked her teeth." It should happen to us! Harker is not the only one who does not object to a vampire overture. In chapter 8, Lucy describes to Mina her memory of how, on a recent night, she met a tall, mysterious man in the shadow of the ruined abbey that looms over Whitby. (This was her first encounter with Dracula.) She speaks of her experience frankly, without shame, because she thinks it was a dream. She ran through the streets to the appointed spot, she says: "Then I have a vague memory of something long and dark with red eyes . . . and something very sweet and very bitter all around me at once; and then I seemed sinking into deep green water, and there was a singing in my ears, as I have heard there is to drowning men . . . then there was a sort of agonizing feeling, as if I were in an earthquake." This is thrilling: her rushing to the rendezvous, her sense of something both sweet and bitter, then the "earthquake."

But Lucy is a flighty girl. The crucial testimony is that of Mina, after Dracula's attack on her. "I did not want to hinder him," this honest woman says. Her statement is echoed by the unsettling notes of tenderness in Seward's description of the event: the kitten at the saucer of milk; Mina's resemblance, with her face at Dracula's breast, to a nursing baby. The mind reels.

Dracula is full of faults. It is way overfull. Many scenes are superfluous. The novel is replete with sentimentality and with oratory. Van Helsing cannot stop making soul-stirring speeches to his fellow vampire hunters. "Do we not see our duty?" he asks. "We must go on," he urges them. "From no danger shall we shrink." His listeners grasp one another's hands and kneel and swear oaths and weep and flush and pale.

To these tiresome characteristics of Victorian fiction, Stoker adds problems all his own. The on-the-spot narration forces him, at times, into ridiculous situations. In chapter 11, Lucy has a hard night. First, a wolf crashes through her bedroom window, splattering glass all over. This awakens her mother, who is in bed with her. Mrs. Westenra sits up, sees the wolf, and drops dead from shock. Then, to make matters worse, Dracula comes in and sucks Lucy's neck. What does she do when that's over with? Call the police? No. She pulls out her diary, and sitting on her bed next to the rapidly cooling body of her mother, she records the episode, because Stoker needs to tell the reader about it.

None of this, however, outweighs the strengths of the novel, above all, its psychological acuity. The last quarter of the book, where the vampire hunters, after the attack on Mina, go after Dracula in earnest, is very subtle, because at that point Mina's dealings with the fiend have rendered her half vampire. At times, she is cooperating with her rescuers. At other times, she is colluding with Dracula. She is a double agent. Her friends know this; she knows it, too, and knows that they know; they know that she knows that they know. This is complicated, and not always tidily worked out, but we cannot help but be impressed by Stoker's representation of the amoral contrivances of love, or of desire. In this bold clarity, *Dracula* is like the work of other nineteenth-century writers. You can complain that their novels were loose, baggy monsters, that their poems were crazy and unfinished. Still, you gasp at what they're saying: the truth.

Each of the annotated editions of *Dracula* has had its claim to attention. Leonard Wolf's *Annotated "Dracula,"* with six hundred notes, was the first, and it also did the job—which somebody had to do eventually—of picking through the psychoneurotic aspects of the novel. The next version, *The Essential "Dracula,"* edited by Raymond T. McNally and Radu Florescu, had its own originality. These two history professors from Boston College had unearthed Stoker's working notes for the novel. They drew no important conclusions from that source, but never mind. They had a sexy new theory: that Stoker based the character of Dracula on a historical personage, Vlad Dracula—also known as Vlad Tepes—a fifteenth-century Walachian prince who, in defending his homeland against the Turks, acquired a reputation for cruelty unusual even among warriors of that period. Tepes means "the Impaler." Vlad's preferred method of dealing with enemies was to skewer them, together with their women and children, on wooden stakes. A fifteenth-century woodcut shows him dining at a table set up outdoors so that he could watch his prisoners wriggle to their deaths. McNally and Florescu's theory gave journalists a lot of exciting things to write about, and their articles were featured. As a result, *The Essential "Dracula"* was very popular. To add to the fun, Florescu claimed that he was an indirect descendant of Vlad's.

The Vlad hypothesis has since been discredited. As scholars have figured out, Stoker, while working on *Dracula*, read, or read in, a book that discussed Vlad, whereupon he changed his villain's name from Count Wampyr to Count Dracula, and moved him from Austria to Transylvania, which borders on Walachia. He picked up other details, too, but not many. This has not put later writers off Vlad's story. Matthew Beresford, in *From Demons to Dracula*, acknowledges that Stoker's character "was not modeled, to any great extent, on Vlad Dracula." Yet he offers a whole chapter on the Walachian prince, including a long description of impalement methods, complete with illustrations.

In 1998 came *Bram Stoker's Dracula Unearthed*, by Clive Leatherdale, a Stoker scholar. This book did not get much attention, but it holds the record for annotation: thirty-five hundred notes, totaling 110,000 words. Leatherdale's edition was also remarkable for its practice—common among fans, if not editors, of cult books—of treating the novel as if it were fact rather than fiction. When Harker, invading the cellar of Castle Dracula, finds the Count sleeping in his dirt-filled coffin, Leatherdale's note asks, "Is he lying on damp earth in his everyday clothes, or in his night-clothes, with no sheeting to prevent earth-stains?" This is a creature who has lived for centuries, and can fly, and raise storms at sea, and Leatherdale is worried about whether he's going to get his clothes dirty? The practice of *Dracula* annotation is both quite serious (Leatherdale, like the others, did a lot of work) and also, unashamedly, an amusement. It is an exercise in showing off—a demonstration of the editor's erudition, energy, interests—and a confession of love for the text.

Leslie Klinger, in his new annotated edition, claims that he has fresh material to go on. He has examined Stoker's typescript, which is owned by a "private collector." This source, he says, has yielded "startling results." In fact, like McNally and Florescu with Stoker's working notes, Klinger draws no important conclusions from his archival discovery, and he admits that he spent only two days studying it. As with the McNally-Florescu version, however, the real sales angle of this edition is not a new source but a new theory. Klinger not only assumes, like Leatherdale, that all the events narrated in the novel are factual; he offers a hypothesis as to how Stoker came to publish them. Here goes. Harker, a real person (with a changed name), like everyone else in the book, gave his diary, together with the other documents that constitute the novel, to Bram Stoker so that Stoker might alert the English public that a vampire named Dracula, also real, was in their midst. Stoker agreed to issue the warning. But then Dracula got wind of this plan, whereupon he contacted Stoker and used on him the methods of persuasion famously at his disposal. Dracula decided that it was too late to suppress the Harker documents entirely, so instead he forced Stoker to distort them. He sat at the desk with Stoker and co-authored the novel, changing the facts in such a way as to convince the public that Dracula had been eliminated. That way, the Count could go on, unmolested, with his project of taking over the world.

Many of Klinger's fifteen hundred notes are devoted to revealing this wicked plot. When Stoker makes a continuity error, or fails to supply verifiable information, this is part of the cover-up. The book says that Dracula's London house is at 347 Piccadilly, but in the 1890s the only houses on that stretch of Piccadilly that would have answered Stoker's description were at 138 and 139. Clearly, Klinger says, Stoker is protecting the Count. Then there's a problem about the hotel where Van Helsing is staying. In chapter 9 it's the Great Eastern; in chapter 11 it's the Berkeley. Again, Klinger concludes, Stoker is covering his characters' traces. He altered the name of the hotel—presumably, he had to prevent readers from running over to the place and checking the register—but then he forgot and changed the name again.

At first, you think that maybe Klinger's book is not actually an annotated edition of *Dracula* but rather, like Nabokov's *Pale Fire*, a novel about a paranoid, in the form of an annotated edition. But no. In the book's prefatory materials, Klinger lays out his conspiracy theory without qualification. So are we to understand that he himself is a maniac whose delusions the editors at Norton thought it might be interesting to publish?

No again. Nestled in those same front-of-the-book materials is a little note titled "Editor's Preface"—exactly the kind of thing that readers would skip—in which he tells us that his great hypothesis is a "gentle fiction." (He used a similar contrivance, he says, in his Sherlock Holmes edition.) Recently, in a book-tour appearance at the New York Public Library, Klinger again admitted that his conspiracy theory was a game. "If you like that sort of thing, there's a lot of that in there," he said. April fool!

That's too bad, first, because it means that a serious novel has been taken as a species of camp, and, second, because it discredits Klinger's non-joke, scholarly footnotes, of which there are many, and carefully researched. Even after the other annotated editions, this volume gives us useful information. Maybe we didn't need to be told what Dover was, or the Bosporus, but when Klinger writes about the rise of the New Woman, or about the popularity of spiritualism in the late nineteenth century, this gives us knowledge that Victorian readers would have brought to the novel, and that could help us. It won't, though, because readers, having had their chain pulled by the conspiracy theory, will disregard those notes, if, improbably, they have bought the book. Every generation, it seems, gets the annotated *Dracula* that it deserves. This is the postmodern version: playful, "performative," with a smiling disdain for any claim of truth. It found the perfect author. A tax attorney would know about gentle fictions.

Whoosh! Why is the curtain blowing so strangely? Oh, my God! There is a man in my study, with a briefcase—he claims he is a lawyer, from Los Angeles—and, by his side, another, taller figure, in black, with pointy teeth. They say they want to help me revise my article. I must break off!

Originally published as "In the Blood," *The New Yorker*, 2009

Evelyn Waugh and his wife, Laura, with their children, c. 1949. Auberon is standing at the back, between his parents.

WAUGH STORIES

Alexander, Arthur, Evelyn, Auberon, and Alexander Waugh

Alexander Waugh, the grandson of Evelyn, has written a book, *Fathers and Sons*, about the father-son relationships—dramas, often, of mutual incomprehension and dismay—in five successive generations of his family. First comes Alexander Waugh (1840–1906), known as the Brute, a surgeon and a paragon of Victorian masculinity in its most unappealing aspects. The Brute loved to whip his dog. On display in his library were repulsive specimens that he had collected in his medical school days, including a congealed substance called the White Blood that everyone in the family was frightened of. The Brute begat Arthur (1866–1943), made by God, it seems, to give pain to his father. Arthur, Alexander tells us, was a mama's boy, "scared of the organ in church, scared of twigs in the garden . . . scared of scissors, scared of lemonade." He grew up to be a man of letters: he wrote biographies of Tennyson and Browning, and he was the managing director of Chapman and Hall, an important publishing house in London. Arthur had two sons, both of them novelists. The first was Alec (1898–1981), who, in the words of his nephew, "wrote many books, each worse than the last." The second was Evelyn (1903–66), the greatest comic novelist of the twentieth century. Evelyn's first son was Auberon (1939–2001), a prolific, vituperative, funny, and famous journalist in London in the closing decades of the century. Auberon sired Alexander (born in 1963), who for some years was a composer and a music critic, then began writing books of general interest, including *Time* (2000), *God* (2002), and now this account of his difficult forefathers.

Fathers and Sons is witty, in the Waugh manner, but it is also poignant, especially regarding the relationship between Arthur and his two sons. No man ever loved a child more than Arthur loved Alec—"son of my soul," as he called him. He seems to have spent almost every hour of his nonwork time talking to the boy, reading to him, taking walks with him. When Alec went away to his father's alma mater, Sherborne, the child and the school fused, in Arthur's mind, into one refulgent idol. He spent every weekend at Sherborne, visiting Alec and his friends, whom he wooed to become his friends. He said that he dreamed every night of being a new boy at the school. He and Alec wrote to each other daily, and Arthur awaited Alec's letters, Alexander says, like a teenager in love. (If a letter arrived after he left for work, his wife would travel across London to bring it to his office.) Alexander thinks that Arthur, because of his tortured relations with the Brute, never had a proper childhood. Now he had one: Alec's.

Then Alec, in his next-to-last year, was caught in flagrante with another boy. (Alexander says they might have been doing nothing more than kissing.) As a courtesy to his father, he was allowed to finish the term before leaving the school, but the other boys were instructed to shun him. Arthur was heartbroken, but he did not reproach Alec. On the contrary, he saw his son as a persecuted Jesus, and himself as the grieving Father. He wrote to Alec of a crucifix he once saw, with the figure of God hovering behind the dying Christ: "The nails that pierce the Son's hands pierce the Father's also: the thorn-crowned head of the Dying Saviour is seen to be lying upon the Father's bosom. And it is always so with you and me. Every wound that touches you pierces my own soul also: every thorn in your crown of life tears my tired head as well. . . . With deep love and unfaltering trust, still and always, your ever devoted and hopeful Daddy."

Two years later, at the age of nineteen, Alec published his first novel, *The Loom of Youth* (1917), which takes place at a school easily recognizable, to those in the know, as Sherborne. Among its evils is the staff's hypocrisy regarding sexual relations between the boys. Everyone knows that this is going on; the only crime is to get caught. *The Loom of Youth* sold many copies and created a scandal. Impassioned letters ran for weeks in the London press. Arthur was publicly humiliated, and many of his friends dropped him. Nevertheless, his cult of Alec remained unshaken. When Alec married and moved to Sussex, Arthur still spent most weekends with him. "I simply go about thinking of your love for me all the time," he wrote to his son. The wonder in all this is that Alec did not recoil from his father's obsessive devotion. One should note that he spent much of his adult life traveling. This started early, and it might have been his way of putting some distance between himself and Arthur. But in his many autobiographical writings he never spoke of his father with anything but love, and apart from publishing books with hot sex scenes (*The Loom of Youth* was only the beginning), he treated the old man kindly until the day he died.

The same cannot be said of Evelyn. Alec was five when Evelyn was born, but he later recalled that he felt like an only child throughout his youth; Evelyn was "no more than an encumbrance in a corner." That is certainly the way Arthur viewed his second son. When Evelyn asked for a bicycle, Arthur went out and bought one for Alec. When Alec wanted a billiard table, it was installed in Evelyn's nursery. (Presumably, it would have taken up too much space in Alec's room.) Alec was sent to prep school at nine. Evelyn didn't go until he was fourteen, and then he went to a school, Lancing, that he considered inferior to Sherborne. (Because of *The Loom of Youth*, he couldn't go to his brother's school.) When Alec, on vacations, returned to the family's home, Underhill, in Hampstead, Arthur hung a banner in the front hall saying WEL-COME HOME TO THE HEIR OF UNDERHILL. Finally, Evelyn asked Arthur, "When Alec has Underhill and all that's in it, what will be left for me?" Arthur put away the banner, but not his preferences.

The situation was due to more than birth order. Arthur, as his Jesus letter shows, was sentimental and self-dramatizing. Also, he never shut up. Several nights a week, after dinner, he would invite the family to join him in his library, where he would read to them at length from his favorite authors, often fixing one member of the family with his eye throughout the recitation. If the text was a play, he would get up and act out the parts. Another opportunity for drama was his chronic asthma. In the throes of an attack, he would cry out to heaven for release, quoting relevant passages from literature. According to Evelyn, Arthur was also a relentless correspondent: "He answered letters that needed no answer, thanking people who thanked him for a present, so that, when he encountered anyone as punctilious as himself, a correspondence was likely to start which ended only in death."

Evelyn was the opposite. From childhood, he had a biting wit and a hyperacute sense of the ridiculous. To Arthur, this was a moral failing, and it no doubt seemed to him more regrettable in that nothing on earth struck Evelyn as more ridiculous than Arthur. Evelyn began insulting him when he was quite young, and when he became a novelist, he went on doing so. The most boring and sinister character in all his fiction—Mr. Todd, who, at the end of *A Handful of Dust* (1934), imprisons the novel's hero, Tony Last, and makes him read Dickens to him every day for the rest of his life—is based in part on Arthur, who worshipped Dickens. (He was the president of the Dickens Fellowship and the editor of two complete sets of Dickens's work. Chapman and Hall was Dickens's publisher.) Even more striking is Mr. Prendergast, a ludicrous clergyman, in *Decline and Fall* (1928). Alexander explains that Evelyn never used a whole person from his life as the basis for a whole character in his fiction; he combined the traits of one acquaintance with those of another. But anyone who knew the Waughs would not have failed to notice that Prendergast displayed a number of Arthur's signal characteristics. Prendergast becomes the chaplain in a prison, where he is beheaded by a lunatic inmate. Paul Pennyfeather, the novel's hero, who is serving time in the prison, finds out about this belatedly, because, as a rule, he is not allowed to speak to the other prisoners. His only chance to communicate with them is during morning hymns. The day after Prendergast's mishap, Paul is in chapel next to his friend Philbrick, who knows the story. The hymn strikes up:

> *"O God, our help in ages past," [sang Paul].*
> *"Where's Prendergast today?"*
> *"What, ain't you 'eard? 'e's been done in."*
> *"And our eternal home."*
> *"Old Prendy went to see a chap*
> *What said he'd seen a ghost;*
> *Well, he was dippy, and he'd got*
> *A mallet and a saw."*
> *"Who let the madman have the things?"*
> *"The Governor; who d'you think?*
> *He asked to be a carpenter,*
> *He sawed off Prendy's head. . . ."*
> *"Time, like an ever-rolling stream,*
> *Bears all its sons away."*
> *"Poor Prendy 'ollered fit to kill*

For nearly 'alf an hour." . . .
"Amen."

Arthur might have given Evelyn more than material. Alec, in
an essay he wrote after his brother's death, claimed that Arthur was
also responsible for the tone of Evelyn's novels. Evelyn, Alec insists,
was a warm, gentle man who made himself seem cold for fear of
being like his father. It is not for nothing, Alec says, that Evelyn's
most sentimental book, *Brideshead Revisited* (1945), was written the
year after Arthur's death: "The warning example was now removed."
Also removed was the danger of pleasing his father, by seeming
tenderhearted.

This is an interesting argument, but it should be added that Evelyn's
rebellion against Arthur is merely one instance of the most notorious
generation gap of the twentieth century, the antagonism between the
young people of the 1920s—known in England as the Bright Young
Things—and their parents, whose values, the children felt, had led to
the pointless slaughter that was World War I. In an essay that Evelyn
wrote while still in high school, he announced this generation's coming:
"They will be above all things clear sighted. The youngest generation
are going to be very hard and analytical and unsympathetic. The young
men of the nineties"—Arthur's generation—"subsisted upon emotion. They poured out their souls like water and their tears with pride;
middle-aged observers will find it hard to see the soul in the youngest
generation. But they will have—and this is their justification—a very
full sense of humor." His prophecy was correct.

In 1922, Evelyn went up to Hertford College, Oxford, where
he soon abandoned his studies in favor of drinking. This time was
not wasted—at the sodden lunch parties that he had daily with his
friends, he refined his comic skills and his ear for witty dialogue—
but he left Oxford in 1924 with no degree and no prospects. During
the next four years, he took various small jobs, failing at most of

them. He published almost nothing, and no one, Alec says, expected him to become a writer. Indeed, few people expected him to become anything. He drank as much as ever and suffered black depressions. In this period, he later recalled, he once tried to commit suicide by swimming out to sea, but he encountered a swarm of jellyfish and hurried back to shore.

Then his luck turned. He got a contract for a biography of Dante Gabriel Rossetti, and he managed to write it. He also fell in love, with a young woman named Evelyn Gardner. Her family wanted no part of him. They were aristocrats; he was middle class, and also penniless. To appease them, and to make some money to get married on, he sat down and in what seems to have been less than eight months wrote his first novel, *Decline and Fall*. In 1928, He-Evelyn and She-Evelyn, as their friends called them, got married. *Decline and Fall* was a success, and it was quickly followed by *Vile Bodies* (1930), which was a bestseller. Both books dealt with the Bright Young Things; together, they constituted that generation's most vivid and accurate portrait. Waugh became a famous writer and remained so for the rest of his life.

The first thing one notices about Evelyn Waugh's fiction is his breath-taking prose. He seems to have had a richer vocabulary, a keener ear, a wider range of effects—all of this supported by the firm bones of a Latinate syntax—than any English prose writer before or since. Even his smallest, transitional passages are exquisitely worked. Here, from *Vile Bodies*, is a carful of drunks returning home from the races:

> Darkness fell during the drive back. It took an hour to reach the town. Adam and Miles and Archie Schwert did not talk much. The effects of their drinks had now entered on that secondary stage, vividly described in temperance hand-books, when the momentary illusion of well-being and exhilaration gives place to melancholy,

indigestion and moral decay. Adam tried to concentrate his thoughts upon his sudden wealth [he thinks he's won some money], but they seemed unable to adhere to this high pinnacle, and as often as he impelled them up, slithered back helplessly to his present physical discomfort.

Waugh was young (twenty-five) when he wrote this, and so he is spreading his plumage a little. Later, his prose became simpler, and more beautiful.

Such writing could become heavy after a while, but it is constantly refreshed by tart dialogue. Waugh, it seems, could do any voice—of any nationality, social class, age, profession, temperament—and make it sound as if it were speaking, that very moment, two feet away. Another balancing factor is Waugh's extreme economy in laying out his story. As good as what he tells us is what he doesn't tell us, or only reveals later, through the mouthpiece of someone who witnessed the event, or heard about it. (See Philbrick's account of the murder of Prendergast.) His use of point of view could pass inspection by Henry James. But his most striking gift is his sheer writerly tact. He knows exactly when to cut something off, and he never explains a joke.

As a result, he was, in the words of his son Auberon, "the funniest man of his generation." People have said that every novelist has only one book in him; if so, Waugh's was a version of *Candide*. In novel after novel, he shows us a naive, good man wandering through a bad world, which, as he tries to make sense of it, reveals itself in all its hilarious nastiness. This was Waugh's favorite joke, a Wildean joke: moral blindness, asserted without shame. In *Black Mischief* (1932), which is set in an African country, the hero, Basil Seal, arrives at the British legation to announce that civil war has erupted in the nation. "I think it's very mischievous of you saying all this," the legate's wife, Lady Courteney, replies. "You're just *talking*. Now go and get yourself some whiskey . . . and I think you might put that dirty gun outside in the lobby." She is English, and upper class, and if the people of this strange, hot country to which her family has been posted have begun killing one another, that is no concern of hers.

This is the soil from which Waugh reaps his comic harvest, but his books wouldn't have lasted if they did not contain a serious moral drama. A year after his marriage, Waugh, sitting in a country inn, writing *Vile Bodies*, received a letter from She-Evelyn saying that she was having an affair and wanted a divorce. He never got over it. In most of his novels, the hero falls in love with a beautiful woman who speedily betrays him. Waugh was loyal to the generation of the 1920s—in English fiction, he was its leader—but he soon began worrying about its morals. Alec recalled that after receiving She-Evelyn's fatal letter, Evelyn said to him, "The trouble about the world today is that there's not enough religion in it. There's nothing to stop young people doing whatever they feel like doing at the moment." In 1930, shortly after the end of his marriage, he converted to Roman Catholicism—an action that probably fortified his gift for comedy. The Church of Rome, more than any other Christian persuasion, sees the world as fallen. Pledged to that faith, Waugh could go on having fun with the world's wickedness. Most of his people behave badly; he likes them anyway, and makes us like them. Nevertheless, he took sin seriously and wondered how goodness could survive against it. This problem underlies all his novels. In some, above all *A Handful of Dust*, from his early period, and his World War II trilogy, published between 1952 and 1961—*Men at Arms, Officers and Gentlemen*, and *Unconditional Surrender* (or *The End of the Battle*, as it was called in its American edition)—the struggle between good and evil is pushed to the forefront, and these are his finest books. They are also his most pessimistic.

But the morals didn't get in the way of the comedy, some of which is directed at people whom, today, we are disposed to rescue from a history of abuse. An important character in *Black Mischief* is known to her friends as Black Bitch. Her countrymen squat on their haunches and polish their teeth with sticks. They all but have bones in their noses. Yet, in his treatment of Africans and other groups foreign to him, Waugh was in complete agreement with most of the people of his time and class. Their views have gone to the grave with them. His have survived, because they are enshrined in his marvelous novels, and therefore we have the opportunity to be shocked by him. Furthermore, Waugh didn't just make fun of today's targeted minorities; he made fun of everyone. Here, from *Decline and Fall*, is his description of a group of Welsh musicians arriving to play at a school festivity:

> Ten men of revolting appearance were approaching from the drive. They were low of brow, crafty of eye and crooked of limb. They advanced huddled together with the loping tread of wolves, peering about them furtively as they came . . . ; they slavered at their mouths, which hung loosely over their receding chins, while each clutched under his ape-like arm a burden of curious and unaccountable shape. On seeing the Doctor they halted and edged back, those behind squinting and mouthing over their companions' shoulders.

In *Black Mischief*, the Europeans, the would-be bringers of civilization, are satirized much more wickedly—and much more pointedly, in moral terms—than the Africans. When, at the end of the book, Lady Courteney's nymphomaniac daughter is eaten for dinner at a tribal gathering, we don't cry for her.

Evelyn was not a good father. The thing he feared most in life was boredom, Alexander tells us, and the six children he had by his second wife, Laura Herbert, often bored him to death. His diaries and letters are filled with unaffectionate references to them. ("Teresa's voice odious, Bron [Auberon] lazy . . . Harriet mad.") When they were home from school, he took dinner in his library. They were glad of this, for they were afraid of him, as was almost everyone he knew. "He spent his life," Auberon later wrote, "seeking out men and women who were not frightened of him. Even then, he usually ended up getting drunk with them, as a way out of the abominable problem of human relations."

That was not the only circumstance in which he was drunk. The cycling depression that he developed in his youth dogged him all his life, and he treated it with alcohol. Auberon recalls that he could tell when his father was at home because of the "miasma compounded of Havana cigar smoke and gin" issuing from the library. Together with the gin, Evelyn dosed himself heavily with chloral bromide, a sleeping medication, and the combination eventually resulted in a spell of paranoid hallucinations—an experience he recorded in his odd and excellent late novel *The Ordeal of Gilbert Pinfold* (1957). He did not learn a lesson from this. He just switched to paraldehyde and gin. Like many first-rate writers of his generation, he was intoxicated most of the day, every day. This no doubt exacerbated his annoyance with his children and the cruelty with which he expressed it.

Auberon, as the oldest boy and hence the child he held to the highest standard, seemed to him a special disappointment—not without reason. By the time Auberon entered puberty, he was, by his own account, "something approaching a professional criminal." While he was at prep school—Downside, run by Benedictine monks—he founded an organization called the Downside Numismatic Society and rented a room for it in the town. There he and his friends went to smoke and play cards. When a group of prefects skeptical of the boys' numismatic interests interrupted their activities, Auberon called the police. He appears also to have set fire to the school, though Alexander says that was an accident. After Downside, he joined the army and was posted to Cyprus, where, one day, he decided that the machine gun attached to his armored car was not functioning properly. He got out, stood in front of the gun barrel, and fiddled with the mechanism—successfully, for the gun resumed firing, and shot six bullets, point-blank, into his chest. He lost his spleen, one of his lungs, two ribs, and part of a hand. When his parents were informed that he would probably die, Laura came to Cyprus, but Evelyn didn't. To him, this was probably just another one of Auberon's derelictions. The boy, at the time, was eighteen.

Auberon later wrote that his father was sometimes capable of great kindness. (Once, when Auberon was in the hospital as a child, recovering from an eye operation, Evelyn arrived with a box of white mice hidden under his overcoat, as a treat.) Furthermore, however much antagonism reigned between father and son when they were living under the same roof, they wrote each other wonderful, entertaining, affectionate letters when they were apart, which was most of the time. In Auberon's letters to Evelyn, he seems to speak to him as an equal, telling him stories, feeding him material, as it were. He did this consciously, he later confessed: "Nothing ever happened to me while he was alive but I mentally sub-edited it into a report which would be sent to him in my next letter." Both of them writers, they were most generous to each other in writing. About five years before his death, Evelyn "lost all terror," Auberon says—he became benevolent, mild—and from then on the two men enjoyed a "distinct cordiality." Auberon does not add that this change in Evelyn was accompanied by another: his writing slipped terribly. Eventually, he put down his pen and devoted his days to crossword puzzles and gin. He longed for death, and at sixty-two he got it, from what is said to have been a heart attack. Auberon, an honest man, recalls that when he received the news, what he felt, mainly, was relief: "His death lifted a great brooding awareness not only from the house but from the whole of existence."

Auberon married young, and the woman he chose, Teresa Onslow, was, like his mother, from a noble family. They had four children, in short order. Auberon published his first novel, *The Foxglove Saga*, when he was twenty, and then he wrote four more, but eventually he decided that they weren't very good. Alexander thinks that he might also have gotten tired of hearing his novels compared unfavorably to Evelyn's. In any case, he gave up on fiction and devoted himself entirely to journalism. Over the years, he worked, it seems, for every newspaper in London, plus several magazines, but his longest stay was at the satirical biweekly *Private Eye*. Though he wrote on many subjects—politics, books, wine, food, nature—his specialty was the short, comic "diary" column, which is what he produced for fourteen years at *Private Eye*. In an entry from December 1981, he notes that two headless bears are said to have been found in the river at Hackney: "Immediately one begins to feel alarmed for several of one's friends. . . . I have not seen Geoffrey Wheatcroft for some time." A week later, he describes *The Spectator*'s Christmas party, where the main speech was given by Sir Peregrine Worsthorne. He adds that Sir Peregrine's father, the Colonel, "used sometimes to be seen in bed with Eartha Kitt although it is thought that no impropriety occurred." Elsewhere, he takes out after Admiral Sir Alexander Gordon-Lennox, the sergeant at arms of the House of Commons, who, understandably, has been reluctant to give Auberon a press pass. When a small bomb goes off in Westminster Palace, Auberon accuses Sir Alexander of having farted.

He did not mince words about what such writing constituted. "Vulgar abuse," he called it, and he stood up for it. "Vituperation is not a philosophy of life nor an answer to all life's ills. It is merely a tool, a device. . . . It redresses some of the forces of deference which bolster the conceit of the second-rate; it also prevents the first-rate from going mad with conceit." He felt that mockery was a British specialty and that this made "life in Britain preferable to life anywhere else." His own leadership in the field endeared him to many, while others responded to his writings with quaking rage and, sometimes, libel suits. Auberon's favorite target was liberal reform, which made a vigorous showing in England in the 1970s. In his columns, he repeatedly insulted the working classes;

he warned against the dangers of breast-feeding. In *Fathers and Sons*, Alexander reports that Auberon always defended corporal punishment in schools, or at least in Catholic schools, where, he argued, it relieved the monks of the strains of celibacy. A beating, he said, was "a small sacrifice for a boy and a great treat for a monk." Once, when, as Auberon tells it, he "repeated an old army joke about the curious trousers worn by men in certain parts of the near East," the British Council Library in Rawalpindi was burned to the ground. That time, he got fired.

People who knew Auberon only from his writings were always surprised, when they met him, to discover what a nice man he was. He also turns out to have been the best father of those surveyed in *Fathers and Sons*. He "was never—well, hardly ever—sharp with us," Alexander writes, and he was huge fun to be with. He loved games; he loved dinner; he would sing Offenbach with a glass of port balanced on his head. Alexander recalls that his school friends often asked Auberon, with horror, what had happened to his left index finger, which the accident in Cyprus had reduced to a stump. He would explain to them that it "had been bitten off by a Royal Bengal Tiger . . . or had dropped off, quite inexplicably, that very morning."

Auberon was also wise, as is clear from his autobiography, *Will This Do?*, which he wrote when he was in his fifties. All the Waugh literary men produced histories of themselves and their family. Auberon's is the best—far better than Evelyn's *Little Learning* (1964), a late, bored book—and one of the finest things in it is his discussion of his mother, Laura. Alexander, too, is very good on Laura. Though she came from an old and rich family, she hated ostentation. Most days, she dressed in trousers belted with twine. If she had to go to a party, she wore an old, largely hairless Astrakhan coat, also belted with twine. (It had had a proper belt, but apparently she lost it.) She cared as little for her family's wardrobe as for her own. Alexander writes that when the time came for her daughters to go to boarding school, it turned out that they owned no underpants. Laura told their nanny to sew up the front of Auberon's old undershorts for them. The nanny, scandalized, sneaked into town and bought them panties with her own money.

Laura deplored the whole circus surrounding Evelyn's fame and almost never attended official occasions with him. Basically, she didn't like human company very much. She kept cows, and "she loved them extravagantly," Auberon writes, "as other women love their dogs or, so I have been told, their children." Next in her affections was her gardener, Mr. Coggins, who would linger with her in the pasture and discuss the cows. After Evelyn died, Coggins vanished. He soon returned—he was just on a bender—but in his absence Laura became convinced that Auberon had murdered him. ("I know where you've hidden the body," she hissed at him during Evelyn's funeral.) Without Evelyn to support her, Laura decided that she had to put the family's grand house—Combe Florey, in Somerset—on the market, but she didn't really want to sell it. So, Alexander says, "when prospective buyers came round she poured buckets of water through the floorboards and ordered her dog, Credit, to shit on the carpets." No one bought Combe Florey. Eventually, Auberon and his family moved in with Laura.

When his mother was not tending to her cows, Auberon says, she occupied herself with jigsaw puzzles, or "retreated into her own private meditations whose direction was not easily to be distinguished from simple misanthropy." In her widowhood, she consoled herself with sherry. Alexander, as a boy, would often visit her in her wing of the house. Together, they would play games with plastic cows on her kitchen table. He recalls, "I particularly liked the smell that attached to all her jerseys—sherry, French cigarettes, and dog baskets all blended into one, a lovely Granny fragrance." Alexander's and Auberon's combined portrait of her is a superb comedy, shaded with sorrow—for her children (she was almost as neglectful a parent as Evelyn) and also for her. She cannot have found it easy to be Evelyn's wife. "Perhaps," Auberon writes, "she would have had a happier life if she had married someone else, but I am not really all that sure how happy anyone's life is, when one comes to examine it." She died at fifty-six, of pneumonia. Auberon, too, died early, at sixty-one, of heart failure. "Better to go," he said, "than sit around being a terrible old bore."

Alexander's and Auberon's books also give us a taste of London journalism, which in Auberon's time was very gloves-off. Stabs in the back, vendettas, letter-writing campaigns, lawsuits: what drama! Writers called people piss pots, poltroons, dog sodomists—almost everything but drunks. (Drunkenness was not considered a vice.) English journalism is much the same today. In that world, Don Imus might have been sued, but he probably wouldn't have been fired.

The rowdiness was not confined to journalism. *Fathers and Sons,* together with Auberon's memoir and Evelyn's novels, puts us back in touch with a vanished world, that of the English upper and upper-middle classes in the years surrounding the First and Second World Wars. These people were extremely insular, and therefore confident. If something seemed silly to them, or even just unusual, they didn't mind making jokes about it. They were not as nice as we are, and they were much funnier. They drank from noon to night and wrote their books young and fast. Even Evelyn, the gloomiest of the lot, seems to have had a capacity for enjoyment (at least in his writing) that we barely understand, and that is not to speak of Auberon. Alexander (the younger) is tamer and tenderer, but he shows the same trait. At one point, he remembers Combe Florey, "a shambling fortress of creaky stairs and alien smells. Chief among its attractions—at any rate to a seven-year-old boy—were a life-sized carved wooden lion in the hall; Victorian painted furniture by William Burges; a stuffed white owl whose wing I could remove by lifting the glass dome that covered it and yanking; . . . a crystal chandelier that tinkled when you punched it; a ferocious gander called Captain, whose attacks we fended off with umbrellas." The Waughs had stuffed owls and homicidal ganders and knickerless children, running wild. That's not what most of us have anymore, but it is impossible to read this passage without thinking of the inherited vigor of English literature—the sheer, knotty concreteness of it, sometimes rude, always robust—from Chaucer on down.

The New Yorker, 2007

Kahlil Gibran, age fourteen, photographed by F. Holland
Day, c. 1897

PROPHET MOTIVE

Kahlil Gibran

Shakespeare, we are told, is the bestselling poet of all time. Second is Lao-tzu. Third is Kahlil Gibran, who owes his place on that list to one book, *The Prophet*, a collection of twenty-six prose poems, delivered as sermons by a fictional wise man in a faraway time and place. Since its publication, in 1923, *The Prophet* has sold more than nine million copies in its American edition alone. There are public schools named for Gibran in Brooklyn and Yonkers. *The Prophet* has been recited at countless weddings and funerals. It is quoted in books and articles on training art teachers, determining criminal responsibility, and enduring ectopic pregnancy, sleep disorders, and the news that your son is gay. Its words turn up in advertisements for marriage counselors, chiropractors, learning-disabilities specialists, and face cream.

The Prophet started fast—it sold out its first printing in a month— and then it got faster, until, in the 1960s, its sales sometimes reached five thousand copies a *week*. It was the Bible of that decade. But the book's popularity should not be laid entirely at the door of the hippies. *The Prophet* was a hit long before the 1960s (it made good money even during the Depression), and sales after that decade have never been less than healthy—a record all the more impressive in that it is due almost entirely to word of mouth. Apart from a brief effort during the 1920s, *The Prophet* has never been advertised. Presumably in honor of this commercial feat, Everyman's Library has now brought out *Kahlil Gibran: The Collected Works*, with a pretty red binding and a gold ribbon for a bookmark. While most people know Gibran only as the author of *The Prophet*, he wrote seventeen books, nine in Arabic and eight in English. The Everyman's volume contains twelve of them.

The critics will no doubt greet it with the same indifference they have shown Gibran ever since his death, in 1931. Even his publisher, Alfred A. Knopf, brushed him off. When Knopf was asked, in 1965, who the audience for *The Prophet* was, he replied that he had no idea. "It must be a cult," he said—an ungrateful response from the man to whom *The Prophet* had been a cash cow for more than forty years. In 1974, a cousin of the poet's, also named Kahlil Gibran, and his wife, Jean, published a good biography, *Kahlil Gibran: His Life and World*. Then, in 1998, came the more searching *Prophet: The Life and Times of Kahlil Gibran*, by Robin Waterfield, a translator of ancient Greek literature. But until the first of those books appeared—that is, for forty-three years after Gibran's death—there was no proper biography of this hugely popular author. Both Waterfield and the Gibrans complain about the literati's lack of respect for their subject; Waterfield blames it on snobbery, but the facts they dug up were not such as to improve his reputation.

Part of the reason there were no real biographies is that little was known about Gibran's life, and the reason for that is that he didn't want it known. One point that seems firm is that he was born in Lebanon, in a village called Bsharri, in 1883. At that time, Lebanon was part of Syria, which in turn was part of the Ottoman Empire. Gibran, by his account, was a brooding, soulful child. From his earliest years, he said, he drew constantly—painting was his first art and, for a long time, as important to him as writing—and he communed with nature. When a storm came, he would rip off his clothes and run out into the torrent in ecstasy. His mother, Kamileh, got others to leave her strange boy alone. "Sometimes," Gibran later recalled, "she would smile at someone who came in . . . and lay her finger on her lip and say, 'Hush. He's not here.'"

Gibran's father was not a good provider. He owned a walnut grove, but he didn't like working it. He preferred drinking and gambling. He eventually got a job as a tax collector, but then he was arrested for embezzlement. Poor before, the family now became destitute. In 1895, Kamileh packed up her four children—Bhutros, Kahlil (then twelve), Marianna, and Sultana—and sailed to America. They settled in Boston, in the South End, a squalid ghetto filled with immigrants from various countries. (Today, it is Boston's Chinatown.) Kamileh, like many other Syrian immigrants, became a pack peddler; that is, she went door to door, selling lace and linens out of a basket she carried on her back. Within a year, she had put aside enough money to set Bhutros up in a dry-goods store. The two girls were sent out to work as seam-stresses; neither ever learned to read or write. Kahlil alone was excused from putting food on the table. He went to school, for the first time.

He also enrolled in an art class at a nearby settlement house, and through his teacher he was sent to a man named Fred Holland Day. In European art, this was the period of the Decadents. Theosophy, espoused by Madame Blavatsky, became a craze. People went to sé-ances, dabbled in drugs, and scorned the ugly-hearted West in favor of the more spiritual East. Above all, they made a religion of art. Day, thirty-two years old and financially independent, was a leader of the Boston outpost of this movement. He wore a turban, smoked a hookah, and read by candlelight. He did serious work, however. He and his friends founded two arts magazines, and he was a partner in a publish-ing house that produced exquisite books. By the 1890s, though, Day's main interest was photography. He particularly liked to photograph beautiful young boys of "exotic" origin, sometimes nude, sometimes in their native costumes, and he often recruited them from the streets of the South End.

When the thirteen-year-old Gibran turned up at Day's door, in 1896, he became one of the models. Day was especially taken with Gibran. He made him his pupil and assistant, and he introduced him to the literature of the nineteenth century, the Romantic poets and their Symbolist inheritors. Robin Waterfield, in his biography, says that this syllabus, with its emphasis on suffering, prophecy, and the religion of love, was the rock on which Gibran built his later style. According to Waterfield, Day also gave Gibran his "pretensions." Imagine what it was like for a child from the ghetto to walk into this world of comfort and beauty, a world, furthermore, where a person could make a life of art. Fortuitously, Gibran already fitted into Day's milieu in a small way: he was "Oriental." Day made a fuss over Gibran's origins, treated him, Waterfield says, like a "Middle Eastern princeling." Gibran looked the part. He was very handsome, and also reticent. A later mentor declared him a mystic, "a young prophet." (This was before he had published anything professionally.) And so he began to see himself that way.

Kamileh and Bhutros would not have failed to notice that Kahlil was spending all his time with people he did not introduce them to. They might also have worried about his exposure to Protestantism—they were Christians of the Maronite sect, allied with the Church of Rome—and, indeed, to Day, who was presumably homosexual. In any case, Gibran, at the age of fifteen, was packed off to a Maronite college in Beirut. In his three years there, he apparently decided that he might be a writer as well as a painter. He and a classmate founded a student literary magazine, and he was elected "college poet."

But in 1902 he returned to the South End, and to his family's troubles. Two weeks before he landed in Boston, Sultana died, of tuberculosis, at the age of fourteen. The following year, Bhutros died, also of TB (it was rife in the South End), and then Kamileh, of cancer. Waterfield says that there is no evidence that Gibran mourned any of them for long. It is hard to escape the thought that this ambitious young man was not inconvenienced by the loss of his slum-dwelling family. One member remained, however: his sister Marianna. She adored him, cooked his dinners, made his clothes, and supported the two of them on her earnings from the dressmaker's shop. Gibran still took no job; art was his job.

Soon, he had something to show. Day held an exhibition of Gibran's drawings in his studio in 1904. They were products of their time, or a slightly earlier time, that of the European Symbolist painters: Puvis de Chavannes, Eugène Carrière, Gustave Moreau. Often, in the foreground, one saw a sort of pileup of faceless humanity, while in the background there hovered a Greater Power—an angel, perhaps, or just a sort of milky miasma, suggestive of mystery and the soul.

Gibran began publishing his writings as well: collections of stories and poems, parables and aphorisms. He had been heavily exposed to Lebanon's political problems: the warring among religious sects, the sufferings of the poor at the hands of a corrupt clergy and the distant Turkish overlords. Anger over this, and also pity—whether for Lebanese peasants or, quite often, for himself—were the main themes of his early writings. They were published in Arabic, and they won him great admiration in the Arab American community. Not only was he standing up for his homeland; he was "making it" in America—and in art, not in dry goods.

He enjoyed this, but he wanted a larger audience, and soon he found the person who would make that possible. Mary Haskell, the headmistress of a girls' school in Boston, was a New Woman. She believed in long hikes, cold showers, and progressive politics. Her school disdained Latin and Greek; it taught anatomy and current events instead. Before Gibran became close to Haskell, in 1908, he had a history of befriending older women who could be useful to him. Haskell, too, was older, by nine years. (She was also taller. Gibran was five feet three, a source of grief to him all his life.) She was not rich, but by careful thrift—the school's cook, who also had some wealthy employers, sneaked dinners to her from their kitchens—she managed to put aside enough money to support a number of deserving causes: a Greek immigrant boy who needed boarding-school tuition, and another Greek boy, at Harvard. Then she met Gibran, who would be her most expensive project.

In the beginning, her major benefaction to him was simply financial—she gave him money, she paid his rent. In 1908, she sent him to Paris for a year, to study painting. Before he went abroad, they were "just friends," but once they were apart, the talk of friendship turned to letters of love, and when Gibran returned to Boston, they became engaged. It was apparently agreed, though, that they would not marry until he felt he had established himself, and somehow this moment never came. Finally, Haskell offered to be his mistress. He wasn't interested. In a painful passage in her diary, Haskell records how, one night, he said that she was looking thin. On the pretext of showing him that she was actually well fleshed, she took off her clothes and stood before him naked. He kissed one of her breasts, and that was all. She got dressed again. She knew that he had had affairs with other women, but he claimed that he was not "sexually minded," and furthermore that what she missed in their relationship was actually there. When they were apart, he said, they were together. They didn't need to have "intercourse"; their whole friendship was "a continued intercourse." More than sex or marriage, it seems, what Haskell wanted from Gibran was simply an acknowledgment that she was the woman in his life. As she told her diary, she wanted people to "know he loved me because it was the greatest honor I had and I wanted credit for it—wanted the fame of his loving me." But he would not introduce her to his friends. "Poor Mary!" Waterfield says. Amen to that.

Later, Gibran told journalists many lies about his childhood, and, according to the Gibrans' biography, he seems to have tried these out first on Haskell. He was of noble birth, he said. His father's family had a palace in Bsharri, where they kept tigers for pets. His mother's family was the richest in Lebanon. They owned immense properties, "whole towns." He, as a young aristocrat, had been educated at home, by English, French, and German tutors.

He was sure that a great destiny awaited him. Haskell believed this even more firmly than he, and in the beginning her adulation was probably as important to him as her money. "Oh Glorious Kahlil!!" she wrote in her diary. "Transcendent, timeless spirit!" When he read to her from an early book of his, she reported that "the invisible" gathered so thickly around her, "lights and sounds came from such far times and spaces, that from center to circumference I trembled with the excessive life-force"—a remarkable response, in view of the fact that the book was in Arabic, a language she did not then understand. She recorded the extraordinary experiences he told her he had had. For instance, he had intuited the theory of relativity before Einstein; he just hadn't written it down. Thousands of times, he said, he had been sucked up into the air as dew, and "risen into clouds, then fallen as rain. . . . I've been a rock too, but I'm more of an air person."

We don't know how much of this Haskell believed. Furthermore, however godlike she found him, she was a schoolmistress, and she tried to educate him. On the pretext of their having a nice literary evening together, she would get him to read to her from the classic authors, exactly as Fred Holland Day had done, and for the same reason—to improve his English. He profited from this, and of course resented it, as he resented the amount of money he had taken from her—by 1913, after five years of friendship, this came to $7,440, equal to almost $150,000 today—but he didn't tell her to stop writing the checks.

Soon after Gibran became "engaged" to Haskell, he told her that he was leaving town. Boston was a backwater. New York was where the action was. Clearly, he had another purpose as well: to get away from Haskell. He also needed to unload Marianna. If he was to become a major artist, how was he going to explain that he lived with this illiterate woman who followed him around the house with a dust rag? And so, in 1911, throwing off the two women who had supported him through his early period, Gibran moved to New York, and to his middle period. He found a studio apartment in an artists' housing complex at 51 West Tenth Street. Haskell paid the rent, of course.

After a few years in New York, during which he published two more books in Arabic, Gibran made a serious decision: he was going to begin writing in English. To do this, he needed Haskell's help, and she rushed to give it. When they were apart, he sent her his manuscripts, and she sent back corrections. When they were together—she visited him often (sleeping elsewhere)—he dictated his work to her. She wrote in her diary that if, during that process, "we come to a part that I question, we stop then and there." Who resolved the question? We don't know. She said that "he always gave every idea, and I simply found the phrases sometimes." But finding the phrases is a large part of writing. For Gibran's first English-language publication, a brief poem, Haskell sent him seven pages of proposed corrections. She probably made substantial changes in his later work as well. Proud of this responsible role in his life, she gave up hoping for more. In 1926, with no objections from Gibran, she married a rich relative. But at night, after her husband went to bed, she would work on Gibran's manuscripts. Until he died, she edited all his English-language books. With the third of these, *The Prophet*, he hit pay dirt.

What made *The Prophet* so fantastically successful? At the opening of the book, we are told that Almustafa, a holy man, has been living in exile, in a city called Orphalese, for twelve years. (When *The Prophet* was published, Gibran had been living in New York, in "exile" from Lebanon, for twelve years.) A ship is now coming to take him back to the island of his birth. Saddened by his departure, people gather around and ask him for his final words of wisdom—on love, on work, on joy and sorrow, and so forth. He obliges, and his lucubrations on these matters occupy most of the book. Almustafa's advice is not bad: love involves suffering; children should be given their independence. Who, these days, would say otherwise? More than the soundness of its advice, however, the mere fact that *The Prophet* was an advice book—or, more precisely, "inspirational literature"—probably ensured a substantial readership at the start. Gibran's closest counterpart today is the

Brazilian sage Paulo Coelho, and his books have sold nearly a hundred million copies.

Then there is the pleasing ambiguity of Almustafa's counsels. In the manner of horoscopes, the statements are so widely applicable ("your creativity," "your family problems") that almost anyone could think that they were addressed to him. At times, Almustafa's vagueness is such that you can't figure out what he means. If you look closely, though, you will see that much of the time he *is* saying something specific—namely, that everything is everything else. Freedom is slavery; waking is dreaming; belief is doubt; joy is pain; death is life. So, whatever you're doing, you needn't worry, because you're also doing the opposite. Such paradoxes, which Gibran had used for years to keep Haskell out of his bed, now became his favorite literary device. They appeal not only by their seeming correction of conventional wisdom but also by their hypnotic power, their negation of rational processes.

Also, the book sounds religious, which it is, in a way. Gibran was familiar with Buddhist and Muslim holy books, and above all with the Bible, in both its Arabic and its King James translations. (Those paradoxes of his come partly from the Sermon on the Mount.) In *The Prophet* he Osterized all these into a warm, smooth, interconfessional soup that was perfect for twentieth-century readers, many of whom longed for the comforts of religion but did not wish to pledge allegiance to any church, let alone to any deity who might have left a record of how he wanted them to behave. It is no surprise that when those two trends—antiauthoritarianism and a nostalgia for sanctity—came together and produced the 1960s, *The Prophet*'s sales climaxed. Nor is the spirit of the 1960s gone from our world. It survives in the New Age movement—of which Gibran was a midwife—and that market may be what Everyman's had in mind when it decided to issue the new collection.

Furthermore, *The Prophet* is comforting. Gibran told Haskell that the whole meaning of the book was "You are far far greater than you know—and All is well." To people in doubt or in trouble, that is good news. (Reportedly, the book is popular in prisons.) Finally, *The Prophet* is short—ninety-six pages in its original edition, with margins you could drive a truck through—a selling point not to be dismissed. And, since the text is in small, detachable sections, you can make it even shorter, by just dipping into it here and there, as some people do with the Bible. My guess is that plenty of its fans have not read it from cover to cover.

There is a better book by Gibran, *Jesus, the Son of Man*, which was published five years after *The Prophet*. This is his second-most-popular work, but way second. That, no doubt, is because it lacks the something-for-everyone quality of its predecessor. *Jesus* is about Jesus. Also, it is not a book of advice or consolation. It is a novel of sorts, a collection of seventy-nine statements by people remembering Christ. Some of the speakers are known to us—Pontius Pilate, Mary Magdalene—but others are inventions: a Lebanese shepherd, a Greek apothecary. They all speak as if they were being interviewed.

Though Gibran thought of himself as an admirer of all religions, he had an obsession with Jesus. He told Haskell that Jesus came to him in dreams. The two of them ate watercress together, and Jesus told him special things—for example, parables that didn't make it into the Gospels. On occasion, Gibran clearly saw himself *as* Jesus, and presumably it was this that inspired his unwise decision, in *Jesus, the Son of Man*, to rewrite long sections of the Bible, for example, the Lord's Prayer: "Our Father in earth and heaven, sacred is Thy name. Thy will be done with us, even as in space."

Much of the book transcends such follies, however. Gibran at one time had hoped to be a playwright, and *Jesus* shows a gift for characterization and "voice"—an insistence, for the moment, on one speaker's point of view—that saves the book from his habitual gassiness. Also, however much he imagined himself as Jesus, in this book alone he drops the oracular tone that is so oppressive in the rest of his work. A number of the speakers have complaints about Jesus. Judas is allowed to justify his crime: "I thought He had chosen me a captain of His chariots, and a chief man of His warriors." Judas's disgraced mother is given a dignified and moving speech: "I beg you to question me no further about my son. I loved him and I shall love him forevermore. If love were in the flesh I would burn it out with hot irons and be at peace. But it is in the soul, unreachable. And now I would speak no more. Go question another woman more honored than the mother of Judas. Go to the mother of Jesus." Hard words.

In contrast to *The Prophet*, which received few and tepid reviews, *Jesus, the Son of Man* was praised by critics, but these were mostly newspaper critics. While the literary journals paid some attention to Gibran early on, they eventually dropped him. This is no surprise. His leading traits—idealism, vagueness, sentimentality—were exactly what the young writers of the twenties were running away from. Consequently, he did not make the scene with Manhattan's better class of artists. He seldom turns up in literary memoirs of the period. Edmund Wilson, in his journal of the twenties, says that "Gibran the Persian" was at a dinner party that a friend of his attended. That's the only mention he gets.

But, if the artists of the time were throwing off idealism and sentiment, ordinary people were not. They wanted to hear about their souls, and Sinclair Lewis was not obliging them. Hence the popularity of *The Prophet* with the general public. After its publication, Gibran received bags of fan mail. He was also besieged by visitors, mostly female. Interestingly, in view of his hunger for fame, he did not enjoy these attentions. He took to spending months of the year in Boston, with Marianna, and though he was now making money, he didn't change his way of living, or even his apartment. He remained in his one-room studio to the end of his life. Apparently, its monastic simplicity pleased him. He called it the Hermitage and lit it with candles.

As his reclusiveness increased, his productivity decreased. After *Jesus, the Son of Man*, he was more or less played out. He produced two more books in English, but they were tired little things, and the reviewers said so. When Gibran was in Paris, he met Rodin, and he later claimed that the famous old sculptor had called him "the William Blake of the twentieth century." This tribute was probably of Gibran's manufacture, not Rodin's, but people at Knopf liked it, and so it was bannered on Gibran's publicity flyers. (Rodin couldn't protest; he was dead.) After *The Prophet*, the critics, already annoyed by that book's popularity, threw the phrase back in Gibran's face. "*Blake?*" they asked.

By his forties, Gibran was a sick man. He had long complained of a periodic illness, which he called the flu. Now he decided that the malady was not in his body but in his soul. There was a great book inside him, greater than *The Prophet*, but he couldn't get it out. He had another difficulty: alcoholism, a situation that might have developed soon after *The Prophet* was published, or while he was writing it. Robin Waterfield thinks that Gibran's basic problem might have been a feeling of hypocrisy, in that his life so contradicted his pose as a holy man. In his last years, he stayed closed up in his apartment, occasionally receiving a worthy visitor but mostly drinking arak, a Syrian liquor that Marianna sent to him, apparently by the gallon. By the spring of 1931, he was bedridden, and one morning the woman who brought him his breakfast decided that his condition was dangerous. Gibran was taken to St. Vincent's Hospital, where he died later that day. The cause of death was recorded as "cirrhosis of the liver with incipient tuberculosis." Waterfield reports that Gibran's admirers have greatly stressed the tuberculosis over the cirrhosis. "Nothing incipient kills people," he objects. His speculation seems to be that Gibran drank himself to death out of a sense of fraudulence and failure.

A black comedy ensued. After mobbed memorial services in New York and Boston, Marianna took the body to Lebanon for burial, as Gibran had wished. In Beirut, the casket was opened, and the minister of education pinned a medal on Gibran's chest. Then began the eighty-mile trek to Bsharri, with an honor guard of three hundred. The road was lined with townspeople, Jean and Kahlil Gibran report in their biography: "Young men in native dress brandished swords and dancing women scattered perfume and flowers before the hearse."

Gibran's will dictated that Marianna be given his money; Haskell his manuscripts and paintings; and the town of Bsharri all future American royalties on the books published during his lifetime. This last provision produced so many difficulties that it was cited in an American textbook on copyright law. Who, among the people in Bsharri, was going to decide how this money would be distributed? Gibran had said that it was to be spent on good causes. To evaluate them, an administrative committee, with members from each of the town's seven leading families, was set up, but this created further problems. "Families split apart in the clamor to win a committee position," *Time* reported. "Age-old feuds gained new fury, and at least two deaths resulted." Meanwhile, the funds were disappearing. The situation became such a scandal that in 1967 Knopf started withholding the royalties, which at that point amounted to $300,000 a year. Marianna eventually sued Bsharri to win control of the copyrights; the judgment went to the Bsharrians, though, in the process, their legacy was substantially reduced, because the fee that their Lebanese American lawyer had negotiated with them was an astonishing 25 percent of future royalties. The Bsharrians then sued the lawyer, and they lost.

In the end, the Lebanese government intervened and, reportedly, put Gibran's estate to rights. His coffin rests in a deconsecrated monastery—Mar Sarkis, in Bsharri—that he chose for that purpose. Robin Waterfield has visited it. He says that he found a crack in the cover of the casket and that, when he looked into the crack, he saw straight through to the back—in other words, that the body had disappeared. This seems a fitting, if sad, conclusion. As Gibran's mother said, "Hush. He's not here."

Agatha Christie

QUEEN OF CRIME

Agatha Christie

They are assembled—maybe eight or nine people—in a small place: a snowbound train, a girls' school, an English country house. Then—oh no! A body drops. Who did this? And why, and how? Among those gathered, or soon summoned, is a detective who says that no one should leave, please. He then begins questioning the people concerned, one by one. In the end, he collects all the interested parties and delivers the "revelation": he names the murderer and the motive and the method. Almost never does the culprit protest. Now and then he'll go off and commit suicide, but as a rule he confesses ("I'm glad I did it!") and exits quietly, under police escort. Anyone who has ever seen a Charlie Chan movie, or played Clue, or, indeed, read a detective story of the past half century will recognize this scenario, created by Agatha Christie, the so-called Queen of Crime, in the 1920s.

The detective story was invented by Edgar Allan Poe, though he wrote only four of them before he lost interest. Other writers picked up where he left off, but the first "career" practitioner of the genre who is still important to us today is Arthur Conan Doyle, whose Sherlock

Holmes series appeared from 1887 to 1927. By Christie's time, at least two conventions had been established. First was the detective's eccentricity. (Holmes, when he is not chasing a criminal, lies on his couch, felled by boredom and drugs, shooting bullets into the wall of his study.) A second rule was the absolutely central role of ratiocination. The detective, when he is working, shows almost no emotion. What he shows—and what constitutes the main pleasure of the stories—is inductive reasoning.

Christie, who began publishing detective fiction thirty-three years after Doyle, generally followed these rules, but she elaborated on them, creating the scenario described above—the small place, the interrogations, the revelation—and used it, fairly consistently, in sixty-six detective novels published between 1920 and 1976. According to a number of sources, her books, in the approximately forty-five languages they have been translated into, have sold more than two billion copies, making her the most widely read novelist in history. There is also a continuing output of books *about* Christie. In the past year, we got two more: *Duchess of Death: The Unauthorized Biography of Agatha Christie*, by Richard Hack, who has previously written lives of Howard Hughes and J. Edgar Hoover, among others; and *Agatha Christie's Secret Notebooks: Fifty Years of Mysteries in the Making*, by John Curran, a devout fan. With Christie, then, we are dealing not so much with a literary figure as with a broad cultural phenomenon, like Barbie or the Beatles.

Christie was born in 1890 and grew up in a large house in Torquay, a seaside resort in Devon. Her father, Frederick Miller, had a modest inheritance, and it sufficed. In her 1977 autobiography, published posthumously, Christie describes her father's day: "He left our house in Torquay every morning and went to his club. He returned, in a cab, for lunch, and in the afternoon went back to the club, played whist all afternoon, and returned to the house in time to dress for dinner." She adds, "He had no outstanding characteristics." Her mother, Clara, did have characteristics. She wrote poetry, and she was interested in the soul. During Agatha's youth, Clara went through Unitarianism, Theosophy, and Zoroastrianism. Agatha adored her, and spent hours poring over her jewelry and ribbons.

When Agatha was a child, she had no companions to speak of. Her sister and brother, Madge and Monty, were more than a decade older. She had no schoolmates, either, because, for the most part, she didn't go to school. (She taught herself, out of books.) She was paralyzingly shy; even as an adult, she wrote, she could hardly bring herself to enter a shop. Her social world consisted mainly of the family's three servants. She also communed, for long periods every day, with imaginary companions: kings, kittens, chickens. Enthusiastically morbid, she adored funerals, and often went to put flowers on the grave of her late canary, Kiki. "I had a very happy childhood," she wrote.

In one respect, it was not happy. When Agatha was five, her father was informed that, apparently as a result of mismanagement, there was almost no money left in his estate. He tried to find a job, but, Christie wrote, "like most of his contemporaries"—she means contemporaries of his class—he "was not trained for anything." He died young (fifty-five) and discouraged. Agatha and her mother soldiered on. Dinner was often rice pudding.

As a young woman, Agatha had no thought of a career. All she wanted was a husband, and when she was twenty-four, she got one: the dashing Archie Christie, a member of the Royal Flying Corps. They married just after the First World War began. Archie was then sent off to France; Agatha worked in the dispensary of a makeshift hospital in Torquay. After the war, the couple settled in a London suburb. They had one child, Rosalind. Archie went to work in the City; Agatha began writing novels. It eventually dawned on her that there was something a little wrong with Archie: he was unapologetically self-serving. She quotes him saying, "I hate it when people are ill or unhappy—it sort of spoils everything for me." As Agatha, in her thirties, lost her youthful looks and became increasingly successful as a writer, he spent more and more time on the golf course.

In 1926, Clara died, plunging her daughter into the kind of sorrow that Archie found so obstructive to his happiness. Agatha moved into her mother's house, to ready it for sale. Archie visited occasionally. One day, he arrived and told her that he had fallen in love with a woman they knew—Nancy Neele, a good golfer—and that he wanted a divorce. Thereafter, he lived mostly at his club. For months, when he was at home, Agatha tried to persuade him to change his mind. Then, one night, she got in her car and drove away. It took the police ten days to find her.

What happened, insofar as it could be pieced together later, is that she abandoned her car near a small town in Surrey, about an hour's drive from home, then took a train to Waterloo Station, in London. There she saw a poster advertising a spa-hotel, in Harrogate, in Yorkshire. That night, she traveled to Harrogate, where she checked into the hotel under the name of Theresa Neele. She spent her days reading and shopping and taking walks.

Meanwhile, a manhunt had been launched. The Surrey constabulary, enlarged to five hundred men, combed the downs and dragged the ponds in the area around her abandoned car. When the weekend came, they were joined by a mob of volunteers, plus bloodhounds. Ice cream vendors set up stands to serve the crowd. Most of the major newspapers carried a daily story on the matter. Christie's fellow guests at the hotel looked at the photos of her in the papers, but none of them made the connection. Indeed, she later recalled playing bridge with them and discussing the strange case of the missing novelist.

Eventually, a reward of £100 was offered. Christie liked to go to the hotel's Palm Court after dinner and listen to the band. After a while, the drummer and the saxophonist recognized her, and they went to the police. The police called Archie; he arrived and stationed himself in the hotel lobby. When Christie came downstairs, he identified her.

A number of theories have been advanced to explain this episode. One is that the disappearance was Agatha's bid to regain Archie's affections. According to another scenario, her flight was a way of boosting sales. Finally, it was hypothesized that she had experienced fugue, a form of amnesia in which a person travels to another place and may assume another identity. This last was the explanation that Christie and her family settled on. She claimed to have no recollection of what had happened, and her autobiography says not one word about the incident. If it was a ploy to get Archie back, it failed. (He persuaded Agatha to give him a divorce. He soon married Neele, and they are said to have been happy for the rest of their lives.) But if Agatha's flight was an effort to get the attention of the public, it was successful. She had produced six detective novels by that time, the last of which, *The Murder of Roger Ackroyd* (1926), was extremely popular. That success, in part, was why her disappearance received so much attention. Conversely, her disappearance, with its interesting link to detective fiction, made her a celebrity. Her earlier novels were reprinted, and they sold out.

For people of Christie's time and class, writing was not an uncommon pastime. Her sister, Madge, had a play produced in the West End long before Agatha did. But why detective stories? Again, this was not a remarkable choice. The period between the First and Second World Wars has been called the golden age of the detective story. Practically everyone who wanted to write had a go at it. Such books were adored by ordinary readers—according to Colin Watson, a historian of the genre, housewives brought them home in the shopping basket—but they were just as popular with educated people. W. H. Auden said that when he picked up a detective story, he couldn't put it down until he had finished it. In T. S. Eliot's *Family Reunion*, the mystery is solved by a character named Agatha.

The intellectuals didn't just read detective stories. They wrote them: G. K. Chesterton; Cecil Day-Lewis; Ronald Knox, the Roman Catholic chaplain of Oxford; S. S. Van Dine, a distinguished Nietzsche scholar. Because the form was so popular, almost any detective novel stood a good chance of getting a contract. That fact was no doubt in Christie's mind as she went to her desk; Archie's salary was small. At the start, she was a clumsy writer. But she was able to offer her readers what they wanted, a whodunit, also called a "puzzle mystery"—a story that is a contest between the author and the reader as to whether the reader can guess who the culprit is before the end of the book.

Though Christie's novels sometimes have colorful settings—Egypt, Mesopotamia—most of them are set in plain old England. The corpse may be discovered in its time-honored location, the library, or it may be stuffed into the cupboard under the stairs, with the tennis rackets. As for the weapon, golden-age mystery writers exercised great ingenuity over this. In the words of Christie's colleague Dorothy Sayers, victims were brought down by "licking poisoned stamps; shaving-brushes inoculated with dread diseases; . . . poisoned mattresses; knives dropped through the ceiling; stabbing with a sharp icicle; electrocution by telephone." Christie was less fanciful. Now and then, the victim is shot or stabbed, and poor Agnes, the one stored with the tennis rackets, does have a skewer driven through her brain, but Christie favored a clean conking on the head or—her overwhelming preference—poison. That choice was surely a product of her war work in the dispensary, with its many shelves of potentially lethal drugs. But poison probably appealed to her also because it did not involve assault. Christie disliked violence. When, in her novels, someone starts to look dangerous, her detective does not pull a gun. He/she doesn't have a gun. Bystanders may wrestle the malefactor to the ground. In one case, the detective squirts soapy water into the murderer's face. It works.

The murder that sets the plot in motion is rarely shocking. For one thing, we almost never see it happen. Furthermore, the victim is ordinarily someone with whom we do not sympathize, even when we feel we should. Christie did not mind bumping off a child or two. One is driven off a cliff; one is drowned while bobbing for apples. In *Murder Is Easy* (1939), little Tommy Pierce, the town sociopath—he tortures animals—is among the victims. "I shall never forget Tommy's face when I pushed him off the window sill that day," says the tenderhearted homicidal maniac who dispatched him. Much more often, however, the victim is a rich, nasty old person who enjoys taunting his prospective heirs with the accusation that they wish him dead so that they can collect their inheritances. He's usually right. Rather boringly, the most common motive for homicide in Christie is money.

This rule—that Christie's murders do not touch the heart—admits of one curious exception: the murder that the culprit commits, after the main murder, in order to get rid of someone who knows too much. Here the victim is often a nice or in any case blameless person, and we do witness the crime, or at least its prelude. In *A Murder Is Announced* (1950), Miss Murgatroyd, who knows that Letty Blacklock wasn't in the dining room when the gun went off, is taking the washing off the line when she hears someone approaching. She turns, and smiles in welcome, obviously to a neighbor. It has started to rain. "Here's your scarf," the visitor says. "Shall I put it round your neck?" Oh no.

Christie created two famous detectives: Hercule Poirot and Jane Marple. Poirot, formerly a member of the Belgian police force, is retired, but he is willing, occasionally, to interest himself in a case. Poirot's most obvious characteristic is his dandyism. He dyes his hair; he smokes thin black Russian cigarettes, often regarded with alarm by those to whom he offers them; he wears pointy patent-leather shoes ill-suited to walking the grounds of the country houses where he must often do his sleuthing. He deplores the English preference for fresh air, thin women, and tea. Poirot says that in interrogations he always exaggerates his foreignness. The person being questioned then takes him less seriously, and in consequence tells him more. His Franglais is a treat. "I speak the English very well," he says proudly.

Christie's other detective, Miss Marple, is the opposite of Poirot. She comes from a sleepy village, St. Mary Mead, and she seems a "sweetly bewildered old lady." She has china-blue eyes; she knits constantly; nobody thinks anything of her. They should, though, because she is a steely-minded detective. When she is on a case, she says, she makes it a rule to believe the worst of everyone—in her words, she has a mind "like a sink"—and she reports with regret that experience has confirmed her in this point of view.

Miss Marple presents the inconvenience that since she is not a professional detective, she cannot interrogate. But, by seeming a dotty old lady, she—like Poirot, with his pointy shoes—tends to be discounted and therefore can get people to say more than they should. Her method is to murmur platitudes. In *A Caribbean Mystery* (1964), we find her at a beach resort, with nothing to do, no homicide in sight. Then she gets the news that Major Palgrave, the old man who has been boring her with recollections of his service in Kenya, died in the night. Hmm! She goes into action. Here she is, having a little chat with Miss Prescott about Mr. Dyson, a fellow guest whom she doesn't like the look of. Miss Prescott speaks:

> "It seems there was some scandal when his first wife was still alive! Apparently this woman, Lucky—such a name!—who I think was a cousin of his first wife, came out here and joined them. . . . And people talked a lot because they got on so well together—if you know what I mean."
>
> "People do notice things so much, don't they?" said Miss Marple.
>
> "And then of course, when his wife died rather suddenly—"
>
> "She died here, on this island?"
>
> "No. No, I think they were in Martinique or Tobago at the time."
>
> "I see."
>
> "But I gathered from some other people who were there at the

time, and who came on here and talked about things, that the doctor wasn't very satisfied."

"Indeed," said Miss Marple with interest.

"It was only gossip, of course, but—well, Mr. Dyson certainly married again very quickly." She lowered her voice again. "Only a month, I believe."

"Only a month," said Miss Marple.

How lovely: the accumulation, the rhythm.

A Christie story goes more or less as follows. By means of interrogation—or, in Miss Marple's case, snooping (she does not eschew field glasses)—the investigator determines two things for each suspect. First, did he have a motive? Was he, for example, the victim's son, and deeply in debt? The second question is whether the person had an opportunity to commit the crime. Where was the impecunious son at the time of the murder?

The answers are rarely definitive. Sometimes, people with motives nevertheless have firm alibis. Conversely, innocent-seeming people may have utterly flimsy alibis. In *Hercule Poirot's Christmas* (1938), when a young man says that he was in the ballroom, by himself, playing records, while the family patriarch was upstairs having his throat cut, Poirot takes this as an indicator of innocence rather than of guilt. It is, he says, "the alibi of a man who did not know that he would be called upon for such a thing." Eventually, this man does come under suspicion, but soon the finger points to someone else instead. This mystification game is a standard device of suspense literature, but nobody did it quite like Christie.

She tries to help the reader, or she pretends to. Often, the detective has a confidant, to whom, as with Holmes and Watson, he or she will summarize the findings so far. Detectives who have no one to tell things to will often make a list (which Christie prints) of the evidence for and against each suspect. By such devices, Christie keeps the readers thinking that they will be able to solve the mystery.

Then she begins confusing them further. A classic trick is the red herring. When Violet faints at the mention of Jim's name, or when Pilar throws her passport out the window, experienced readers know that they should ignore this. It is too showy. But when Poirot notices that, since Roger Ackroyd's death, a chair has been moved in his study—that is, when the occurrence is trivial but nonetheless mentioned—this is potentially a real clue. Or it may be a red herring, masquerading, by its modesty, as a real clue.

A related subterfuge is the "double bluff." Here, Christie gives us, near the beginning of the book, an obvious culprit. In *The Murder at the Vicarage* (1930), the town vicar arrives home one evening and sees Lawrence Redding, a local painter, running out of the vicarage looking pale and shaken. The vicar then enters his house, goes to his study, and finds the town's widely hated magistrate, Colonel Protheroe, slumped over the desk with a bullet in his head. Christie seems to be telling us that Redding is the culprit. But we know her tricks by now, so we say to ourselves that Redding is too obvious—and too obvious too early in the book—and so we cross him off our list. Soon, it seems, we are justified. Redding goes to the police and confesses to the crime. Then Anne Protheroe, the colonel's wife, confesses, saying that Redding, her lover, was only trying to shield her. But then the suspicion shifts again, and again—until it comes full circle. The murderers, it turns out, were indeed Redding and Anne. Of course, the double bluff may be a triple bluff. In guessing that Christie is fooling us, we can be fooled, as with the red herring.

But, in truth, the guessing that we are asked to do is almost fruitless, because the solution to the mystery typically involves a fantastic amount of background material that we're not privy to until the end of the book, when the detective shares it with us. Christie's novels crawl with impostors. Letty is not really Letty; she's Lotty, the sister of Letty. And Hattie isn't Hattie. She's a piece of trash from Trieste, who, with her husband, Sir George, killed Hattie (who was married to him) and assumed her identity. The investigator digs up this material but doesn't tell anyone until the end.

In response to protests that the resulting denouements were unguessable, and therefore "unfair," Christie replied that the reader should have been able to figure them out. The culprit, she said, was always the most obvious person; he just didn't seem so. That is a brazen falsehood. In most of Christie's books, the killer turns out to be a most unlikely person. In one, the guilty party is a dead man; in another, a child. In yet another, amazingly, it is Poirot. In one virtuoso performance, all twelve suspects, together, committed the crime. This is not to speak of a more common problem: killers who are likable people and whom, therefore, we don't suspect. I read all sixty-six of Christie's detective novels, and I have guessed exactly two of the culprits. I'll bet that this is a fairly typical record.

How did Christie come up with these ingenious plots? In John Curran's recently published *Agatha Christie's Secret Notebooks*, the notebooks in question are school exercise books in which Christie worked out her puzzles. In many of her notebooks, some pages had already been used. In one, her daughter had done her penmanship practice; in another, the family had recorded their bridge scores. But Christie was a thrifty woman, and she used the remaining blank pages to devise her plots. She made lists of possible victims, culprits, and MOs. Then she picked the combinations that pleased her. Curran thinks that this shows the fertility of her imagination; I think it shows her willingness to work by formula, and thereby to forgo depth in favor of the puzzle. If she had given her characters any psychological definition, we could have solved the mystery. But as long as they are kept suspended, opaque—as they must be, in order for the book to be a puzzle—any one of them could be the culprit.

This practice exposed her to the contempt of some critics. Edmund

Wilson wrote of detective stories, "I finally got to feel that I had to unpack large crates by swallowing the excelsior in order to find at the bottom a few bent and rusty nails." The same point is actually made by Christie, via Mrs. Ariadne Oliver, a recurrent character who is a detective-story writer. "When it all comes out," Mrs. Oliver says, the killer "seems, somehow, so inadequate. A kind of anticlimax." If a character isn't interesting, who cares if he killed Colonel Protheroe?

But the readers did care. They wanted the pleasure of a puzzle. And usually Christie gave them a comedy as well. When characters are informed of a murder, they tend to say things like "Very unpleasant" or "Most distressing for you, Elspeth." That may sound like standard post-Wildean wit, but Christie can work it up into lovely scenes. In *4.50 from Paddington* (1957), a decomposing corpse has been found in the barn of a great estate. The family's grandson, Alexander, is home from school on vacation, with a friend. The two boys, thrilled by the news, come tearing up to the barn on their bicycles in the hope of seeing the body. The policeman at the door says no. Alexander pleads:

> "Oh sir, please, sir. You never know. We might know who she was. Oh please, sir, do be a sport. It's not fair. Here's a murder, right in our own barn. It's the sort of chance that might never happen again. Do be a sport, sir." . . .
>
> "Take 'em in, Sanders," said Inspector Bacon to the constable who was standing by the barn door. "One's only young once!"

The murderers, too, are funny. One of them worries that he may botch the job of eliminating his chosen victim, so he kills someone else first—the town rector!—as a practice run.

A year after Christie's divorce from Archie, she went on a trip to the Middle East and visited the famous dig at Ur, in Iraq. There she met an archaeologist, Max Mallowan, whom, soon afterward, she married.

She was thirty-nine. Mallowan was fourteen years younger, but she saw no impediment. He was an intelligent and easygoing man, and it was an affectionate marriage. For years, Christie went with him on digs in Iraq and Syria, countries that she came to love. At most of these outposts, a writing room was erected for her. She was also given responsible jobs to do, removing dirt from the relics (she used facial cleanser) and photographing them. At night, the whole team dressed for dinner, and the cooks produced nice things, like walnut soufflés.

Max and Agatha made this yearly migration until 1960. In his later years, Max held a chair at the University of London; then he was elected a fellow at All Souls, Oxford. Christie, of course, grew old sooner than he. In her memoir she depicts herself as "thirteen stone"—182 pounds—"of solid flesh and what could only be described as 'a kind face.'"

Some people say that Christie's shining period was her middle years. I find that she wrote her best books, in alternation with her worst books, until near the end. She was not a great writer, and some of her admirers, including Janet Morgan—in the *authorized* biography—say that she wasn't even a particularly good writer. I disagree. She could produce a bad book, and when she did, she usually knew it. Halfway through *Death Comes as the End* (1944), she wrote to Max that she was "despondent about it." (This is indeed her worst detective novel.) But, from the beginning, she was perfectly fitted to her genre. Not only were her plots tight, but she wrote excellent, natural dialogue. As the years passed, she developed a good feel for detail. In one book, the bishop of Westchester, meeting Miss Marple in a hotel lobby, has a sudden memory of his childhood, in a Hampshire vicarage. He remembers himself calling out, "Be a crocodile now, Aunty Janie. Be a crocodile and eat me." The vision flashes, then vanishes.

When Christie was in her mid-forties, however, she began to tire of writing. For a long time, she had been averaging at least one novel a year. She felt like a "sausage machine," she said. She now described Poirot as an "ego-centric creep." Like Arthur Conan Doyle with Sherlock Holmes, she tried to eliminate him, but the fans, and hence the publishers, protested. She also lost her taste for sin, perhaps because of the Second World War, next to which her little murders might have seemed to her frivolous. Wickedness, she says in a novel of 1961, has "no black and evil splendour."

As she lost interest in fiction, she turned to drama—and then to film and television—for which she adapted her novels and stories. But much of the time, in her late years, she didn't want to do any writing at all. She drafted her books, Janet Morgan writes, "in interludes between other occupations—gardening, cooking, outings, helping Max—and she would willingly abandon a chapter for a walk." You can tell. The characters get thinner; the pace slackens; some of the plots are preposterous. (In one, a house labors under a Gypsy curse.) Eventually, delirium set in. She died in 1976, at eighty-five.

In her last years, ironically, she became more and more popular. Her books, even in hardcover, sold between forty and fifty thousand copies in their first few weeks of publication. She received the CBE in 1971. The Nicaraguan government put Poirot's face on a postage stamp.

For today's readers, one pleasure of Christie's books is her portrait of the times, the period between the two world wars, and, above all, the changes that took place after the second war. Her people are upper-middle class or, sometimes, upper class. They gaze with astonishment at housing developments and supermarkets. They complain about how heavily they are taxed and how they can no longer afford to maintain the grand houses they once saw as their birthright. Eventually, they sell these huge piles to the nouveaux riches. (Christie's own home in Devon, a lovely Georgian house on the river Dart, was turned over to the National Trust in 2000.) In a wonderful scene, a visitor to the apartment of an old major sees large rectangles of high polish on the parquet. That is where the Oriental rugs were that the major has just been forced to sell.

Social inequality seems to have meant nothing to Christie, or to most other golden-age detective novelists. Julían Symons, in his *Bloody Murder*, an erudite and witty history of the detective story, sums it up: "The social order in these stories was as fixed . . . as that of the Incas." On the other hand, if we consider Christie within the context of her time and social class, she was a proto-feminist. Miss Marple is far from the only plucky female investigator in her novels. And though Poirot is allowed to make condescending remarks about women ("Women are never kind"), such comments, like his pointy shoes, are part of her satire of his silly, Frenchy ways. Furthermore, his aspersions are as specks compared with Christie's portrayal of the difficulty of being a woman. "I always had brains, even as a girl," one of her old ladies says. "But they wouldn't let me do anything." (She is the one who pushed Tommy Pierce out of the window.) Another woman, accused of being a gold digger, answers, "The world is very cruel to women. They must do what they can for themselves—while they are young. When they are old and ugly no one will help them."

Racism, antisemitism, and xenophobia turn up constantly in Christie's books. In one, a hostess serves a special dessert called Nigger in His Shirt (chocolate pudding covered with whipped cream). We also get dagos, wogs, and Eye-ties. Most frequently commented on are the Jews. In an early novel, *The Secret of Chimneys* (1925), Herman Isaacstein, who is, of course, a financier with a big nose, is invited to a political meeting at a country estate. When the host, Lord Caterham, is told who Isaacstein is, he says, "Curious names these people have." Caterham starts calling him Nosystein. The others take this up and shorten it to Nosy.

The treatment, then, is intended as comic. It is part of Christie's satire, from book to book, of her countrymen: their obsession with their gardens and their dogs; their stiff upper lips; their cucumber sandwiches; their inimitable village names (Much Deeping, Chipping Somerton). After the Second World War, some readers, especially Americans, found themselves unamused by her characters' views on ethnic difference. Christie's publishers received letters, including one from the Anti-Defamation League. Her agent probably figured that such letters would seem ridiculous to her. In any case, he didn't forward them to her. He simply gave Dodd, Mead, her American publishers, permission to delete any potentially offensive references to Jews or Catholics in her novels.

Some people have come up with subtle explanations for Christie's popularity and for the general enthusiasm for the detective novel in her time. Auden thought that the fundamental appeal was religious. At least in Protestant countries, he wrote, the solution of the crime vicariously relieves our guilt, restores us to innocence. Others have said that the solace is political. The interwar years were marked by terrible political upheaval. The detective story might have reassured people that disruptive forces lay not in the social order but just in one bad person, who could be removed. According to John G. Cawelti in *Adventure, Mystery, and Romance*, a probing history of the detective story, the genre is still doing that duty. Another proposal is that the loss and the recovery are literary—that readers from the twenties onward, assaulted by modernism, were grateful to find in detective literature sentences with subjects and predicates, and stories with a beginning, a middle, and an end. Borges said that after you read a detective novel, other fictions seem to you shapeless. At bottom, all these arguments are the same: the appeal of the detective story is the restoration of order.

Miss Marple doesn't quite agree. Or, in her view, order is restored only until the next time. She says that since the Second World War you don't know who your neighbors are, but she doesn't really believe that there's a cause of modern unease. "You could blame the war (both the wars)," she thinks, "or the younger generation, or women going out to work, or the atom bomb, or just the Government—but what one really meant was the simple fact that one was growing old." As for crime, she seems to think that it's been around forever and that small, stable communities offer no protection. "One does see so much evil in a village," she says. She enjoys describing the poisonings, clubbings, stickups, and so on that have occurred in St. Mary Mead. This is comical, and the comedy is there, as the theorists have claimed, to tame evil. But always, in Christie, there is a melancholy note, a skepticism. In *The Body in the Library* (1942), the body belongs to Ruby, a dance instructor in a hotel. She has been strangled with the satin waistband of her party dress. "She may, of course, have had some remarkable qualities," a police commissioner says of the girl. "Probably not," Miss Marple answers.

The New Yorker, 2010

J. R. Ackerley with Queenie, late 1950s or early 1960s

A DOG'S LIFE

J. R. Ackerley

J. R. Ackerley (1896–1967) was known, in his time, mainly as the literary editor of *The Listener*, the ambitious weekly review of culture published by the BBC. Many people regarded him as the best editor in London. He was able to persuade E. M. Forster, Clive Bell, John Maynard Keynes, Leonard and Virginia Woolf, Cecil Day-Lewis, Louis MacNeice, Christopher Isherwood, and W. H. Auden, among other front-rank writers, to contribute to *The Listener*, in return for little pay, not much space, and no byline. Today, however, Ackerley is remembered primarily as a memoirist and a bombardier. He produced four books: three memoirs—*Hindoo Holiday* (1932), *My Dog Tulip* (1956), *My Father and Myself* (1968)—and a novel, *We Think the World of You* (1960), all of which are now in print from New York Review Books. In them, he wrote candidly and profoundly about homosexuality, a sensitive topic at the time. (In England, until 1967, one could still be sentenced to life in prison for homosexual acts. Forster, who was Ackerley's best friend, refused to write an introduction for his first book.) But eventually homosexuality was overshadowed in Ackerley's work by another subject: his passion for his dog, a German shepherd named Queenie. He describes her:

> Her ears are tall and pointed, like the ears of Anubis. How she manages to hold them constantly erect, as though starched, I do not know, for with their fine covering of mouse-gray fur they are soft and flimsy; when she stands with her back to the sun it shines through the delicate tissue, so that they glow shell-pink as though incandescent. Her face also is long and pointed, basically stone-gray, but the snout and lower jaw are jet black. Jet, too, are the rims of her amber eyes, as though heavily mascara'd, and the tiny mobile eyebrow tufts that are set like accents above them.

This passage, with its echoes of Renaissance poetry, might be considered comical. With the erect pink ears, it might also seem faintly obscene. In a 1958 essay on *Lolita*, Lionel Trilling argued that Nabokov chose a subject as shocking as pedophilia for want of any more potent image of forbidden love. Ackerley might have chosen the love of a dog—like Humbert Humbert's emotion, a true passion—for the same reason, to confront his readers with the image of a wild love, a crazy love, something that could make them truly uncomfortable. (Incest has been used for that purpose in our time, I think. See Arundhati Roy's *God of Small Things*.) Homosexuality, however taboo, was not extraordinary in Ackerley's time, whereas, even in England, a romantic passion for a dog would have been regarded as odd.

Joe Randolph Ackerley was the child of Netta (Janetta), who had been an actress, and Roger, who, born into the working class, had made a fortune as a fruit importer. (He was known locally as "the banana king.") Roger was a good-natured libertine. He loved women—he and his friends, Ackerley says, socialized by telling off-color jokes—and he liked food and drink almost as much. When told by his doctor that if he gave up claret he could add ten years to his life, he replied, "I'd sooner have the claret." He died of cerebral syphilis, at sixty-six. To Ackerley, he was an image of unachievable virility and spiritual waste.

Ackerley was remarkably handsome. At school, the other boys begged to get into his bed. He says he fought them all off, with a few exceptions—for example, a certain Jude, who undid the seams of his pants pockets and invited the occupants of neighboring seats to feel him up during class. When the First World War began, Ackerley enlisted in the army, and in France in 1917 he was wounded and captured by the Germans. Still, he had an easy time of it compared with others, notably his older brother, who had his head blown off. Probably during the war, but unquestionably afterward, when he was at Cambridge, Ackerley realized that he was homosexual. He says that he was proud of it, identifying himself with the ancient Greeks—Socrates and so on. Soon, he began his quest for what he called the Ideal Friend. This man, he wrote, should be "normal," that is, heterosexual, or, in any case, not effeminate. (Ackerley loathed pansies, as he called them.) "He should be physically attractive to me and younger than myself—the younger the better, as closer to innocence; finally he should be on the small side, lusty, circumcised, physically healthy and clean." Ackerley didn't like smells. (One man, to accommodate him, kept his boots on in bed.) During sex, Ackerley always remained fully clothed and insisted that the other man be naked.

By the standards of the day, he was fantastically promiscuous. In the words of his superb biographer, Peter Parker, he spent a good deal of his leisure time "lurking in bars and bushes" in London's pickup centers. He liked working-class men best: policemen, waiters, soldiers. He was also fond of petty criminals. He congratulated himself on the fact that in the circles he frequented, he made no secret of his homosexuality. Lytton Strachey, whom he knew only slightly, closed a letter to him as follows:

With best regards to
The Army

The Navy
and The Police Force.

Ackerley condescended mightily to these young men. After all, he
paid for their services. ("A pound was the recognized tariff for the Foot
Guards then," he wrote. "The Horse Guards cost rather more.") Furthermore, he had the class consciousness of his time and place. He and
his friends passed the boys around and compared notes. At one party, a
guardsman was given to a guest as a gift. "It would be the blackest in-
gratitude to disparage the Guards," Ackerley wrote. "These brave soldiers
are of incalculable use to a great many lonely bachelors in London." And
yet, mysteriously, he often became madly infatuated with someone he
had picked up. P. N. Furbank, in his introduction to the NYRB edition
of *We Think the World of You*, recalls that "every three weeks or so, he
would have found the love of his life," and though the beloved typically
had little material for conversation with a Cambridge-educated literary
man, Ackerley dreamed of a glorious future with him. In *We Think the
World of You*, the hero, Frank, a thinly disguised version of Ackerley,
begs his former boyfriend, Johnny, to come back to him. Remember
how happy we were, he says to Johnny. Couldn't it be that way again?
Sure, says Johnny (who often borrows money from Frank). By this time,
Johnny is married, with three children. He is also in prison, for burglary.

After finishing at Cambridge, Ackerley tried to make a career as
a writer. His indulgent father gave him a large allowance and boasted
of every small success he had. The successes were small indeed: a few
poems, published here and there. He received some encouragement.
E. M. Forster—seventeen years older, and a famous man—wrote to
him out of the blue to praise a poem of his. (That's how their friendship
began.) But not many people noticed him. Forster, who had experienced a literary rebirth in India, heard that the maharaja of Chhatar-
pur, in central India, was looking for a secretary, and he urged Ackerley
to take the job. Ackerley did, in 1923, and stayed there for half a year.
The maharaja kept a pack of good-looking boys who danced naked for

him and also performed, often for his eyes alone, plays that he wrote about the Hindu gods. Ackerley had only a chaste good time—kisses, endearments—with the prince's harem, but he wrote a diary that became the basis for *Hindoo Holiday.*

Back in England, he had a success with a play, *The Prisoners of War* (1925), about a love between two soldiers. This drama seemed poignant and brave to many homosexual men. (In Parker's book, as in many other biographies of early twentieth-century English writers, it seems that almost every man in literary London at the time was homosexual.) Nor did you have to be a partisan to like this play. The war was of recent memory. Nevertheless, Ackerley soon decided that he had no real talent for writing, and in 1928 he took a job, or, as he later put it, "imprisoned" himself, at the BBC. He stayed there for three decades. With his excellent taste and his curiosity and boldness—he liked strong-minded writers, fresh-looking art—he unquestionably raised the level of English culture in his period. At the same time, the energies he spent on that were subtracted from his own work as an artist. He did go on writing, but sporadically. In his thirty years at the BBC, he published only two books, *Hindoo Holiday* and *My Dog Tulip.* This was not just because he came home tired from the office. He was a relentless self-editor, and therefore a slow writer.

Most important, however, was his acquisition, in 1946, of a beautiful German shepherd, Queenie, his first (and last) dog. Queenie became the love of his life and the brilliant, bounding subject of most of the rest of his work. She didn't give him much time to write, however. He baked her dog biscuits. He stood in line to buy her horse meat. Most days, he got home by four in the afternoon so that he could take her for a *three*-hour walk.

In almost all Ackerley's work, one question is foremost: How much can we say? How far can we go in telling the truth about our lives? Throughout his years at the BBC, he had to wrestle with conservatism—stiffly worded memos in which his superiors wondered why he was so interested in incomprehensible modernist poetry and left-wing commentators. (He was a self-declared Socialist.) The publishers of his books forced him again and again to make changes, lest they be sued. It cannot be claimed that he eventually chose a dog as his primary subject in order to slip under the wire of censorship. Nevertheless, the fact that Queenie was not human did allow him to say things that could not otherwise be said. When, in *My Dog Tulip*, Tulip (Queenie) goes into heat, we hear about the hordes of male dogs stampeding across the park to take advantage of her availability. None of them achieved their goal. Still, Ackerley writes, these were not wasted encounters, for Tulip "clearly enjoyed being pleasured by their little warm tongues." Canine cunnilingus! In 1956, English readers probably did not expect to be hearing about this. Most of Ackerley's books, though popular with the critics, had poor to mediocre sales when they were published. They became better known, in the United States as well as in Britain, after his death. Amazingly, *My Dog Tulip* was a Book of the Month Club selection.

Other descriptions of Tulip's biological processes seem touching in their fidelity to nature's facts. Ackerley liked to see her defecate, he said: "She lowers herself carefully and gradually to a tripodal attitude with her hind legs splayed and her heels as far apart as she can get them so as not to soil her fur or her feet. Her long tail, usually carried aloft in a curve, stretches rigidly out, parallel with the ground; her ears lie back, her head cranes forward, and a mild, meditative look settles on her face." Other passages are undisguisedly funny. When, during Tulip's heats, the hopeful males in the park fail to mount her (German shepherds are tall), they do not give up easily. After her forays on the common, she returns to Ackerley "with sundry dogs clinging to her bottom"—a marvelous image. (This persistent undernote of comedy is what was missing from the 2009 animated film of *My Dog Tulip*. The movie was charming, but too charming.) Comic or shocking, Ackerley's unashamed descriptions of Queenie's physical functions are part of his answer to the question about how much can be told. A lot more than we tell, he is saying.

Was Queenie a substitute for a human love? Yes, Ackerley says, or she was at the start. She gave him everything that his lovers wouldn't, above all constancy, "a background," he wrote to a friend, "of secure, unalterable devotion, which my nature needed." As he worked at his desk at night, she sat in his easy chair and gazed at him unceasingly. By his account, the fifteen years he spent with her were the happiest of his life, and his relationship with her made him ashamed of his earlier erotic history, of which he wrote, in his diary,

> Twenty-five years of emotional fidget, when I could scarcely ever conclude or even start a journey, but must always be impulsively leaping off the bus as it went, or leaving the train at some intermediate station, or getting on to a train that was going heavens knows where, to follow, to get a closer look at, to make myself known to, that sailor, that soldier, that young workman, whom I had seen pass in the street below.

That's not to say that he swore off sex. When, rarely, he was on vacation outside England, he would pick up someone now and then, but he doesn't seem to have cared much anymore.

Something that is hard to explain is why Ackerley fell in love with a female dog. He was decidedly misogynist, and yet he not only chose a girl; he stressed her girlishness. In his books, he speaks of Queenie's coquetry, and of her jealousy, which he regards as a female characteristic. He describes her sexual anatomy in embarrassing detail. P. N. Furbank offers the theory that she was a needed substitute, in disguised, furry form, for what Ackerley really wanted: a woman. I don't believe that. I think it's more likely that what he wanted was just a piece of the feckless, date-canceling boyfriend, Freddie Doyle (the incarcerated Johnny of *We Think the World of You*), who was Queenie's owner when Ackerley first set eyes on her. She was a female, and so Ackerley, in buying her from Freddie, acquired a female. Only when he learned to love her did he love her femininity.

All this made some readers wonder whether Ackerley had sex with Queenie. We should not be shy about bringing up this matter. He wasn't. In *My Father and Myself*, he recalls that a friend of his asked him the question and that he was glad to be able to answer without a fuss. When Queenie was in heat, he said, he pressed his hand "against the hot swollen vulva she was always pushing at me at these times, taking her liquids into my palm." That was all. According to Peter Parker, another friend is reported to have asked Ackerley the same question, and got a slightly fuller answer. "A little finger-work," Ackerley said.

When Ackerley wrote *My Father and Myself*, which he worked on for the last thirty-four years of his life, he reached a new level of candor, and not about a dog but about human beings, a more difficult matter. The book's very subject was candor, or the lack of it, between his father and himself. Ackerley, by his own account, was disturbed that he never told his father that he was homosexual. He tried, he says, but his father cut him off: "It's all right, old boy. I prefer not to know. So long as you enjoyed yourself, that's the main thing." Roger no more wanted to tell than to hear. In his office, after he died, Ackerley found a letter addressed to him. In it, Roger revealed that for close to two decades he had had a second family: Muriel, a former barmaid, and their three children. This was just the beginning of the revelations. Soon, Ackerley found evidence that his father, who had been a member of the Guards in his youth, was a special friend of a certain extravagantly homosexual Count de Gallatin, and received financial favors from him. Had the skirt-chasing Roger therefore been one of the guards who Ackerley said were of "incalculable use to a great many lonely bachelors"? Ackerley scanned newspaper files; he interviewed people who had known his father or the count. He never found proof, but he makes a strong cir-cumstantial case. On this subject, too, Ackerley grieves over the lack of confidentiality between the two of them: "He was no real use to me nor I to him." This and the revelation of the second family are the only occasions of professed candor in Ackerley's work where I find him uncandid. What is there to be shocked about in the fact that he and his father didn't confide in each other about their sex lives? I believe that Ackerley's purpose in writing a book about his and his father's failure to share their secrets was to show that his father, like him, had had secrets.

Nevertheless, the telling of these things gives Ackerley the occasion to engage in other, true acts of honesty. As a counterpoint to what he guesses was his father's experience, he puts in a whole chapter on his own "sexual psychology," in the course of which he offers a great deal of concrete information about what he and his partners did in bed— "kisses, caresses, manipulations, intercrural massage"—and about what they didn't do, for example, fellatio, which he found disgusting. He also attaches an appendix on premature ejaculation, which seems, pretty much, to have ruined his sex life. Again, we get the details, the stains. The interest of such material is not just prurient (though, God knows, it is that). Moral questions are involved. How do you survive the humiliation of always having your body go against your will? Do you have to succeed at sex in order to feel that you have succeeded in life? And how do you tell your partner, who at that moment is innocently taking off his clothes, that the act for which he is preparing has already been completed? Eventually, the premature ejaculation led to impotence, because of the attendant worry: "Why had I taken him to the pub first? it was getting late, I must hurry. . . . Why had I not taken him to the pub first? he was bored, I must hurry. . . . Then the slow collapse, and nothing that he could do, or I could do in the way of furious masturbation, could retrieve the wretched failure."

The real fruit of Ackerley's candor, however, is the power it lent his writing: the richness of characterization, the tartness of metaphor, the protection that honesty gives against sentimentality, or just a stupid simplicity. His portrait of his mother, whom he loved, is a study in wit and indirection. Netta was a sweet, kind, ineffectual, hypochondriacal, garrulous, silly woman. Early in the marriage, she barred Roger from her bedroom. Sex was bad for him, she said. She spent the rest of her life taking suppositories and talking to her terriers. In her old age, she drank, and lost whatever sanity she had. She kept a favorite housefly in her bathroom, and she would place crumbs on the edge of the bathtub for it. When she died, she left several cartons, intriguingly marked "private." They were all found to contain wastepaper, together with a few other things:

> Some aged feathers and other trimmings for hats, empty jewel-cases, empty boxes, empty tins, old cosmetic and powder containers, buttons, hairpins, desiccated suppositories, decayed De Reszke and Melachrino cigarettes, old and used sanitary towels done up in tissue paper, stumps of pencils, orangewood sticks, Red Lavender lozenges.

That catalog is Ackerley's metaphor for the contents of his mother's mind.

But no one benefits more from his unflinchingness than his greatest character, Queenie. He knows that there is a measure of comedy in this passion of his for a dog and that, to observers, the comedy was magnified by the fact—which he reveals only gradually—that Queenie was a nightmare to have around. Possessive of Ackerley, she would bark furiously at any person who entered a room he was in, and, as he explained, "people seem to resent being challenged whenever they approach their own sitting or dining rooms." Her tail swept teacups off tables. Ackerley's friends stopped inviting him over. He stopped inviting them, because it upset her.

Queenie had always been, for him, not just a source of devotion but an image of vitality. "She welcomed life like a lover," he wrote. But he never disguises the fact that her animal spirits are animal. Once, he takes her out for a walk, and she begins chasing rabbits, a skill she has perfected:

She must engirdle the crafty, timid creature and confuse it with her swiftness so that it knows not which way to turn. And barking is unwisdom, she has discovered that too, for although it may add to the general terrorizing effect of her tactic, it also hinders her own hearing of the tiny, furtive movement in the midst of the bush. Silently, therefore, or with only a muted whimpering of emotion, she rises and falls, effortlessly falls and rises, like a dolphin out of the green sea among the silver masts.

Ackerley hears a tiny scream. Then: "I hear the crunch of the tender bones and the skull, bone still warm with the lust of the young creature's life. She devours it all, fur, ears, feet." Queenie is beautiful, like a dolphin in the green sea, and she is a practiced killer. Ackerley can keep two opposing ideas in mind at the same time, and the counterpoise of comedy and violence only makes the lyrical, the beautiful, more so.

He retired from the BBC, in 1959, at the age of sixty-three, and thereafter spent much of his time holed up in his apartment, in Putney. His sister, Nancy, by all accounts a monster, moved in and picked fights with him daily. His aunt Bunny also joined the household. He liked her, but she was failing. She became incontinent, and the whole apartment stank. It was also too small for three, nor could Ackerley, on his small pension, afford to support them all, which he was doing.

He and Queenie both developed disabling arthritis. Queenie grew deaf. Her teeth rotted; she could not eat by herself. Ackerley said that he would keep her alive as long as she went on holding him in her gaze— the thing he so loved. Finally, too ill to care anymore, she turned her face to the wall, and he had her put down. According to Peter Parker, he never forgave himself. Always a drinker, he now drank more, starting in the morning. He had blackouts, took falls. He looked forward to death, the "dear dark angel," as he called her. In 1967, when he was seventy, she came.

The New Yorker, 2011

E. B. White with his dachshund, Minnie, at *The New Yorker*

THE ENGLISH WARS

Prescriptive and Descriptive Dictionaries

For a long time, many English speakers have felt that the language was going to the dogs. All around them, people were talking about "parameters" and "lifestyles," saying "disinterested" when they meant "uninterested," "fulsome" when they meant "full." To the pained listeners, it seemed that they were no longer part of this language group. To others, the complainers were fogies and snobs. The usages they objected to were cause not for grief but for celebration. They were pulsings of our linguistic lifeblood, proof that English was large, contained multitudes.

The second group was right about the multitudes. English is a melding of the languages of the many different peoples who have lived in Britain and North America; it has also changed through commerce and conquest. The fact that it has always been such a ragbag encouraged further permissiveness. In the past half century or so, however, this situation has produced a serious quarrel, political as well as linguistic, with two combatant parties: the prescriptivists, who were bent on instructing us in how to write and speak, and the descriptivists, who felt that all we could legitimately do in discussing language was to say what the current practice was. This dispute is the subject of *The Language Wars: A History of Proper English*, by the English journalist Henry Hitchings, a convinced descriptivist.

In England, the most important and thorough prescriptivist volume of the twentieth century was *A Dictionary of Modern English Usage*, written by H. W. Fowler, a retired schoolteacher, and published in 1926. Its first edition is 742 pages long, and much of it has to do with small questions of spelling and pronunciation. Fowler's true subject, however—his heart's home—is a set of two general principles, clarity and unpretentiousness, that he felt should govern all use of language. The book's fame derives from the articles he wrote in relation to those matters—"genteelism," "mannerisms," "irrelevant allusion," "love of the long word," to name a few. Fowler defines "genteelism" as "the substituting, for the ordinary natural word that first suggests itself to the mind, of a synonym that is thought to be less soiled by the lips of the common herd, less familiar, less plebian, less vulgar, less improper, less apt to come unhandsomely betwixt the wind & our nobility." As is obvious here, Fowler was dealing not just with language but with its moral underpinnings, truth and falsehood. To many people, he seemed to offer an idealized view of what it meant to be English—decency, fair play, roast beef—and to recommend, even to prescribe, those things. Accordingly, Hitchings deplores the book.

England did not. *A Dictionary of Modern English Usage* sold sixty thousand copies in its first year. Its most famous descendant was George Orwell's 1946 essay "Politics and the English Language." Published just after the Second World War—that is, just after most of the world had been nearly destroyed by ideologues—the essay said that much political language, by means of circumlocution and euphemism and other doctorings, was "designed to make lies sound truthful and murder respectable." (Orwell repeated the point three years later, in *1984*.) Orwell was thus the most urgent prescriptivist possible. To him, our very lives depended on linguistic clarity. Hitchings nods at Orwell respectfully but still has questions about the campaign for plain English to which the great man contributed so heavily.

What the plain-English manifestos have been to Britain, *The Elements of Style*, by William Strunk Jr. and E. B. White, is to the United States. Strunk was an English professor at Cornell, and *The Elements of Style* began life as a forty-three-page pamphlet that he wrote in 1918 and distributed to his students in the hope of reforming what he saw as their foggy, verbose, and gutless writing. His goals were the same as Fowler's: clarity and unpretentiousness. He also had a mania for conciseness.

A year after the pamphlet appeared, E. B. White, the twenty-year-old son of a piano manufacturer, enrolled in Strunk's course. After graduation, he forgot his teacher's manual for many years, during which time he became a professional essayist, renowned for his clarity and unpretentiousness. Then, one day, a friend from college sent him a copy of Strunk's pamphlet, thinking that it might amuse him. Impressed by its wisdom, White agreed to revise the manual for readers of his own time. The volume, now widely known as "Strunk and White," was published in 1959. It is not without faults: the passive voice, frowned on in the book, occurs eleven times just on page 16 of the fourth edition. Nevertheless, *The Elements of Style* is the most trusted style manual in the United States.

White appended an essay to the manual, "An Approach to Style," which carried the question of usage beyond correctness, into art. After the book's many pages of rules, he says that excellence in writing depends less on following rules than on "ear," the sense of what *sounds* right. Also, White stressed morals even more than Fowler did. "Style takes its final shape more from attitudes of mind than from principles of composition," he says. "This moral observation would have no place in a rule book were it not that style *is* the writer, and therefore what a man is, rather than what he knows, will at last determine his style." In short, to write well, you had to be a good person.

Strunk and White, together with Fowler and, to some extent, Orwell, addressed their remarks to people who had had an education similar to theirs. Hence their ease, their wit, and their willingness to prescribe. None of them had any interest in telling steelworkers how to use English. But in the middle of the twentieth century their pre-scriptivist assumptions came up against violent opposition, at least in the academic world. The newly popular theory of structural linguistics held, in part, that you couldn't legislate language. It had its own, inter-nal rules. The most you could do was catalog them. A second important objection came from the reform politics of the late twentieth century. In a world changed by immigration, and intolerant of the idea of an elite, many people felt that prescriptive style manuals were exclusionary, even cruel. Why should we let some old Protestant men tell us how to write our language?

Also on the level of taste and tone, the books seemed to some readers—for example, Hitchings—provincial and small-minded. "The idea of Fowler," he writes, "is part of that nimbus of Englishness that includes a fondness for flowers and animals, brass bands, cups of milky tea, net curtains, collecting stamps, village cricket, the quiz and the crossword." The idea of Strunk and White, too, was a little discomfort-ing. The book became a cult object. A ballet based on it, by Matthew Nash, had its New York premiere in 1981. Nico Muhly composed a song cycle on the subject, and performed it at the New York Public Library in 2005, in conjunction with the publication of Maira Kal-man's *illustrated* edition of *Elements*. In 2009, Mark Garvey, a journal-ist, brought out a book, *Stylized: A Slightly Obsessive History of Strunk & White's "The Elements of Style,"* that quotes the correspondence between White and his publishers, reproduces testimonials by celebrated writers, and describes Garvey's feelings—all his feelings—about the book: "I love its trim size. I love the trade dress of the 1979 third edition: The authors' last names fill the top half of the honey-mustard cover in a stocky, crimson, sans serif typeface." For some, such fetishism was a bit nauseating—and also clubbish. Strunk and White could be associated with what some readers saw as the pipe-and-slippers tone of *The New Yorker*, where White was a celebrated contributor for decades.

The crucial document of the language dispute of the past half century was *Webster's Third New International Dictionary*, published in 1961. This 2,662-page revised edition of the standard unabridged dictionary of American English was emphatically descriptivist. "Ain't" got in, as did "irregardless." "Like" could be used as a conjunction, as in "Winston tastes good like a cigarette should." Some of these items had appeared in the preceding edition of the unabridged *Webster's* (1934), but with plentiful "usage labels," characterizing them as slang, humorous, erroneous, or illiterate. In the new edition—*Web. 3*, as it was called— usage labels appeared far less often; they bore more neutral names, such as "nonstandard" and "substandard"; and they were defined in subtly political terms. "Substandard," the dictionary tells us, "indicates status conforming to a pattern of linguistic usage that exists throughout the American language community but differs in choice of word or form from that of the prestige group in that community." Two examples that the dictionary gave of words acceptable throughout the American language community except in its prestige group were "drownded" and "hisself."

On many sides, *Web. 3* was met with fury. A number of readers had no memory of having heard "drownded" or "hisself" said by anyone, ever, prestigious or not. Some people—including the influential critic Dwight Macdonald, in an acidulous 1962 essay, "The String Untuned"—went so far as to accuse the editors of equivocating, misleading, and concealing, for political reasons. Even the middle-of-the-road *Times* ridiculed *Web. 3*. Rex Stout's beloved detective Nero Wolfe threw the book into the fire because of its failure to distinguish between "imply" and "infer." This was the closest thing to a public scandal that the quiet little world of English-language manuals had ever seen.

Out of it a new lexicon was born: *The American Heritage Dictionary of the English Language*, published in 1969. The *AHD* was a retort to *Web. 3*. It was unashamedly prescriptive and also, strictly speaking, elitist. In the words of its editor, William Morris, the book was written to provide "that sensible guidance toward grace and precision which intelligent people seek in a dictionary." Intelligent people, dictionary consulters: that's not everybody. Still, the *AHD*'s makers did their best to keep the doors open. They had put together a "usage panel" of about a hundred people, mostly professional writers and editors, whom they consulted—indeed, they asked them to vote—on controversial words and phrases. The editors then arrived at their decisions, but for many words they added not just a usage label but also a usage "note," giving the voting results, which were sometimes close. Here, for instance, is the entry on "ain't": "Nonstandard. Contraction of *am not*." But this is followed by an eighteen-line usage note, saying that while "ain't" is strongly condemned, "ain't I" is a little more tolerable than "ain't" combined with any other word. Actually, 16 percent of the panel thought that "ain't I" was acceptable in speech. (Don't try it in writing, though. Only 1 percent approved this.) Such polling could be viewed as a preemptive defense against a charge of exclusiveness, but it can also be seen as an attempt to purvey common sense, rather than snobbery or defensiveness, and, in the end, just to tell the truth. In every quarter of society, there is an elite. *Web. 3* tried to make that fact go away. The *AHD* did not, but it also demonstrated that occupants of the upper tier often—even usually—disagreed. So this was an elite that you might be able to join. You didn't need a secret password.

In making the case for the language as it was spoken, the descriptivists did at least one great service: they encouraged studies of the vernacular. Dictionaries of slang have been around for a long time. In

2010, the Bodleian Library, at Oxford, brought out what its editors claim is the first specimen, a 1699 volume titled *A New Dictionary of the Terms Ancient and Modern of the Canting Crew, in Its Several Tribes of Gypsies, Beggers, Thieves, Cheats, &c.*—"cant" means slang—whose author is listed only as B.E. I did not know, though I was glad to learn, many of its listings: "Louse-land" (Scotland), "Suck your face" (drink), "Hogen-mogen" (a Dutchman). The grandfather of twentieth-century slang books is considered to be Eric Partridge, whose *Dictionary of Slang and Unconventional English* (1937) shocked many people of the time. Since then, there have been national slang books, theoretical slang books, slang books covering tweets and texts and emails (Julie Coleman's *Life of Slang*). Two years ago, a new contestant lumbered into the field: *Green's Dictionary of Slang*, a three-volume, six-thousand-page lexicon. It covers the street talk not only of England—home of the book's author, the language scholar Jonathon Green—but of most other English-speaking countries and of numerous subcultures within them: the gay, the incarcerated, the military, and so on. An important event in lexicography this year was the publication of the fifth and final volume of Joan Houston Hall's *Dictionary of American Regional English*, with such items as "too yet" (also); "we-uns" (we, us); "toe jam," in wide use; and the "toe social," a party where the women stand behind a curtain, sticking their toes out beneath it, and the men, after appraising the toes, bid for a companion for the evening.

Unsurprisingly, sex is the richest contributor to slang. Jonathon Green claims to have found fifteen hundred words for copulation and a thousand each for "penis" and "vagina." There have been books strictly limited to obscenity. Green wrote one, *The Big Book of Filth* (1999). More recent is Ruth Wajnryb's *Expletive Deleted* (2005). Wajnryb breaks no ground in her discussion of the reasons for dirty talk: obscenity enhances your vivacity; it cements fellowship within the group doing the talking. But she does discuss ethnic variations. Arabic and Turkish, she says, are justly praised for elaborate, almost surrealist curses ("You father of sixty dogs"). Bosnians focus on the family ("May your mother fart at a school meeting"). Wajnryb gives generous treatment to the populations, such as the Scots and the African Americans, who hold actual competitions of verbal abuse, and she offers memorable examples:

> *I hate to talk about your mother, she's a good old soul,*
> *She got a ten-ton pussy and a rubber asshole.*

For many years, the filthiest word in English was "fuck." Even the dauntless Partridge had to use "f*ck." (In Norman Mailer's 1948 war novel, *The Naked and the Dead*, the GIs use "fug." In what may be an apocryphal story, Mae West, meeting Mailer at a party, said, "Oh, you're the guy who can't spell 'fuck'!") According to Wajnryb, "fuck" has ceded first place to "cunt."

While most discussions of slang focus on the lower and lower-middle classes, the gentry, too, have their argot. "U and Non-U: An Essay in Sociological Linguistics," written in 1954 by the scholar Alan S. C. Ross, was an early and notorious study of this. For many years, language manuals had provided double-column lists of correct and incorrect words. Ross and his colleagues offered parallel columns of upper-class (U) speech versus the speech of (non-U) middle-class people trying to attain, or pretend to, upper-class status. Here is a sample:

U	Non-U
Expensive	Costly
False teeth	Dentures
Pregnant	Expecting
House (a lovely)	Home (a lovely)
What?	Pardon?
Napkin	Serviette
Awful smell	Unpleasant odor
Rich	Wealthy
Curtains	Drapes

Some of the distinctions, such as "house" versus "home" and "curtains" versus "drapes," are still in force.

Note how well the non-U words conform to Fowler's definition of genteelism: the choice of the fancier, rarer, or more euphemistic word. Americans have made their own contributions to non-U. Today, "discomfit" often turns up where "discomfort" should be.

Ross insisted that he did not endorse the U and non-U rules. He was a blameless professor at the University of Birmingham, and his essay was written for an obscure journal of philology in Helsinki. But it was swiftly leaped upon by people in England who did endorse such rules and were happy to talk about them. The essay was reprinted, in modified form, several times—for example, in *Noblesse Oblige*, a volume edited by Nancy Mitford. Here, various contributors added their own notes on U ways. Mitford told us that any sign of haste is non-U. Whenever possible, she said, she avoided airmail.

However descriptive Professor Ross's intentions, his essay brings us to the obvious vice of the prescriptivists: many of them are indeed snobbish, as the descriptivists charge. The problem is not that they believe in the existence of elite groups—anyone who denies this is fooling himself—but that they are willing to scold us for not belonging to one. The novelist Kingsley Amis, who wrote a very Fowlerian manual called *The King's English* (1997), instructed us that "medieval" was to be pronounced in four syllables, as "meedy-eeval." To pronounce it in three syllables was "an infallible sign of fundamental illiteracy."

Moving to a higher level, can we justly conclude that clear English is significantly related to moral worth? Unclarity, E. B. White says, is "a destroyer of life, of hope." Such statements are intended, in part, as comical hyperboles, but how funny are they, in the end, since most people would like to be on the side of life and hope? It must be said that the writers in question are not oppressing the masses. No, the object of prescriptivist scorn is Ross's non-Us, the aspiring middle class. It is always rewarding, Amis writes, "to spot a would-be . . . infiltrator." Amis's father was a clerk in a mustard-manufacturing firm, so his pleasure in spotting arrivistes is understandable. But is it okay?

The descriptivists' response to such statements is one of outraged virtue, and that is *their* besetting sin: self-righteousness. Hitchings sometimes casts himself as Candide, viewing with dismay the vile underbelly of the linguistic world. The rules are relative, he tells us. (Can it *be*?) They express the rule makers' social class, education, and values. (No!) Accordingly, they are also grounded in the rule makers' politics. (Really!) Having arrived at this last conclusion, the main point of his book, Hitchings ceases to be the shocked idealist and becomes an avenger. Purists are bullies, he writes. Even the soft-spoken language manuals are agents of tyranny. Of Strunk and White's restraint, he says that "with so much that masquerades as simplicity, it is really a cover for imperiousness." Linguistic rigidity, he writes, is the product of its proponents' "anxieties about otherness and difference." You know what that means.

To support his points, Hitchings applies a great deal of faulty reasoning, above all the claim that since things have changed before, we shouldn't mind seeing them change now. Usages frowned on today were once common. (Dr. Johnson split infinitives; Shakespeare wrote "between you and I," and just about anything else he wanted.) Conversely, words considered respectable now were once decried. (Fowler took a firm stand against "placate" and "antagonize.") And people have been complaining about the bad new ways, as opposed to the excellent old ways, for millennia. Why should we be so tedious as to repeat their error? Hitchings thinks that many of the distinctions that prescriptivists insist on—not just small things like "disinterested"/"uninterested" but big things like "who"/"whom"—"may already have been lost."

It is not hard to see the illogic of this argument. What about the existence of a learned language, or a literary language? If Milton took from Virgil, and Blake from Milton, and Yeats from Blake, were those fountains dry, because they were not used by most people? As for the proposition that if something was good enough for Dr. Johnson, it should be good enough for us, would we like to live with the dentistry, or the penal codes, or the views on race, of Johnson's time?

But the most curious flaw in the descriptivists' reasoning is their failure to notice that it is now they who are doing the prescribing. By the eighties, the goal of objectivity had been replaced, at least in the universities, by the postmodern view that there is no such thing as objectivity: every statement is subjective, partial, full of biases and secret messages. And so the descriptivists, with what they regarded as their trump card—that they were being accurate—came to look naive, and the prescriptivists, with their admission that they held a specific point of view, became the realists, the wised-up.

In the same period, the reformism of the sixties became, in some quarters, a stern, absolutist enterprise. Hitchings acknowledges the tie between political correctness (he calls it that) and the descriptive approach to language study. Faithful to his book's thesis, he steps up to defend the enforcers, who were, he says, decent-minded people "demonized by the political right." But he has a difficult time reconciling their views with his proclaimed antiauthoritarianism. Things get awkward for him as the book progresses.

Once you check his sources, things get worse. In the prescriptivists' books, you will find that, contrary to Hitchings's claims, many of them, or the best ones, are not especially tyrannical. Those people really wanted clear, singing prose, much more than rules, and they bent rules accordingly. White, addressing the question of "I" versus "me," in *The Elements of Style*, asks, "Would you write, 'The worst tennis player around here is I' or 'The worst tennis player around here is me'? The first is good grammar, the second is good judgment." Kingsley Amis, for all his naughty jokes, is often philosophical, even modest. His preference for "all right" over "alright," he tells us, is probably just a matter of what he learned in school. But it is Fowler, that supposedly starchy old schoolmaster, who is the most striking opponent of rigidity. In his *first* edition, he called the ban on prepositions at the end of a sentence "cherished superstition," and said that those who avoid split infinitives at the cost of awkwardness are "bogy-haunted creatures." Even more interesting is to watch him deal with matters of taste. One of his short essays, "Vulgarization," has to do with overusing a fancy word. It's wrong to do this, he says, but "nobody likes to be told that the best service he can do to a favourite word is to leave it alone, & perhaps the less said here on this matter the better." This almost brings a tear to the eye. He doesn't want people to lose face.

Nowadays, everyone is moving to the center. The big fight produced some useful discussions of linguistic history, including Guy Deutscher's *Unfolding of Language* (2005). These books, by demonstrating how language changes all the time, brought about some concessions on the part of the prescriptivists, notably the makers of the *AHD*'s later editions. First, the editors changed the makeup of their advisory panel. (The original hundred advisers were not dead white men, but most of them were white men, and the average age was sixty-eight.) Some definitions were made more relativist.

Most important is that the editors tried to pull descriptivists over to their side. In the most recent edition, the fifth, they have not one but two introductory essays explaining their book's philosophy. One is by John R. Rickford, a distinguished professor of linguistics and humanities at Stanford. Rickford tells us that "language learning and use would be virtually impossible without systematic rules and restrictions; this generalization applies to all varieties of language, including vernaculars." That's prescriptivism—no doubt about it. But turn the page and you get another essay, by the cognitive psychologist Steven Pinker. He tells us more or less the opposite. There are no rules, he declares. Or they're there, but they're just old wives' tales—"bubbe meises," as he puts it, in Yiddish, presumably to show what a regular fellow he is. And he attaches clear political meaning to this situation. People who insist on following supposed rules are effectively "derogating those who don't keep the faith, much like the crowds who denounced witches, class enemies, and communists out of fear that they would be denounced first." For the editors of the *AHD* to publish Pinker's essay alongside Rickford's is outright self-contradiction, in service of avoiding a charge of elitism.

But the *AHD*'s run for cover is not as striking as the bending over of certain descriptivists, notably Hitchings. Having written chapter after chapter attacking the rules, he decides, at the end, that maybe he doesn't mind them after all: "There *are* rules, which are really mental mechanisms that carry out operations to combine words into meaningful arrangements." We should learn them. He has. He thinks that the "who"/"whom" distinction may be on its way out. Funny how we never see any confusion over these pronouns in his book, which is written in largely impeccable English.

No surprise here. Hitchings went to Oxford and wrote a doctoral dissertation on Samuel Johnson. He has completed three books on language. He knows how to talk the talk. As for walking the walk, he'd rather take the Rolls. You can walk, though.

The New Yorker, 2012

The princess confronts her determined suitor. Detail from illustration by Walter Crane, 1875

ONCE UPON A TIME

Grimms' Fairy Tales

Among Grimms' fairy tales there is a story called "The Stubborn Child" that is only one paragraph long. Here it is, in a translation by the fairy-tale scholar Jack Zipes:

> Once upon a time there was a stubborn child who never did what his mother told him to do. The dear Lord, therefore, did not look kindly upon him, and let him become sick. No doctor could cure him and in a short time he lay on his deathbed. After he was lowered into his grave and covered over with earth, one of his little arms suddenly emerged and reached up into the air. They pushed it back down and covered the earth with fresh earth, but that did not help. The little arm kept popping out. So the child's mother had to go to the grave herself and smack the little arm with a switch. After she had done that, the arm withdrew, and then, for the first time, the child had peace beneath the earth.

This story, with its unvarnished prose, should be clear, but it isn't. Was the child buried alive? The unconsenting arm looks more like a symbol. And what about the mother? Didn't it trouble her to whip that little arm? Then we are told that the youngster, after this beating, rested in peace. Really? When, before, he had seemed to beg for life? But the worst thing in the story is that, beyond disobedience, it gives us not a single piece of information about the child. No name, no age, no pretty or ugly. We don't even know if it is a boy or a girl. (The Grimms used *ein Kind*, the neuter word for "child." Zipes decided that the child was a boy.) And so the tale, without details to attach it to anything in particular, becomes universal. Whatever happened there, we all deserve it. A. S. Byatt has written that this is the real terror of the story: "It doesn't feel like a warning to naughty infants. It feels like a glimpse of the dreadful side of the nature of things." That is true of very many of the Grimms' tales, even those with happy endings.

Jacob and Wilhelm Grimm were born to a prosperous couple (the father was a lawyer), Jacob in 1785, Wilhelm in 1786. The family lived in a big house in the Hessian village of Hanau, near Kassel, and the boys received a sound primary education at home. But when they were eleven and ten, everything changed. Their father died, and the Grimms no longer had any money. With difficulty, the brothers managed to attend a good lyceum and then, as their father would have wished, law school. But soon afterward they began a different project, which culminated in their famous book *Nursery and Household Tales* (*Kinder- und Hausmärchen*), first published in two volumes, in 1812 and 1815, and now generally known as *Grimms' Fairy Tales*.

The Grimms grew up in the febrile atmosphere of German Romanticism, which involved intense nationalism and, in support of that, a fascination with the supposedly deep, pre-rational culture of the German peasantry, the *Volk*. Young men fresh from reading Plutarch at university began sharing stories about what the troll said to the woodcutter, and publishing collections of these *Märchen*, as folktales were called. That is the movement that the Grimms joined in their early twenties. They had political reasons, too—above all, Napoleon's invasion of their beloved Hesse, and his installation of his brother Jérôme as the ruler of the Kingdom of Westphalia, a French vassal state. If ever there was a stimulus to German intellectuals' belief in a German people that was culturally and racially one, and to the hope of a politically unified Germany, this was it.

Two things sustained the Grimms. First, their bond as brothers. For most of their lives, they worked in the same room, at facing desks. Biographers say that they had markedly different personalities—Jacob was difficult and introverted, Wilhelm easygoing—but this probably drew them closer. Wilhelm, when he was in his late thirties, made bold to get married, but the lady in question simply moved into the brothers' house and, having known them for decades, made the domestic operations conform to their work schedule.

That was their other lodestar: their work. Eventually, their specialties diverged somewhat. Wilhelm remained faithful to folklore, and it was he who, after the second edition of *Household Tales* (1819), did all the editorial work on the later editions, the last of which was published in 1857. Jacob branched out into other areas of German history. Independently, Jacob wrote twenty-one books; Wilhelm, fourteen; the two men in collaboration, eight—a prodigious output. Though their most popular and enduring book was *Household Tales*, they were serious philologists, and in the last decades of their lives what they cared about most was their *German Dictionary*, a project on the scale of *The Oxford English Dictionary*. Wilhelm died at seventy-three. Jacob carried on for four more years, and brought the dictionary up to *F*. Then he, too, died. Later scholars finished the book.

There are two varieties of fairy tales. One is the literary fairy tale, the kind written, most famously, by Charles Perrault, E. T. A. Hoffmann, and Hans Christian Andersen. Such tales, which came into being at the end of the seventeenth century, are original literary works—short stories, really, except that they have fanciful subject matter: unhappy ducks, princesses who dance all night, and so on. To align the tale with the hearthside tradition, the author may also employ a certain naivete of style. The other kind of fairy tale, the ancestor of the literary variety, is the oral tale, whose origins cannot be dated, since they precede recoverable history. Oral fairy tales are not so much stories as traditions. In the words of the English novelist Angela Carter, who wrote some thrilling Grimm-based stories, asking where a fairy tale came from is like asking who invented the meatball. The premodern tale tellers might be thought of as descendants of the scops of the Anglo-Saxon Dark Ages or of the griots of West Africa—men whose job it was to carry stories—or of the Yugoslavian bards studied in the twentieth century by Milman Parry and Albert Lord, in the effort to understand how the Homeric epics were composed. One might even look to Irish American bars in New York or Boston, where the most masterful joke teller will have told the most detailed and witty version of a priest-rabbi-and-minister joke, until the next aspirant comes along. Scholars tend to associate fairy tales with women, at home, telling stories to one another to relieve the tedium of repetitive tasks such as spinning (which often turns up in these narratives). Each woman would add or subtract a little of this and that, and so the story changed. But when the story is told in public, or to a sizable audience, it tends to be told by a man.

In the Grimms' time, industrialization was starting to simplify or eliminate certain domestic chores. For that reason, among others, the oral tale was beginning to disappear. Intellectuals considered this a disaster. Hence the many fairy-tale collections of the period, including the Grimms'. They were rescue operations. The Grimms, in the introduction to their first edition, assert that almost all their material was "collected" from oral traditions of their region and is "purely German in its origins." This suggests that the tales were supplied by humble people, and the brothers say that their primary source, Dorothea Viehmann, was a peasant woman from a village near Kassel. They claim that they did not change what Viehmann or the others said: "No details have been added or embellished."

Most of this was not true. The people who supplied the first-edition tales were largely middle class: the brothers' relatives, friends, and friends of friends. As for Viehmann, she was not a peasant but the wife of a tailor. She was also a Huguenot. In other words, her culture was basically French, and she was no doubt well acquainted with French literary fairy tales, Perrault's and others'. So much for the material's being "purely German in its origins." But at least Viehmann was an oral source. Many items in the Grimms' first edition came not from interviewees but from other fairy-tale collections. Most important, the brothers, especially Wilhelm, revised the tales thoroughly, making them more detailed, more elegant, and more true to Christian orthodoxy, as one edition followed another. In the process, the stories sometimes doubled in length. The folklore scholar Maria Tatar supplies three sentences from the brothers' original draft of "Briar Rose," which we call "The Sleeping Beauty":

> [Briar Rose] pricked her finger with the spindle and immediately fell into a deep sleep. The king and his retinue had just returned and they too, along with the flies on the wall and everything else in the castle, fell asleep. All around the castle grew a hedge of thorns, concealing everything from sight.

And here, after seven successive revisions, is how that passage reads in the final edition of *Household Tales*:

> [Briar Rose] took hold of the spindle and tried to spin. But no sooner had she touched the spindle than the magic spell took effect, and she pricked her finger with it. The very moment that she felt the prick she sank down into the bed that was right there and fell into a deep sleep. And that sleep spread throughout the entire palace. The king and the queen, who had just come home and entered the great hall, fell asleep, and the whole court with them. The horses fell asleep in the stables, the dogs in the courtyard, the pigeons on the roof, and the flies on the wall. Even the fire that had been flaming on the hearth stopped and went to sleep, and the roast stopped crackling, and the

cook, who was about to pull the kitchen boy's hair because he had done something wrong, let him go and fell asleep. And the wind died down and not a single little leaf stirred on the trees by the castle.

All around the castle a briar hedge began to grow. Each year it grew higher, and finally it surrounded the entire castle and grew so thickly beyond it that not a trace of the castle was to be seen, not even the flag on the roof.

That was a considerable change.

As Tatar has pointed out in her book *The Classic Fairy Tales* (1999), what the Grimms produced falls somewhere between the oral and the literary tale. But the brothers should not be reproached for departing from the original. First of all, whose original? Perrault had written a famous version of "The Sleeping Beauty" more than a century before—Wilhelm, in expanding "Briar Rose," probably drew on it—and the story was older than Perrault. Most literary tales were derived in some measure from folk sources, and once they were published, they in turn influenced folk versions. Finally, oral tales, when transcribed faithfully, are often barely readable. Tatar offers an example from the first draft of the Grimms' first edition. This is part of a sentence:

> Early the next morning the forester goes hunting at two o'clock, once he is gone Lehnchen says to Karl if you don't leave me all alone I won't leave you and Karl says never, then Lehnchen says I just want to tell you that our cook carried a lot of water into the house yesterday so I asked her why.

Though a scholar might publish this in, say, the *Journal of American Folklore*, nobody else would try to get anyone to read it.

The Grimms, however, changed more than the style of the tales. Their first edition was not intended for the young, nor, apparently, were the tales told at rural firesides. The purpose was to entertain grown-ups, during or after a hard day's work, and rough material was part of the entertainment. But the reviews and the sales of the Grimms' first edition were disappointing to them. Other collections, geared to children, had been more successful, and the brothers decided that their second edition would take that route. In the introduction, they dropped the claim of fidelity to folk sources. Indeed, they said more or less the opposite: that, while they had been true to the spirit of the original material, the "phrasing" was their own. Above all, any matter unsuitable for the young had been expunged.

As with most rating committees in charge of such cleanups, what they regarded as material unsuitable for the young was information about sex. In the first edition, Rapunzel, imprisoned in the tower by her wicked godmother, goes to the window every evening and lets down her long hair so that the prince can climb up and enjoy her company. Finally, one day, when her godmother is dressing her, Rapunzel wonders out loud why her clothes have become so tight. "Wicked child!" the godmother says. "What have you done?" What Rapunzel has done goes unmentioned in the second edition. Such bowdlerizing went on for half a century. By the final edition, the stories were far cleaner than at the start.

But they were not less violent. The Grimms were told by friends that some of the material in the first edition was too frightening for children, and accordingly they made a few changes. In a notable example, the first edition of "Hansel and Gretel" has the mother and the father deciding together, during a period of famine, to abandon the children in the woods. In later editions, it is the *stepmother* who makes the suggestion, and the father repeatedly hesitates before he finally agrees. Apparently, the Grimms could not bear the idea that the mother, the person who bore these children, would propose such a thing, or that the father would readily consent.

This is an admirable scruple, but a puzzling one, because it is largely absent from other Grimm tales, many of which feature mutilation, dismemberment, and cannibalism, not to speak of regular homicide, often inflicted on children by their parents or guardians. Toes are chopped off; fingers are severed. A typical, if especially appalling, case is "The Juniper Tree." As usual, there is a stepmother who hates her stepchild, a boy. He comes home one day and she asks him if he wants an apple. But no sooner does the boy lean over the trunk where the apples are stored than she slams the lid down and cuts off his head. Now, however, she starts to worry. What if somebody figures out what happened? So she props up the boy's body in a chair, puts his head on top, and ties a scarf around the neck to hide the wound. In comes Marlene, the woman's own, beloved daughter. The girl comments that her stepbrother looks pale. Well, give him a slap, the mother says. Marlene does so, and the boy's head falls off. "What a dreadful thing you've done. But don't breathe a word," the stepmother says. "We'll cook him up in a stew." Then the husband comes home and she serves him the stew. He loves it. "No one else can have any of it," he says. "Somehow I feel as if it's all for me." You can hardly believe what you're reading.

You get used to the outrages, though. They may even come to seem funny. When, in a jolly tale, a boy sees half a man fall down the chimney, are you supposed to get upset? When you turn a page and find that the next story is titled "How Children Played Butcher with Each Other," should you worry? Some stories do tear you apart, usually those where the violence is joined to some emphatically opposite quality, such as peace or tenderness. In "The Twelve Brothers," a king who has twelve sons decides that if his next child is a girl, he will have all his sons killed. That way, his daughter will inherit more money. So he has twelve coffins built, each with a little pillow. Little pillows! For the little sons whom he is willing to murder!

In sum, the Grimm tales contain almost no psychology—a fact underlined by their brevity. However much detail Wilhelm added, the stories are still extremely short. Jack Zipes's translation of "Rapunzel" is three pages long, "The Twelve Brothers" five, "Little Red Riding Hood" less than four. They come in, clobber you over the head, and then go away. As with sections of the Bible, the conciseness makes them seem more profound.

Since the Second World War, some people have argued that the violence of the Grimm tales is an expression of the German character. Louis Snyder, in his book *Roots of German Nationalism* (1978), has a whole chapter on what he sees as the Grimms' celebration, and encouragement, of pernicious national traits: "obedience, discipline, authoritarianism, militarism, glorification of violence," and, above all, nationalism. Of course, the Grimm tales *were* nationalist: the brothers hoped to make their young readers feel and be more German. But in the nineteenth century there were fervent nationalist campaigns in most European countries. That is how the Western empires fell. And though ethnic pride was the Nazis' chief justification for their movement, that wasn't necessarily the fault of ethnic pride. Nazism fed on many trends that, previously, had been harmless—for example, the physical culture movement of the early twentieth century, the fad for going on nature hikes and doing calisthenics. This became a feature of Nazism—an argument for purity, strength, the soil—but it existed also in countries that fought the Nazis, notably the United States.

Nevertheless, the Grimms are premier representatives of the nationalism that became Aryanism in the 1920s and '30s, and the Nazis were grateful to them. Hitler's government demanded that every German school teach the Grimms' book. After the war, accordingly, the Allies banned the Grimm tales from the school curricula in some cities. Still today, certain people, notably feminists, would like to move them to the back shelves of the library, because, so often, the villain is a woman, doing violence to girls, and also because the girls seldom resist. When, in "Snow White," the heroine is being hunted down by the terrible queen-stepmother, she does almost nothing to save herself. Finally, she sinks into utter passivity, immobilized in a glass coffin, waiting for her prince to come and awaken her with a kiss. In the words of Sandra Gilbert and Susan Gubar, in *The Madwoman in the Attic*, she is "patriarchy's ideal woman."

Gilbert and Gubar actually defend the wicked stepmothers, whose arts, they say, "even while they kill, confer the only measure of power available to a woman in a patriarchal culture." That is, these women at least have some gumption, unlike the sweet, mild girls they are trying to eliminate. Such feelings are widespread. On a rock at the edge of Copenhagen harbor sits a bronze statue of Hans Christian Andersen's Little Mermaid (who, unlike Disney's, does not get her man). Over the years, her head has been sawed off repeatedly; she has been blasted off her rock with explosives. A dildo was once affixed to her hand, apparently in celebration of International Women's Day. At the same time, some writers have recommended that the feminist critics look more closely at the Grimm collection. According to the novelist Alison Lurie, an expert on children's books, it is primarily the most popular tales, especially the ones adapted by the Disney Company in its early years, that feature the wilting violets. Others of the stories have spunkier heroines.

But you do not have to be a member of any special political camp to object to the Grimm tales. You only need to be a person interested in protecting children's mental health. After the Second World War, there was a powerful movement in the United States for realism and wholesomeness in children's books. No more cannibal stews but, rather, "Judy Goes to the Firehouse." (This is the trend that Maurice Sendak, to the outrage of many, was bucking with *Where the Wild Things Are*, in 1963.) Writers reluctant to part with the Grimm tales suggested that we go on reading them to our children but point out the poisonous stereotypes they contain. Presumably, as your child is nodding off, you are supposed to give her a shake and tell her how the prince's rescue of Snow White reflects the hegemony of the patriarchy.

Other writers have proposed that we revise the tales again. Why not? Why should the Grimms have the last word? Jack Zipes, in his book *Breaking the Magic Spell* (1979), addresses "Rumpelstiltskin," the story in which, as the Grimms tell it, a king offers to marry a miller's daughter if she can spin straw into gold. She has no idea how to do this. A gnome, Rumpelstiltskin, offers to do the job for her. But, once she marries, he says, she must give him her first child. When, at the end, she reneges on the deal, he becomes so angry that he tears himself in two. With apparent sympathy, Zipes quotes a writer, Irmela Brender, who, saddened that Rumpelstiltskin is destroyed, when all he ever wanted was a little companionship, has proposed a version in which the miller's daughter, instead of denying Rumpelstiltskin the baby, invites him to move in with the royal family:

> "We could do a lot of things together. You'll see how much fun we can have." Then Rumpelstiltskin would have first turned pale and then blushed for joy. He would have climbed on a chair and would have given the queen a kiss on her cheek. . . . And they would have been happy with each other until the end of their days.

W. H. Auden once described the Grimm sanitizers as "the Society for the Scientific Diet, the Association of Positivist Parents, the League for the Promotion of Worthwhile Leisure, the Cooperative Camp of Prudent Progressives."

Then there are those who believe that the Grimm tales, whatever their cruelty, are good for us. One camp here consists of the psychoanalytic critics, most notoriously Bruno Bettelheim, whose 1976 book, *The Uses of Enchantment*, dropped like a hot brick into the tepid waters of children's literature of that period. Bettelheim argued that fairy tales, by allowing children to attach their unsavory repressed desires to villains (dragons, witches) who were then conquered, helped the children to integrate and control such desires. To Bettelheim, a Freudian, the most important conflict was the Oedipus complex. In his view, it was because of that nasty struggle that the Grimm tales so often featured a wicked stepmother. Children are thereby given the opportunity to hate their mother (in the form of the stepmother) and still, as they do in life, love her (the real mother, conveniently absent from the tale).

Such an interpretation makes some sense. Bettelheim went further, though. In "The Frog Prince," he says, the reason the princess dislikes the amphibian in question is that the "tacky, clammy" feel of a frog's skin is connected to children's feelings about their sexual organs. This seems a perfect example of the psychoanalytic critics' habitual indifference to the obvious. Many human beings—and no doubt princesses, especially—don't like things that are sticky and warty. To provoke such recoil, you do not have to be a sexual organ. Furthermore, this particular frog has been stalking the princess day and night. Finally, he invades her bed. In response, she picks him up and hurls him against a wall, whereupon he explodes and his little guts dribble down the plaster. Fortunately, this causes him to turn into a handsome prince, but even if he hadn't, many of us would have endorsed her action.

While Bettelheim tells us that fairy tales help us adjust, Jack Zipes has said the opposite: that the value of fairy tales is that they teach us *not* to adjust, because the oppressive society in which we live is something we should refuse to adjust to. Zipes, a professor emeritus of German and comparative literature at the University of Minnesota, has written sixty books on or of folktales: critical studies, collections, translations. His newest entry is *The Irresistible Fairy Tale: The Cultural and Social History of a Genre*, but it does little more than repeat the theory of fairy tales that Zipes has been putting forth for several decades. Zipes is a Marxist of the Frankfurt school. He was also heavily influenced by the German philosopher Ernst Bloch and by the student movement of the 1960s. In keeping with those positions, he believes that fairy tales, because they are grounded in a naive morality, offer us a "counterworld," which encourages us to step back, consider the dubious morality of our own world, and take steps to reform it. As he puts it, fairy tales may "expose the crazed drive for power that many individual politicians, corporate leaders, governments, church leaders, and petty tyrants evince and . . . the hypocrisy of their moral stances." This interpretation leads to expectable conclusions. In "The Ugly Duckling," for example, the duck, in envying the swans, shows "a distinct class bias if not racist tendencies."

If some of this seems comical, it should be said that Zipes, in his books, shows a real love of fairy tales, especially the Grimms'. Such are the mysteries of literary criticism. His views, however dated, are still, like Bettelheim's, endorsed by some writers. Maria Tatar seems to be inheriting the position of dean of fairy tales, and in her *Annotated Brothers Grimm* (2004)—it is one of Norton's series of copiously annotated classics—she apparently feels that she can afford to be nice to everyone. This makes some of the notes in her edition bewilderingly latitudinarian; she nods to Zipes, to Bettelheim, to Gilbert and Gubar, you name it. Accordingly, she seems clueless at times. She tries to find some basis for what seems to her the surprising appearance of antisemitic feeling in some of these nineteenth-century stories. Had Wilhelm been consorting with the wrong people? In any case, she says, such characterizations are unfair to Jews. You don't say.

Still, her edition is the one I would recommend. The book is dazzlingly illustrated, by Walter Crane (the best), Arthur Rackham, Gustave Doré, Maxfield Parrish, and others. Another virtue of Tatar's edition is that she has isolated, at the end, a group of "Tales for Adults"—stories that she feels should be examined by parents before they are read to children. Included in this section is "The Stubborn Child," with the little arm sticking up through the dirt, and such items as "The Hand with the Knife" and "The Jew in the Brambles." Still, "The Juniper Tree," which Tatar herself describes as "probably the most shocking of all fairy tales," is not placed among "Tales for Adults," presumably because it is too characteristic, too echt Grimm, to be cordoned off in a special section. (In my opinion, parents should simply not read it to children. If they give the child the book, they should get an X-Acto knife and slice the story out first.)

In truth, most of the Grimms' tales cannot be made wholly

respectable. The rewritings that seem most persuasive are sometimes more unsettling than the Grimm versions—for example, Angela Carter's "Company of Wolves," inspired by "Little Red Riding Hood." This story stresses the eroticism of the girl's encounter with the wolf. When she enters her grandmother's cottage, she almost immediately understands what her situation is, but she decides not to be afraid. She asks the wolf what she should do with her shawl. He answers:

> Throw it on the fire, dear one. You won't need it again.
> She bundled up her shawl and threw it on the blaze, which instantly consumed it. Then she drew her blouse over her head; her small breasts gleamed as if the snow had invaded the room.

And so on with the rest of her clothes. Then she laughs in the wolf's face, rips off his shirt, and throws that, too, into the fire:

> She will lay his fearful head on her lap and she will pick out the lice from his pelt and perhaps she will put the lice into her mouth and eat them, as he will bid her, as she would do in a savage marriage ceremony.
> The blizzard will die down.
> The blizzard died down, leaving the mountains as randomly covered with snow as if a blind woman had thrown a sheet over them, the upper branches of the forest pines limed, creaking, swollen with the fall. . . .
> See! sweet and sound she sleeps in granny's bed, between the paws of the tender wolf.

Does the violence in the Grimm collection need a symbolic reading? The fairy-tale scholar Marina Warner, in her book *From the Beast to the Blonde* (1994), says that most modern writers ignore the Grimms' "historical realism." Among the premodern populations, she records, death in childbirth was the most common cause of female mortality. The widowers tended to remarry, and the new wife often found that her children had to compete for scarce resources with the children of the husband's earlier union. Hence the wicked stepmothers. As for the scarcity of resources, Robert Darnton has written that a peasant's basic diet around that time consisted of a porridge of bread and water, sometimes with a few homegrown vegetables thrown in. Often, there was not even porridge. In the Grimm story "The Children Living in a Time of Famine" (Tatar moved this, too, into "Tales for Adults"), a mother says to her two daughters, "I will have to kill you so that I'll have something to eat." The little girls beg to live. Each goes out and somehow finds a piece of bread to bring back. But this is not enough. The mother again says to the girls that they must die: "To which they responded, 'Dearest Mother, we'll lie down and go to sleep, and we won't rise again until Judgment Day.'" So they lie down together and die. This is a hair-raising story, but also, I think, a wishful fantasy—that the children might die without crying.

And so you could say that the Grimm tales are no different from other art. They merely concretize and then expand our experience of life. The main reason that Zipes likes fairy tales, it seems, is that he thinks they provide hope: they tell us that we can create a better world. The reason that most people value fairy tales, I would say, is that they do not detain us with hope but simply validate what is. Even people who have never known hunger, let alone a murderous stepmother, still have a sense—from dreams, from books, from news broadcasts—of utter blackness, the erasure of all safety and comfort and trust. Fairy tales tell us that such knowledge, or fear, is not fantastic but realistic. Maybe, after this life, we will go to heaven, as the two little girls who starved to death hoped to. Or maybe not. Though Wilhelm tried to Christianize the tales, they still invoke nature, more than God, as life's driving force, and nature is not kind.

The New Yorker, 2012

God calls Job's attention to the marvels he has created: Behemoth and
Leviathan. Engraving by William Blake, 1825–1826

WHY ME?

The Book of Job

The book of Job, in the Old Testament, opens with words both majestic and once-upon-a-time-ish: "There was a man in the land of Uz, whose name was Job; and that man was perfect and upright, and one that feared God, and eschewed evil." Job has ten children, three thousand camels, seven thousand sheep, and many servants. He is the richest man in the East. He doesn't take his good fortune for granted, however. Always, the Bible says, he gets up early and makes burnt offerings to God.

As the action begins, God is being visited by angels, together with Satan, who at this point in the Bible is not the agent of all evil but a sort of officer of God. (A note in *The HarperCollins Study Bible* says that he is something like a CIA operative.) God boasts to Satan, Have you seen my servant Job, so pious, so devoted to me? Satan answers, Why shouldn't he be devoted? You have given him everything a person could ever want: "But put forth thine hand now, and touch all that he hath, and he will curse thee to thy face." Well, God says, let's see about that, and he gives Satan permission to destroy Job's life.

This test is the subject of the book of Job. Is there such a thing as disinterested faith? Will people go on believing in God if they are not rewarded—indeed, if they are unjustly punished? And why *should* they be faithful to a God who allows the wicked to triumph and the innocent to suffer? Mark Larrimore, the director of the religious studies program at the New School, has published *The Book of Job: A Biography*, which is a "reception history," chronicling the answers given to that riddle by commentators from the midrash—the rabbinical meditations that were first compiled in the third century—down to Elie Wiesel.

When God first unleashes Satan on Job, he tells him that he must not assault the man physically. So Satan just kills Job's children, servants, and livestock. In response, Job tears his robe, shaves his head, falls to the ground—and worships God! "The Lord gave, and the Lord hath taken away," he says. "Blessed be the name of the Lord." Satan returns to God and complains that as long as Job remains physically unharmed, the test isn't valid: "But put forth thine hand now, and touch his bone and his flesh, and he will curse thee to thy face." God, presumably annoyed by this additional challenge, gives Satan permission, and soon Job is covered with boils from head to toe. "My flesh is clothed with worms and clods of dust," he says. "My skin is broken, and become loathsome. . . . My life is wind." He sits down in a pile of ashes. His wife tells him to give up: "Curse God, and die." But Job stands firm: "Shall we receive good at the hand of God, and shall we not receive evil?"

Three of Job's friends—Eliphaz, Bildad, and Zophar—come to visit him, and what they say is, basically, what Satan said. God and human beings give to each other as they receive. If Job is afflicted in this way, then he must have sinned. But I didn't, Job says. Nor, he now realizes, does God administer that kind of justice. It doesn't matter what you do. The world makes no moral sense.

Almost the entire middle section of the book of Job is taken up with the debate over this riddle. Again and again, the friends tell Job that God must have had a reason for destroying his life, and Job says it's not so. This could get boring, but for the fact that there is a tense internal drama. Everyone becomes increasingly passionate and bitter— above all, Job. "Miserable comforters are ye all," he says to the three men. His language is now furious. "I am a brother to dragons," he cries. Meanwhile, he sees the wicked prosper:

> Their houses are safe from fear, neither is the rod of God upon them.
>
> Their bull gendereth, and faileth not; their cow calveth, and casteth not her calf.
>
> They send forth their little ones like a flock, and their children dance.

The "little ones" are especially hard to read about. Job's children can't dance; they're dead. His feelings about his loss of status are also poignant. He had been proud of his wealth, proud of being able to feed others at his table and to help the needy. People respected him. Now "I called my servant, and he gave me no answer. . . . My breath is strange to my wife." Still, Job will not curse God: "Though he slay me, yet will I trust in him." Nevertheless—and this is crucial—"I will maintain mine own ways before him." That is Job's answer to Satan's challenge. He acknowledges God's greatness, but he will not give up the idea that he has not sinned.

Now comes a striking event. God appears, in a whirlwind. Throughout the Old Testament, as Freud claimed, God takes the part of the angry father. Here he surpasses himself, by pointing out to the four men what he is and they are not: the creator of all things. "Where wast thou when I laid the foundations of the earth? . . . When the morning stars sang together, and all the sons of God shouted for joy?" He proudly inventories the wonders he fashioned. Most thrilling, perhaps, is his portrait of the warhorse:

> Hast thou given the horse strength? hast thou clothed his neck with thunder?

Canst thou make him afraid as a grasshopper? the glory of his nostrils is terrible.

He paweth in the valley, and rejoiceth in his strength: he goeth on to meet the armed men. . . .

He swalloweth the ground with fierceness and rage: neither believeth he that it is the sound of the trumpet.

He saith among the trumpets, Ha, ha! and he smelleth the battle afar off, the thunder of the captains, and the shouting.

"Ha, ha!" That is the spirit of God's answer to Job. I am power itself, he says. How dare you question me?

Job immediately apologizes: "I abhor myself, and repent in dust and ashes." Now God addresses the three friends, who told Job that God is just. He punishes them for presuming to say that they understand his ways. Then he turns to Job and tells him that he alone has spoken the truth—apparently, that God is not understandable. For this, God rewards him.

The story is bewildering, from beginning to end. How could God, being God, allow Satan to destroy a good man? More important is the moral: that we have no right to question him for doing such things. (God, for all that he says from the whirlwind, never answers Job's questions.) Furthermore, the book of Job seems to claim that all wrongs can be righted by property. If everything was taken away from Job, the problem is settled by God's giving it all back, mostly twofold—fourteen thousand sheep for his seven thousand, and so on. As for the ten dead children, in this case Job gets only ten back, but the new daughters are more beautiful than any other women in the land.

For people who take the Bible seriously as an explanation of life and as a guide to right conduct, all this is mysterious. It is certainly not the first instance in which God inflicts appalling misery on his people. In Genesis, he killed every creature on earth except those on Noah's ark. But Job is highly individualized—a person like us. He is probably the character in the Old Testament we sympathize with most closely. (David is his only competition.) Therefore, his struggle to go on believing in God is something that theologians and moralists have had to think about. Their conclusions are the subject of Mark Larrimore's book.

Discouragingly, it begins by listing all the things that we don't know about Job. In our lifetime, Job has been regarded as a sort of Jewish saint, a symbol of suffering Jewry, but, in fact, we don't know whether he was Jewish. (No lineage is provided, and neither Job nor his friends have Jewish names.) Nor is there any certainty about whether the book was written by Jews. We know nothing about the setting of the tale (where is Uz?), or about how it came to be written. Scholars think that it, or parts of it, was handed down over centuries as an oral tale, and finally recorded sometime after the seventh century BC.

The text we have is clearly corrupt in many places. The central section—where Job speaks to his friends, and God speaks to them all—is in verse, and its language is impassioned: pleading, sweeping, vaulting. The outer sections are written in prose, and in a blunt, matter-of-fact manner. This stylistic contrast, together with the subject matter, underlies the main puzzle of the book: the profound nature of Job's complaint and of God's answer versus the cynicism of the outer sections, where God bargains with Job's life and then, at the end, pays him off. Many modern scholars believe that the outer sections might have been written independently of the central section—perhaps slapped on to make it a story, with a beginning and an ending. More daringly, some writers have suggested that God's speeches are interpolations. God rarely makes such a grand appearance in the Old Testament. Why here, in his most dazzling entry, is he not given any sort of introduction? (All we get is "Then the Lord answered Job out of the whirlwind.") And why is this proud, thundering deity so different from the cold executive of the opening and closing sections? Also, his pronouncements from the whirlwind are often inconsistent with what he says elsewhere in the Bible. As Larrimore puts it, "The pious asseverations of Job's friends, condemned by God, are the passages of the book that best square with other texts accepted as scriptural."

That is by no means the end of the textual problems. Sometimes you can't figure out what's happening. Job will make a statement to his friends that doesn't seem to be addressed to them. Passages have apparently been moved or omitted or inserted. Immediately before God's arrival, we suddenly hear, at length, from a man named Elihu, who adds little to the discussion and is never mentioned again. But Job's text was not questioned until the Renaissance, and the investigation didn't really get going until the nineteenth century, at German universities. For many centuries before that, philosophers and theologians took the book as canonical and analyzed it as such. Not surprisingly, their main question was the one debated by Job and his friends: Why does God allow evil in the world?

The first single commentator to whom Larrimore gives serious attention is Pope Gregory I, or Gregory the Great (540–604), who wrote a six-volume study of Job. His book, as Larrimore explains it, is our introduction to many centuries of allegorical interpretation of the book of Job—indeed, of the entire Old Testament—as parallel to the New Testament. In particular, Job's torment was thought to presage the sufferings of Jesus. Some modern readers find this sort of thinking far-fetched, but it certainly wasn't confined to the Middle Ages, or to Roman Catholics. Luther's Bible, one of the earlier vernacular testaments, had illustrations that combine, in the same frame, events in Job that occurred many verses apart. This was not to save money on woodcuts. It was an expression of the view of time that had been held for many centuries, by both Jewish and Christian commentators. To them, the Old Testament was divinely inspired, and if it seemed to contain contradictions or errors, that was not its fault but ours. We needed to dig for deeper, subtler meaning.

According to Larrimore, this was also, essentially, the opinion of the great Jewish scholar Maimonides, in the twelfth century, and of the formidable Saint Thomas Aquinas, in the thirteenth. Aquinas, emboldened by the dispute between Job and his friends, treated the book as a *quaestio*, or debate, the primary mode of learning at the University of Paris, where he was a celebrated professor. (Job won the debate, of course.) As Larrimore points out, such a method has the problem of omitting the matter of the hero's extreme suffering. Maimonides, in his *Guide for the Perplexed*, from 1190, is less certain, but he, too, obedient to the tradition, says that we must yield to the text's divine authority. In Job, he believes, we can understand God's message only in glimpses. In 1536, John Calvin wrote his *Institutes of the Christian Religion*, with meditations on Job. Calvin's view was the most radical, in terms of theodicy—that is, the attempt to reconcile the existence of evil with a benevolent and omnipotent God. Calvin said that God had a higher justice, veiled to human eyes. Other thinkers did not buy that. (After all, the Old Testament shows God issuing codes of justice for us—the Ten Commandments, for example.) The problem was stated most succinctly two centuries later, by David Hume: "Is he willing to prevent evil, but not able? Then he is impotent. Is he able, but not willing? Then he is malevolent. Is he both able and willing? Whence then is evil?"

One logical answer is that there is no God. But before the eighteenth century, and during most of it, atheism was not an option, even for the most strong-minded. To choose between two positions, a person must have two to choose from. Before the Enlightenment, the vast majority of Europeans did not. Larrimore quotes the French historian Lucien Febvre, writing in the early twentieth century:

> Today we make a choice to be Christian or not. There was no choice in the sixteenth century. One was a Christian in fact. One's thoughts could wander far from Christ, but these were plays of fancy, without the living support of reality. One could not even abstain from observance. Whether one wanted to or not, whether one clearly understood or not, one found oneself immersed from birth in a bath of Christianity from which one did not emerge even at death.

What Febvre said of the sixteenth century was also true of the eighteenth century and most of the nineteenth. Bold minds might question God's care of us, but few doubted his existence. Larrimore quotes a passage from Voltaire's *Candide* (1759): "'What difference does it make,' said the dervish, 'if there is good or evil? When His Highness sends a ship to Egypt, does he worry about whether or not the mice are comfortable on board?'" Voltaire said that Candide was "Job brought up to date."

Many philosophers, probably without meaning to, inched their way toward the same position. Kant said that all we could do with doubts about God was admit them. For Kant, Larrimore writes, "the book of Job shows that the problem of evil must remain an open wound." Larrimore thinks that's still true: that the dispute between Job and his friends epitomizes modern thought. There are no answers, only riddles. In the face of that impasse, the discussion often shifts from content to style. In the eighteenth and nineteenth centuries, a number of people who wrote on Job—the German theorist Johann Gottfried von Herder, the Anglican bishop Robert Lowth—stopped trying to figure out God's plan, and instead focused on his poetry, whose sublimity, they felt, was meaning enough. Indeed, the ambiguity boosted the sublimity. This position was undoubtedly reassuring, but the new aestheticism could also be seen as a failure of moral seriousness. Furthermore, it placed God at a very far remove from humankind. One of the reasons that Job complains so bitterly is that he thought that he and God had a relationship. Now it is sundered: "I cry unto thee and thou dost not hear me."

His sense of abandonment is a great part of the poignance of the book. But as the Enlightenment, whose efficient universe had little place for a punishing God, yielded to Romanticism, with its worship of passion, many thinkers had less need for a pleasant, companionable God. An excellent example is William Blake, who between 1805 and 1810 produced a series of twenty-one watercolor illustrations for the book of Job. Blake did not need God to make sense. He wanted him to be a figure of pure energy, like the "Tyger, burning bright." Nor did Blake mind conflicts. Larrimore quotes his *Marriage of Heaven and Hell*: "Without Contraries is no progression. Attraction and Repulsion, Reason and Energy, Love and Hate, are necessary to Human existence."

Blake's thunderbolt was bracing, but soon it, too, was not enough. In the twentieth century, the most pressing new influence on the interpretation of Job's story was the Shoah, after which, Larrimore writes, Job "became Jewish." The person most responsible for his conversion was Elie Wiesel, an Auschwitz survivor. Wiesel began lecturing about Job as early as 1946. He regards the book as a great text, and a great torture. For many, Job epitomized the suffering of the Jews during the Second World War and also their perceived response to it, which, in the 1960s, Hannah Arendt described as going like lambs to the slaughter. As God played dice with his life, Job grieved and protested, but he didn't take any action. This interpretation anguished Wiesel. An alter ego in one of his novels never ceases to resent Job. "That biblical rebel should never have given in," he says.

Eventually, Wiesel decided that Job *hadn't* given in. This, to my knowledge, is the beginning of the modern recasting of the book of Job. Wiesel, in his *Messengers of God: Biblical Portraits and Legends* (1976), argues that, contrary to the usual reading, Job did not submit when God told him that he must. You can tell, Wiesel says, because, in the text that we have, he submitted so fast. He was just pretending. The true ending, Wiesel preferred to believe, was lost. Later, he again changed his mind, and settled on the idea that Job merely chose silence, not submission. Job, he wrote, had "learned that he lived in a world that was cold and cynical—a world without true friends," but one, nevertheless, in which "God seeks to join man in his solitude."

Wiesel has had many heirs, speaking not necessarily for the Jews but for any suffering people. Postmodern critics, by favoring certain political positions and by welcoming self-contradictory, ambiguous texts, have abetted this trend, arguing that the insistence on Job's submission is a vote for authoritarianism. This is something like the upheaval in New Testament studies after the discovery, in 1945, of the Nag Hammadi manuscripts, a collection of gospels from Christian communities which seem to have been judged too eccentric—or too dangerous doctrinally—to be included in the so-called canonical Gospels. With Job, the danger was that human beings could legitimately ask God why he ran the world the way he did.

But objections to Job's capitulation came from many ideological quarters. The American rabbi Richard Rubenstein has said that we should think not just of Job, who was able to have his argument with God and be saved, but also of his barely mentioned children, slaughtered because of God's bet with Satan. As Larrimore summarizes Rubenstein's position, the death of Job's children

> should put us in mind of the frequency of divine infanticide in the Bible. The track record of the God of the Jews is, in fact, too awful to contemplate. Rubenstein imagines that a modern-day comforter might counsel Job to admit to guilt, even though he was innocent. Lie, or the truth will out, that God is a demon—if he exists at all.

Rubenstein was the chaplain for Jewish students at several leading colleges from the 1950s through the 1970s. He no doubt had considerable influence.

Such teachings might not have been necessary. An honest modern study of Job should take into account the fact that, at least in the West, theodicy is not the issue that it once was. However much people may grieve over the undeserved suffering of others—not just Jews, but Cambodians, Bosnians, Tutsis, Syrians, Afghans—they are less inclined to ask God why he will allow this. Many of them don't believe in God, or if they do, they are less likely to regard him as a benevolent intercessor, enforcing justice in the world. They have seen too much evidence to the contrary.

Not all the objections issue from grief and anger. Another heir of Wiesel's, or at least of the long-term quarrel over Job, is the translator Stephen Mitchell. In his popular rendering of the book of Job, the hero, again, does not submit. Instead, he undergoes a "spiritual transformation": "He has let go of everything and surrendered into the light." Therefore, where the King James Version has Job, at the end, saying to God that he will "repent in dust and ashes" (other English-language translations have wording close to this), Mitchell's hero—blissfully aware now that he is part of the infinite—says, "I will be quiet, comforted that I am dust." Mitchell studied Zen Buddhism for many years and, with his wife, Byron Katie, has written books—*Loving What Is* (2002), *A Thousand Names for Joy* (2007)—on how to relieve your suffering by challenging the thoughts that create it.

In all this, Larrimore maintains a supremely tolerant position. He approves of the wealth of "interpretative openings and opportunities." Everything is okay with him, and he thinks that whatever disagreements there are may lead to community. (This is interesting, since an absolutely crucial aspect of Job's trial is that he suffers alone.) Such a latitudinarian approach is perhaps appropriate to a reception study, telling who thought what, and who, after them, thought something else, but eventually it comes to seem anti-intellectual. At times, Larrimore sounds like a kindly Unitarian minister, or like Mister Rogers.

If, for many Westerners, the question of why God allows good people to be tortured is no longer a pressing issue, why is it that Job appears to be the most fascinating book of the Old Testament? I can't think of a single character in the Bible, apart from Jesus or David, who is quoted more often than the dramatis personae of the book of Job are.

This is without doubt due, in part, to the book's amorality. I believe that if you woke a lot of people in the middle of the night, and asked them why they cared about the book of Job, they would name the most troubling, least sympathetic character in that document: God. He, not Job, is the star of the book, and though he is not loving or fair, that seems to be part of the attraction. Once God appears and speaks, you are almost blown to the ground. "Hast thou an arm like God?" he demands. Then, in a rolling magnificat, he names the things that he has created: the earth, the sea, the night, the light, the constellations, the clouds, the winds, the dew, the rain, the snow, the hail, the frost, the thunder and lightning. He goes on to the animals: the goats, the asses, the hinds, the peacocks, the ostriches, the grasshoppers. In two celebrated passages, he describes with pride the monsters he created: Behemoth and Leviathan, Behemoth's counterpart in the sea. "His breath kindleth coals, and a flame goeth out of his mouth." God's description of the warhorse is even more exalted, because this creature is unquestionably real, not fantastic. Likewise the eagle: "She dwelleth and abideth on the rock, upon the crag of the rock, and the strong place. From thence she seeketh the prey, and her eyes behold afar off." She brings pieces of flesh back to her children. They feed on the blood.

God's speech slaughters the moral, the what-should-be, nature of the rest of the book of Job. It is the knife flash, the leap, the teeth. It is like an action movie, or a horror movie. Of course, Job is important in the story, but today he seems the pretext, the one who is like us, and makes the argument that we would make. As for God, he makes the argument that, at least as far as nature is concerned, is true.

The New Yorker, 2013

Grendel's mother pulls Beowulf down into her dark swamp. Illustration by Henry Justice Ford, 1899

GRENDEL HATES MUSIC

J. R. R. Tolkien and *Beowulf*

In the 1920s, there were probably few people better qualified to translate *Beowulf* than J. R. R. (John Ronald Reuel) Tolkien. He had learned Old English and started reading the poem at an early age. He would declaim passages of it to the private literary club that he had founded with his schoolmates. "Hwæt!" (Lo!) he would begin. (He did the same, later, as a professor, at the beginning of his Old English classes. Some of the students thought "Hwæt!" meant "Quiet!") He also loved stories, especially medieval ones, with lots of wayfaring and dragon slaying—activities prominent in his books *The Hobbit* and *The Lord of the Rings*. In 1920, he began teaching Old English at the University of Leeds. He needed money—by now he had a wife and children—and he supplemented his income by marking examination papers. Anyone could have told him that he should translate *Beowulf*. How this would advance his reputation! Finally, he sat down and did it. He finished the translation in 1926, at the age of thirty-four. Then he put it in a drawer and never published it. Now, forty years after his death, his son Christopher has brought it out, and it is a thrill.

Beowulf was most likely written in Britain—by whom, we don't know—in around the eighth century. (That is Tolkien's date. Some scholars put it later.) The plot is simple and exalted. Beowulf is a prince of the Geats, a tribe living in what is now southern Sweden. He is peerlessly noble, brave, and strong. Each of his hands has a grip equal to that of thirty men. He is alone in the world; he was an orphan, and he never acquires a wife or children. Partly for that reason—because he has no one to behave toward in an intimate way—he has no real psychology. Unlike Anna Karenina or Huckleberry Finn, he is not a filter, a point of view, standing between us and his world.

This unself-consciousness gives that world a sparkling vividness. Here are Beowulf and his men, after a journey, sailing back to Geatland (this and all uncredited translations are by Tolkien):

> Forth sped the bark troubling the deep waters and forsook the land of the Danes. Then upon the mast was the raiment of the sea, the sail, with rope made fast. The watery timbers groaned. Nought did the wind upon the waves keep her from her course as she rode the billows. A traveller upon the sea she fared, fleeting on with foam about her throat over the waves, over the ocean-streams with wreathéd prow, until they might espy the Geatish cliffs and head-lands that they knew. Urged by the airs up drove the bark. It rested upon the land.

The boat must have been enormous; it carries Beowulf and what seems to have been at least a dozen knights, plus their horses, their battle gear, and heaps of treasure. The timbers groan. Yet the boat fairly flies, gathering a ruff of sea foam. Then, suddenly, the men see the cliffs of their homeland and, mirroring their eagerness, the boat lands in five short words.

That passage is speed incarnate. Others, many others, are portraits of dark or light, such as the description of dinnertime at Heorot, the king of Denmark's mead hall:

There was the sound of harp and the clear singing of the minstrel; there spake he that had knowledge to unfold from far-off days the first beginning of men, telling how the Almighty wrought the earth, a vale of bright loveliness that the waters encircle; how triumphant He set the radiance of the sun and moon as a light for the dwellers in the lands.

Not everyone loves the light, however. Outside the hall there lurks a monster, Grendel. Grendel hates music, and for twelve years he has been coming to Heorot after dark, to prey on the Danish knights. The poet describes one of Grendel's visits:

The door at once sprang back, barred with forgéd iron, when claws he laid on it. He wrenched then wide, baleful with raging heart, the gaping entrance of the house; then swift on the bright-patterned floor the demon paced. In angry mood he went, and from his eyes stood forth most like to flame unholy light. He in the house espied there many a man asleep, a throng of kinsmen side by side, and band of youthful knights. Then his heart laughed.

He seized one sleeping man, "biting the bone-joints, drinking blood from veins, great gobbets gorging down. Quickly he took all of that lifeless thing to be his food, even feet and hands." How lovely, the bright-patterned floor. How appalling, Grendel's dinner.

Beowulf is the story of the hero's defeat of three successive monsters. The first is Grendel. The Geats are allies of the Danes, and Beowulf, who by then seems to be about thirty, decides to go to Denmark and rid it of this menace.

It is hard to say what Grendel looks like. He is apparently about four times the size of a man. He has claws; he does not speak. But he also has human qualities. He has to enter Heorot by a door. When wounded, he bleeds, as Beowulf soon discovers. With his powerful hands, the hero grabs Grendel's wrist and tears off his arm and shoulder. His shoulder! He then hangs the whole business—shoulder, arm, hand—from the rafters of the mead hall. Imagine the Danish knights drinking their mead as half of Grendel's torso drips blood onto them. Grendel is the most real of the monsters. (It means something that he is the only one of the three who has a name.) As Seamus Heaney, another *Beowulf* translator, has written, Grendel "comes alive in the reader's imagination as a kind of dog-breath in the dark." Almost with embarrassment, you pity him somewhat. Tolkien describes how, after the fight with Beowulf, Grendel, "sick at heart," dragged himself home, "bleeding out his life." He is also a bit childlike. It is no surprise that John Gardner, in his 1971 novel *Grendel*, portrays the monster as a boy.

One reason Grendel seems childlike is that he has a mother. When her son comes home to die, Grendel's mother goes on a rampage. So Beowulf must suit up again. The mother lives in a chamber beneath a stinking swamp: "The water surged with gore, with blood yet hot." Beowulf dives right in, with his helmet on. His knights, afraid to join him, stand at the edge of the water. Grendel's mother is waiting for him—with helpers, a gang of sea monsters, which tear at him with their tusks, to soften him up. Finally, she takes over. Demon or not, she clearly loved her son, and she goes at Beowulf with a blinding fury. The hero finds that his famous—and previously invincible—sword, Hrunting, is of no use against her plated hide. It bounces off her. But he sees, close by, another sword, forged by giants, which no man can pick up—except him. He waves it through the air, piercing the monster's throat and breaking her neck bone. This is more horrid even than Beowulf's removal of Grendel's arm and shoulder, or, at least, it feels more painful. (It also shows a man killing a woman.) Before he leaves the den, Beowulf beheads Grendel's corpse, lying nearby. Normally, the poet says, it would have taken four men to pick up that head. But Beowulf carries it alone, to the surface, and hands it to his knights.

When they get back to the mead hall, they tug it around by its hair, as a game.

Beowulf's third fight, which takes place back home, in Geatland, is with a dragon who, unlike Grendel and his mother, is less a monster than a symbol. He is not sad or weird. Indeed, he is rather glamorous. He is fifty feet long and breathes fire. He has wings—he can fly—and he doesn't live in a nasty fen. He has a nice cave, where he guards a treasure that has been his for three hundred years and that he feels strongly about. But now someone has come and stolen a jeweled cup. This enrages him, and he begins incinerating the Geatish countryside.

Many years have passed since Beowulf killed Grendel and his mother. He has become the king of the Geats and has ruled them for fifty years. He is about eighty years old now, and tired. Still, to protect his people he must eliminate this menace. He sets out, but "heavy was his mood." Speaking to his knights, he reviews his great deeds. He bids them farewell. In what is probably the poem's most iconic image, he goes and sits on a promontory that juts out over the sea. (This says everything. Beowulf will soon be part of nature—the land, the sea.) As always, he insists on going into the contest alone. His knights, relieved, slink off into the forest. The dragon emerges from the cave, "blazing, gliding in loopéd curves." Beowulf brings his huge sword down on the monster's body, but, as with Grendel's mother, it doesn't make a dent. The dragon sinks his teeth into the hero's neck. His blood "welled forth in gushing streams."

Will he lose the fight? No. Not all his men ran into the forest. One young knight, Wiglaf, stayed back and, unbeknownst to the king, followed him close behind. Seeing Beowulf wounded, Wiglaf rushes forth and stabs the dragon "a little lower down." As the poet is too polite to say, Wiglaf took better aim than Beowulf did, and thus weakened the dragon to the point where the old man could go in for the kill. Beowulf has not lost his touch: "He ripped up the serpent." That's the end of the dragon—the Geatish knights unceremoniously dump the body over the cliff—but it's also the end of Beowulf. Wiglaf unclasps the king's helmet, and bathes his wounds, to no avail. In the final lines of the poem, we see the knights, in tears, riding their horses in a circle around Beowulf's tomb. "Thus bemoaned the Geatish folk their master's fall, comrades of his hearth, crying that he was ever of the kings of earth . . . most generous and to men most gracious, to his people most tender and for praise most eager."

Tolkien might have put away his translation of *Beowulf*, but about a decade later he published a paper that many people regard as not just the finest essay on the poem but one of the finest essays on English literature. This is "*Beowulf*: The Monsters and the Critics." Tolkien preferred the monsters to the critics. In his view, the meaning of the poem had been ignored in favor of archaeological and philological study. How much of *Beowulf* was fact, and how much fancy? What was its relationship to recent archaeological finds?

Tolkien saw all this as an evasion of the poem's true subject: death, defeat, which come not only to Beowulf but to his kingdom, and every kingdom. Many critics, Tolkien says, consider *Beowulf* something of a mess artistically—for example, in its mixing of pagan with Christian ideas. But the narrator of *Beowulf* repeatedly says that, like the minstrels who entertain the knights, he is telling a story from the old days. "I have heard," he says. "I have learned." Tolkien claims that the events of the poem, insofar as they are real, occurred in about AD 500. But the poet was a man of the new days, when the British Isles were being converted to Christianity. This didn't happen overnight. And so, while he tells how God girded the earth with the seas, and hung the sun in the sky, he again and again reverts to pagan values. As in the *Iliad*, none of the people in the poem care anything about modesty, simplicity (they adore treasure, they count it up), or humility (they boast of their valorous deeds). And death is regarded as final. No one, including Beowulf, is said to be going to a better place.

Another aspect of *Beowulf* that critics seeking a tidier poem deplore is the constant switching of time planes: the time-very-past, in which a noble tribe created the treasure that becomes the dragon's hoard; the times-less-past (there are several), in which we are told of the greatness and the downfall of legendary kings and heroes; the time-present, in which Beowulf kills the monsters; the time-future, when other peoples, hearing of Beowulf's death, will make bold to move against the Geats, and will conquer them, pressing them into slavery. Geatish maidens scream as they imagine it. They know that it will come to pass. This is like something out of *The Trojan Women*.

As the time planes collide, spoilers proliferate. When Beowulf goes to meet the dragon, the poet tells us fully four times that the hero is going to die. As in Greek tragedy, the audience for the poem knew the ending. It knew the middle, too, which is a good thing, since the events of Beowulf's fifty-year reign are barely mentioned until the dragon appears. This bothered many early commentators. It did not bother Tolkien. The three fights were enough. Beowulf, Tolkien writes in his essay, was just a man:

> *And that for him and many is sufficient tragedy.* It is not an irritating accident that the tone of the poem is so high and its theme so low. It is the theme in its deadly seriousness that begets the dignity of tone: *lif is læne: eal scæceð leoht and lif somod* (life is transitory: light and life together hasten away). So deadly and ineluctable is the underlying thought, that those who in the circle of light, within the besieged hall, are absorbed in work or talk and do not look to the battlements, either do not regard it or recoil. Death comes to the feast.

According to Tolkien, *Beowulf* was not an epic or a heroic lay, which might need narrative thrust. It was just a poem—an elegy. Light and life hasten away.

Few people—indeed, few literary scholars—can read *Beowulf* in the original Old English. Most of them can barely refer to it. The characters in the *Iliad* and the *Odyssey,* poems that were written down more than a millennium before *Beowulf,* are known even to people who haven't read their source. Achilles, Hector: in some parts of the world, babies are given these names. But people do not know the names of the characters in *Beowulf,* and if they did, they still wouldn't know how to pronounce them: Heoroweard, Ecgtheow, Daeghrefn. That is because Old English, as the standard language of the Anglo-Saxons, preceded the Norman invasion, in 1066, when the French, and their Latinate language, conquered England. Here are the lines, at the opening of *Beowulf,* that Tolkien used to shout out to his literary club:

> *Hwæt wē Gār-Dena in geār-dagum*
> *þēod-cyninga þrym gefrūnon,*
> *hū ðā æþelingas ellen fremedon.*

This sounds more like German than like English. If you don't know German, it doesn't sound like anything at all.

Old English did not become an object of academic study until the mid-nineteenth century, and by that time there was little chance of its being included, with Greek and Latin, as a requirement in university curricula. Also, little of the surviving Old English literature is artistically comparable to what Greece and Rome produced. In consequence, it was treated as a sidelong matter. In Tolkien's time, Oxford required that students specializing in English literature know the language well enough to be able to read, and translate from, the first half of *Beowulf.* That is why Tolkien had a job: at Oxford, for decades, he taught the first half of *Beowulf.*

Then there were the conventions of Old English poetry. *Beowulf* does not rhyme at the ends of its lines, and it doesn't have a rhythm as regular as, say, Shakespeare's iambic pentameter. Instead, each line has a caesura, or a division in the middle, and the two halves of the line are linked by alliteration. (Look at the opening line that Tolkien recited to his literary club: "Hwæt wē Gār-Dena in geār-dagum.") The pattern of the consonants creates the stresses, and thereby the rhythm.

What is the modern translator to do with this? It is hard, in discussing Tolkien's translation, not to compare it with Seamus Heaney's famous 2000 version. Heaney was a poet by trade—indeed, a Nobel laureate in literature—and to him it would probably have been unthinkable to translate *Beowulf* as anything but verse. He also chose to obey the *Beowulf* poet's prosody: the caesura, the alliteration. As for tone, he says that the language of *Beowulf* reminded him of his family's native Gaelic: solemn, "big voiced." This magniloquence, it seems to me, is the leading edge, linguistically, of Heaney's poem. It is an Irish-sounding translation, and he wanted it that way.

To achieve all this, he had to make some compromises. Consider the lines where Tolkien shows us Grendel eating a knight. The monster seizes the man, "biting the bone-joints, drinking blood from veins, great gobbets gorging down. Quickly he took all of that lifeless thing to be his food, even feet and hands." In Heaney's translation, the monster, picking up the knight,

> *bit into his bone-lappings, bolted down his blood*
> *and gorged on him in lumps, leaving the body*
> *utterly lifeless, eaten up*
> *hand and foot.*

Here, for the sake of alliteration and rhythm, we lose, among other things, the great gobbets (what a phrase!), the idea of using a man as food, and, most unfortunately, the picture of Grendel eating the feet and hands. Heaney's "hand and foot" seems to mean just that Grendel went from the top of the man to the bottom. We don't have to imagine, as we do in Tolkien's translation, the monster crunching on the little bones and the cartilage—harder to swallow, no doubt, than the "great gobbets." We're forced to think about what it would be like to eat a man.

The same problems arise from line to line. Heaney, to his credit, took responsibility for this poem, and turned it into something that regular people would want to read, and enjoy. (Who knew that a translation of a poem more than a thousand years old, about people killing dragons, could reach the top of the *Times* bestseller list?) In the words of Andrew Motion, in the *Financial Times*, Heaney "made a masterpiece out of a masterpiece." I have no doubt that Heaney grieved over some of the choices he had to make, but by his rules he had to act as an artist, create a new poem. This is the sacrifice always made in a "free" translation. For those who could read Old English, he reproduced the original on facing pages.

Tolkien, though he wrote poetry, did not consider himself primarily a poet, and his *Beowulf* is a prose translation. In the words of Christopher Tolkien, his father "determined to make a translation as close as he could to the exact meaning in detail of the Old English poem, far closer than could ever be attained by translation into 'alliterative verse,' but with some suggestion of the rhythm of the original." In fact, the alliteration is there throughout. Consequently, you can tap out the rhythm, with your foot, line by line. But Tolkien doesn't insist on any of this.

Such acts of faithfulness do not make his poem more accessible to the modern reader than Heaney's free translation. Especially because Tolkien reproduces the *Beowulf* poet's inversions ("Didst thou for Hrothgar king renowned in any wise amend his grief so widely noised?"), his translation is probably harder to read. But you get used to the inversions; you can understand the sentence even if you have to read it twice. And what is won by the archaism—or just by the willingness to sound strange, as in the "feet and hands"—is a rare immediacy.

Why did Tolkien never publish his *Beowulf*? It could be said that he didn't have the time. As he was finishing his translation, he got the appointment at Oxford and had to move his family. Such a disruption can put a writer off his feed. A few years later, he began *The Hobbit*, which, with its three sequels, in *The Lord of the Rings*, took up many of his remaining healthy years. It has also been argued, by Tolkien's very sympathetic biographer, Humphrey Carpenter, that he was too much of a perfectionist to let the poem go. Christopher Tolkien, in the introduction to his edition of *Beowulf*, says that the typescript he worked from—and this was a "clean" copy, a retyping from preceding marked-up copies—was full of changes, plus marginal notes suggesting other, possible changes. Christopher also supplies a commentary consisting of Tolkien's lectures on *Beowulf* and the notes he wrote to himself before and after the lectures. This material, which Christopher says he cut substantially, is longer than the poem: 217 pages, as opposed to 93. So although Tolkien told his publisher in 1926 that he had finished the translation, he in fact went on fiddling with it for a long time. When he published *The Hobbit*, in 1937, a number of his colleagues said to him, "Now we know what you have been doing all these years!" But he wasn't just writing *The Hobbit*. He had never stopped working on *Beowulf*.

Was this really due primarily to perfectionism? *Beowulf* was only one of Tolkien's several translations from Old English, and he gave a number of them, such as *Pearl* and *Sir Gawain and the Green Knight*, the same treatment that he gave *Beowulf*. Both *Pearl* and *Sir Gawain* were actually set in print, but Tolkien could not bring himself to write the introductions, and so the contracts lapsed. Nor should it be thought that Tolkien's problem was that he feared criticism from other scholars of Old English. *The Hobbit*, too, though it was not an academic enterprise, was laid aside for years, until a representative of the publisher George Allen & Unwin went to Oxford to see Tolkien, borrowed the typescript, read it, and prevailed upon him to complete it.

Another possible explanation for Tolkien's putting *Beowulf* aside—a theory that has been advanced in the case of many unpublished manuscripts—is that the work was so important to him that if he finished it, his life, or the life of his mind, would be over. I think this makes some sense. *Beowulf* was Tolkien's lodestar. Everything he did led up to or away from it. This idea suggests another. Tolkien was a serious philologist from the time he was a child. He and his cousin Mary had a private language, Nevbosh, and wrote limericks in it. One of their efforts went like this:

> *Dar fys ma vel gom co palt "Hoc*
> *Pys go iskili far maino woc?*
> *Pro si go fys do roc de*
> *Do cat ym maino bocte*
> *De volt fact soc ma taimful gyroc!"*

("There was an old man who said 'How / Can I possibly carry my cow? / For if I were to ask it / To get in my basket / It would make such a terrible row!'") Later, he made up a private alphabet, and then another, to use in writing his diary.

As an adult, Tolkien could read many languages—and he made up more, including, for the elves of Middle-earth, several Elvish tongues—but the number is not the point. Even in secondary school, Carpenter says, "Tolkien had started to look for the bones, the elements that were common to them all." Or, in the words of C. S. Lewis, his closest friend, for a time, in adulthood, he had been *inside* language. Perhaps he couldn't come back out. By this I don't mean that he couldn't talk to his wife and children, but that Old English, or at least that of *Beowulf*, was where he was happiest. He knew how it worked, he loved its ways: how the words joined and separated, what came after what. Old English is where he spent most of the day, in his reading, writing, and teaching. He might have come to think that this language was better than our modern one.

The sympathy might have gone even deeper. Like Beowulf, Tolkien was an orphan. (He was taken in by his grandparents.) He grew up in the West Midlands, and said that the *Beowulf* poet, too, was probably from there. He did not have difficulty living in a world of images and symbols. (He was a Roman Catholic from childhood.) He liked golden treasure and coiled dragons. Perhaps, in the dark of night, he already knew what would happen: that he would never publish his beautiful *Beowulf,* and that his intimacy with the poem, more beautiful, would remain between him and the poet—a secret love.

Originally published as "Slaying Monsters," *The New Yorker,* 2014

Marilynne Robinson, 2007

LONESOME ROAD

Marilynne Robinson

Marilynne Robinson's new novel, *Lila*, opens in about 1920, and it begins with a shocking action: a woman steals a child. Not that anybody seems to care much. The child, a girl who looks to be four or five, has been deposited by someone (there is no mention of parents) in a house for migrant workers somewhere in the Midwest. Most of the time, she hides under a table, but occasionally she cries, and then she gets pushed out onto the front steps. One night, a woman named Doll, the sole denizen of the house who appears ever to have paid any attention to the girl, returns from work and finds her on the stoop. This time, instead of settling her back inside, Doll carries her off to another cabin, where an old woman grudgingly lets them in. The two women feed the girl some corn bread and then try to clean her up:

> The old woman held her standing in a white basin on the floor by
> the stove, and Doll washed her down with a rag and a bit of soap,
> scrubbing a little where the cats had scratched her, and on the chigger

bites and mosquito bites where she had scratched herself, and where there were slivers in her knees, and where she had a habit of biting her hand. The water in the basin got so dirty that they threw it out the door and started over. Her whole body shivered with the cold and the sting. "Nits," the old woman said. "We got to cut her hair." She fetched a razor and began shearing off the tangles as close to the child's scalp as she dared—"I got a blade here. She better hold still." Then they soaped and scrubbed her head, and water and suds ran into her eyes, and she struggled and yelled with all the strength she had and told them both they could rot in hell.

Despite the chiggers and the curses, the scene is pure Rembrandt. We can almost see the ray of heavenly light coming through the side window. Ever since the publication of Robinson's thrilling first novel, *Housekeeping* (1980), reviewers have been pointing out that for an analyst of modern alienation she is an unusual specimen: a devout Protestant, reared in Idaho. For years she taught at the Iowa Writers' Workshop, where she was accustomed to interrupting her career as a novelist to produce essays on such matters as the truth of John Calvin's writings. But Robinson's Low Church allegiance has hugely benefited her fiction. It is certainly responsible, in part, for her extreme directness. In that bath scene, in *Lila*, the author lays out, right at the start, all the novel's main themes: abandonment, forgiveness, rescue, and then, in bracing counterpoise, the question of whether one actually *wants* to be rescued, or can be. The scene also contains the book's governing metaphor, water, which will wash away our sins—or not. And there, in the middle of the water, naked and screaming, is the book's heroine. She does not speak except to curse, Doll reports. She has no name that she can tell them. Eventually, the old woman says, "I been thinking about 'Lila.' I had a sister Lila. Give her a pretty name, maybe she could turn out pretty." After a few weeks, Doll and Lila take off down the road and join a work crew.

———

Some of us have met Lila before. Since *Housekeeping*, Robinson has written three novels—*Gilead* (2004), *Home* (2008), and now *Lila*—centered on Gilead, Iowa, a dusty, no-account little town where dogs take naps in the middle of Main Street. Gilead, however, was once at the heart of a great passion. It was a stop on the Underground Railroad and, in time, a hot spot of the Union army's cause, under the town's Congregationalist minister, a fiery-eyed man who had audible conversations with Jesus. That man's son and then his grandson succeeded to his pulpit, and it is the grandson, John Ames, who is the most important figure in the series so far. In *Gilead*, Ames, as a young man, marries the girl whom everyone in town expects him to marry. She dies in childbirth, and the baby dies with her. Ames goes on alone. By day, he writes his sermons and reads books of philosophy, theology, and history. At night, he eats a fried-egg sandwich, listens to the radio, and goes to bed. This continues for forty years, and he expects it to continue for the rest of his life. But then, one Sunday, while he is preaching—he is now sixty-seven—the back door of the church opens, and a woman slips into the sanctuary, to get out of the rain. Her dress is shabby. Her eyes are sad. She didn't grow up to be pretty. It is Lila.

Their circumstances could not be more different. He is almost twice her age. Furthermore, he is an erudite man, however isolated and obscure, while she is a transient worker. With her bedroll and a small suitcase (she owns two dresses), she goes from place to place, asking at houses in the towns and the countryside for a day's work. She was on her way to Sioux City when, approaching Gilead, she spotted an abandoned shack. She has been camping out there for a few weeks when, as she is walking in the town, a storm breaks and she ducks into Ames's church.

As Ames tells us in *Gilead*, he falls in love instantly, and though he is too modest to say that she seems attracted to him also, he hints at this. She asks him about the possibility of baptism. "No one seen to it for me when I was a child," she says. "I been feeling the lack of it." Most suggestively, she starts turning up in the garden behind his house, to tend to it—pull weeds, plant roses. (She has a special talent with roses.) At first, she makes sure to come when she knows he won't be there. Eventually, she omits that caution. Then, one evening, according to Ames, "when I saw her there, out by the wonderful roses, I said, 'How can I repay you for all this?' And she said, 'You ought to marry me.' And I did." It is like a miracle: sudden, inexplicable.

Ames is a kind of character that people say novelists can't create, an exceptionally virtuous person who is nevertheless interesting. As it happens, he has a few failings. He is sometimes bitter about the fact that he has spent his life stuck in Gilead, baptizing babies (his brother became a professor, and an atheist), and he grieved terribly that he had no children. His best friend, Robert Boughton, the town's Presbyterian minister, fathered eight. At times, when Boughton's children were still young, Ames couldn't bear to enter his friend's house. (If the two men were working together on a project, Boughton's wife would pack a dinner for them to eat in Ames's kitchen.) Then comes Lila and, in short order, a child, Robby, named after Boughton. But no sooner does Ames receive these gifts than he is told that he must lose them. The doctor says that he has angina pectoris and won't live long. That would be hard enough, but Ames is desperately worried about how Lila and Robby are going to fare without him. Boughton has a son, Jack, who could be a character out of Dostoevsky. In childhood Jack liked to steal things, break things, and then smile when he was caught. As a young man, he got a fifteen-year-old country girl pregnant and promptly left town. Now, after twenty years, Jack has returned to Gilead, and Ames thinks he sees him hanging around Lila and Robby. What rises in his heart is not just anxiety but hatred.

Ames is a sort of visionary—a trait that would appear to mark him as saintly—but, as with other saints, not all of his visions are beautiful. In *Gilead*, he remembers a windy night when he walked beneath a row of oaks:

> They were dropping their acorns thick as hail almost. There was all sorts of thrashing in the leaves and there were acorns hitting the pavement so hard they'd fly past my head. All this in the dark, of course. I remember a slice of moon, no more than that. It was a very clear night, or morning, very still, and then there was such energy in these things transpiring among those trees, like a storm, like travail. I stood a little out of range, and I thought, It is all still new to me.

It's as though he had seen a ghost.

With such matters in his head, plus the learned books, he can sometimes fail to notice what is in front of his face. When he speaks of his coming together with Lila, which he regards as the most glorious event of his life, what appears to please him most is the idea that he gave her a settled existence, a settled mind. "It seemed that all the wondering about life had been answered for her, once and for all," he says. "If that is true, it is wonderful."

It isn't true. The most forceful piece of technical machinery operating in Robinson's Gilead books is point-of-view narration. *Gilead* is written in the first person: Ames speaking to us, or, rather, to Robby (it is a letter for the boy to read when he is grown). *Lila*, like *Home*, employs what is called third-person limited. As Henry James put it, the narrative emerges from a "central intelligence." (Lila is "she," not "I," but everything is recorded as she alone sees it.) Each of the three Gilead books can stand on its own. I didn't hear anybody complaining, when *Gilead* was published, that we were getting only Ames's side of the story. Who cared about another side? Ames's point of view was truer, or at least more interesting, than any purportedly real truth. But now Robinson has followed up *Gilead* with *Home* and *Lila*, which often, while covering the same events as *Gilead*, contradict that book, and each other, too. Or, if they don't actually catch each other in lies, they still manage, by omission or inclusion or shading, to cast a different light on matters. Robinson is now very obtrusively using point of view. To what end?

Few people who have read *Gilead* will forget Ames's description of his and Lila's decision, among the roses, to get married—the speed, the wildness of it—but I hope nobody ever asks me to choose between that and the version that Lila, in *Lila*, gives of the same event. In her telling, she is not in a nice, symbolic garden. She is walking down a dusty road, with Ames beside her. She didn't invite him to accompany her, and yet, once he does, she tells him that he should marry her. It's crazy, but so is his answer: "You're right. I will." Her rejoinder is equally crazy: "All right. Then I'll see you tomorrow." In fact, they have no plans to meet the next day. She is just saying that so that she can get away from him for a moment.

In Lila's life, one emotion trumps all others, and that is shame: over her poverty, her lack of beauty, her ignorance, and, since these facts determined her choices in life, her life. She was ditched not just once but several times. She did a stint in a brothel, though she wasn't a very good prostitute—she couldn't see the point of high heels, for example—and she eventually switched to being the institution's cleaning lady. That was right before she went to Gilead. When she attends Ames's Sunday services, she always sits in the back row so that no one can see her, judge her. But how, if she is so filled with shame, could she have proposed marriage to Ames? There lies the secret of Lila, as a character: boldness, the perception and expression of truth, combined with a certainty, based on her past experience, that she will be cast aside.

That is what she expects from Ames, and after saying that she will see him tomorrow, she scrupulously avoids him. A few days later, curious as to whether he is engaged, he goes to her shack, and finds her coming up from the river, barefoot, with a catfish that she has just caught. He says that he has brought her a gift, his mother's locket:

> She felt her face warm. And the fish kept struggling, jumping against her leg. She said, "Damn catfish. Seems like you can never quite kill 'em dead. I'm going to just put it here in the weeds for a minute." And there it was, flopping in the dust. She wiped her hand on her skirt. "I can take that chain now, whatever it is."
>
> He said, "Excellent. I'm—grateful. You should put it on. It's a little difficult to fasten. My mother always asked my father to do it for her."
>
> Lila said, "Is that a fact," and handed it back to him. He studied her for a moment, and then he said, "You'll have to do something with your hair. If you could lift it up." So she did, and he stepped behind her, and she felt the touch of his fingers at her neck, trembling, and the small weight of the locket falling into place. Then they stood there together in the road, in the chirping, rustling silence and the sound of the river.

After this radiant scene, the only episode in *Lila* that you could call a sex scene, Ames says, "So. Are we getting married or not?" Lila answers that she doesn't think it's a good idea. The abstemious Robinson allows Ames only a tiny, and therefore especially poignant, reaction. ("His face reddened and he had to steady his voice.") Lila tries to explain. If she married him, she says, she would be the preacher's wife, and people would look at her all the time, to see if she measured up. She couldn't bear that. That's why she can't even get baptized. Ames protests that if she wants to get baptized, they don't need a church. They can do it right there, in the field, with water from her bucket. Yes? she says. Then hold on. And she goes to her shack and changes into a clean blouse. Then he baptizes her, resting his hand three times on her hair. She bursts into tears. Ames lends her his handkerchief.

"Wait," she says to him. "Can you still get married to somebody you baptized?" "No law against it," he says. She tells him that she wants him but that she doesn't trust him not to discard her. ("I done some things in my life"; she mentions the brothel.) Nor does she trust *herself* not to walk away from him. This long scene overflows with lyricism and tenderness and sensuousness—the locket, the tears, the trembling fingers—but buried in the middle is some dark, ugly business that you can't fully see: Lila's and Ames's loneliness, endured for so many years, and probably largely ineradicable. As they embrace, the slimy catfish wriggles in the dirt, ready to die. When the afternoon is over, the two have agreed to marry, and you feel as though you have to go lie down.

But Lila and Ames are not just a couple of people in Iowa. As much as Natasha Rostova and Andrei Bolkonsky, they represent their country's history, and that is the second department in which Robinson has made point-of-view narration work for her powerfully. In *Gilead*, Ames tells us that his grandfather preached the town "into the war," the Civil War, with the result, Robinson suggests, that most of the young men in Gilead died. This turned the grandfather's son, Ames's father, into a pacifist. On Sundays, he would not attend his father's services; he went to the Quakers instead, creating a terrible breach within the family. That is a flashback; *Gilead* is set mostly at the beginning of the civil rights movement. *Home* takes place in the year of the Montgomery bus boycott, 1956. Boughton and Ames watch the events on Boughton's new appliance, a television.

Lila is less concerned with race than with poverty—indeed, starvation—among the migrant workers of the Midwest. We hear what they ate, when they had anything to eat: basically, fried mush. When Lila is abandoned for the second time, it is by a decent person, the head of the work crew that she and Doll joined at the beginning of the book. The crew can't afford to feed her anymore. Robinson didn't need point-of-view narration in order to delineate these matters, but she certainly makes it enrich the situation. In *Home*, Boughton, watching the Montgomery riots, says that the rioters are unwise to make such a fuss. He doesn't know that his son Jack is married to a Black woman whom he met after he left Gilead. Jack, returning to Gilead, asks Ames, Could he and his wife and their son make a home in that town? Ames says no, for which he has a solid, political reason (a small Black community was forced out of Gilead some years earlier) and also a selfish, personal reason (Ames wants Jack nowhere near Lila). This is the way politics operates in our lives, on the bone.

Robinson's use of politics is also, to some extent, a weakness of the Gilead novels. It is in these matters that we start to get clichés, so foreign, otherwise, to her work. Discussing the victims of the dust bowl, she apostrophizes: How can that be? "People only trying to get by, and no respect for them at all, even the wind soiling them." If I am not mistaken, what we are getting here is Robinson's moral-essayist voice, in opposition to her novelistic voice. Both *Home* and *Lila* sag in the middle as Robinson shakes her finger at whoever she thinks needs to learn a lesson. Great novelists have done this before (see *War and Peace*), but it didn't necessarily benefit their work. Robinson writes about religion two ways. One is meliorist, reformist. The other is rapturous, visionary. Many people have been good at the first kind; few, today, at the second kind.

The second kind is Robinson's forte. She knows this, and works it. She inverts time, she loops it, she dispenses with whole chunks of it. (We never find out what Lila did for most of her adult life, before arriving in Gilead.) When Robinson likes an image, she'll use it as many times as she wants to. If the young Lila gets ditched more than once, other children, too, are abandoned. Married and pregnant, Lila, in *Lila*, revisits her old shack and finds that it has been taken over by a boy, maybe twelve years old, who has been thrown out by his father. (The father chased him down the road, throwing rocks at him. "The way you'd chase off a dog," the boy says.) Winter is coming. Lila, after hearing the boy's story, goes back to town to get him some warm clothes and food. While she is gone, he takes fright and runs away, with nothing. A blizzard arrives, shutting Lila and Ames in their house. Sitting in their kitchen, playing cards and waiting for their baby to come, they are in a sort of daze—thrilled that their child is about to be born, but aware that another child, the renegade boy, is out there, in the snow, probably dying. Add one boy; take one away. *Lila*—like *Home*—is in many ways a realistic novel. It tells us how to make biscuits and harness a mule. At the same time, Robinson shows us griefs that go far beyond the bounds of realism. In *Housekeeping*, there's a woman who is certain that she sees the ghosts of naked little children by the road at night, hungry and crying. She puts out food for them. The dogs eat it. She puts out more. In a way, that's Marilynne Robinson.

But most of the time Robinson's people aren't actually starving; they're just alone. That is the final meaning of her insistence on her characters' own point of view: because they don't see the same reality, they are consigned to solitude. Lila tells us that, as Ames's wife, she was just as lonely as she had been before she married him. And the horrible, or at least extremely arresting, thing is that Robinson doesn't entirely regret the situation. Lila, soon after the birth of her son, begins having fantasies of opening her front door and walking back out into her old life, taking the baby with her:

> But she imagined the old man, the Reverend, calling after them, "Where are you going with that child?" The sadness in his voice would be terrible. *He* would be surprised to hear it. You wouldn't even know your body had a sound like that in it. And it would be

familiar to her. She didn't imagine it, she remembered that sadness from somewhere, and it was as if she would understand something if she could hear it again. That was what she almost wanted.

Life without comfort, without love, that is the real life, and Lila would like to understand why. This is an unflinching book.

The New Yorker, 2014

From *Richard Pryor: Live on the Sunset Strip,* 1982

FLAMETHROWER

Richard Pryor

This year is the tenth anniversary of Richard Pryor's death, and a new biography has been published: *Becoming Richard Pryor*, by Scott Saul, a professor of English at Berkeley. Saul says of Pryor that "the secret of his genius must be located within the story of his life." That's what they all say, the biographers, but in Pryor's case it seems to be truer than usual. Early on, he created a skit about a baby trying to be born. The baby tries and tries and pushes and pushes. Finally, he pops his head out, looks around, and begins shrieking. Pryor said that his work was based on fear, and as Saul has shown, there was plenty to frighten him.

There must be such a thing in the world as a quietly run whorehouse, but Pryor's childhood home—one of the three brothels owned by his grandmother Marie in Peoria, Illinois—was not such a place. Pryor said that one of the reasons he liked movies as a boy was that you were never in doubt as to why the women in them were screaming. As for the sounds that Richard heard in the middle of the night in his room on the top floor of one of Marie's businesses, he had no idea what was happening to those girls. A number of times, he saw his mother,

Gertrude, one of the women in Marie's employ, nearly beaten to death by his father. Gertrude left when Richard was five. He later registered no resentment over this. "At least Gertrude didn't flush me down the toilet," he said. (This was not a joke. As a child, Pryor opened a shoebox and found a dead baby inside.)

The person he seems to have regarded as his mother—and he called her "Mama"—was Marie, a woman of great personal force. (A photo of her, looking like a pre-Columbian deity, can be found, together with many other interesting things, on a website of archival materials related to Saul's biography.) She was six feet tall, weighed two hundred pounds, and stored a straight razor permanently in her bra. The family was into other enterprises besides prostitution: they had a tavern, a pool hall, a bootlegging operation. Marie's recessive husband and her son Buck (Richard's father) worked the easier jobs. She was the heavy. In his film *Richard Pryor: Live in Concert*, Pryor describes what it was like for him, as a boy, to be beaten by her. She made him go out, to the trees nearby, and select a switch for her to whip him with. (In the movie, he imitates the sound of the switch cutting through the air—the clean, sinister whistle.) But he clearly felt that she punished him because she cared about him. He said that when he was young, people who were "sensitive" were "something to eat." His grandmother, he implied, and a few others tried to spare him such a fate. They succeeded, for a while, and then he was eaten.

Pryor was expelled from school at the age of fifteen. (He had taken a swing at the science teacher.) As soon as he could, he enlisted in the army and was sent to a base in Germany, but he got kicked out of there, too. At a screening of Douglas Sirk's movie *Imitation of Life*, about an African American girl who, to her grief, passes for white, a white soldier in the audience laughed. On his way out of the show, Pryor stabbed the offender with a switchblade. He got a month in the brig.

He broke into comedy in the usual way, step by little step: school plays, community "youth center" dramatics. Once he left school, he had bartending jobs where the management would let him improvise at the mike in the breaks between the musicians' sets. Eventually, he landed bit parts in movies. His breakthrough was in television. Both Merv Griffin and Ed Sullivan loved him and made him a regular. At the time, Pryor's idol was Bill Cosby, three years his senior. Pryor wanted a mainstream audience such as Cosby had. In his view, to be confined to Black audiences, and hence to Black subject matter, was to be a victim of racism all over again. "For about a year I was Bill Cosby," he later said.

Maybe, but not for a minute longer. The two comics' temperaments could not have been more different. Then there was the class difference: Cosby was college educated and, at least on the surface, a family man who would produce five children with one woman and keep them under one roof. Pryor had no such bona fides. But the crucial point was how the two men regarded themselves. In his stand-up comedy and, later, on *The Cosby Show*, Cosby put himself before us just as a *man*, a person who had a job and went to the dentist and so on. By contrast, Pryor almost always presented himself specifically as a Black man, and he peopled his stages with specifically Black characters—the local pimps, the take-no-guff wives, and so on. He claimed that the relations between Blacks and whites in America were utterly ruled by racism. Asked on a talk show, in 1968, if he feared that George Wallace, the outspoken segregationist governor of Alabama, might become president, Pryor answered, "Wallace *is* president. Wallace has always been president."

His absolutism, his in-your-face-ness, was a product not just of intelligence and anger but also of drugs. From his twenties through his forties, Pryor was heavily dosed, most days, with stimulants and alcohol. In his mature years, he seems to have pretty much lived on cocaine and Courvoisier. Cocaine is notorious for promoting violence. Whatever he did for Black people, Pryor regularly beat up women. On his first day in the writers' room for Mel Brooks's *Blazing Saddles*, he broke out his stash of coke, snorted, and invited the others to share. ("Never before lunch," Brooks said gamely.) Norman Steinberg, one of the men who wrote the screenplay with Pryor, recalled that once, while the writers were working, a woman with her hand in a cast came into the room and asked Pryor for money, which he gave her. After she left, Steinberg asked Pryor how the woman had hurt her hand:

> "I punched her," Richard said.
> "You punched her in the hand?"
> "She put it in front of her face."

In a fight with a night clerk at his apartment building, he put out the man's left eye. Another time, his wife, hearing gunshots, ran to their bedroom and found him lying in the darkness with water and glass and little, struggling fish all over the floor. The man had actually shot his fish tank.

That's not to speak of the damage he did to his work: the last-minute cancellations, the no-shows. In a famous story, he walked onstage at the Aladdin in Las Vegas, went to the mike, said, "What the fuck am I doing here?" and walked off. In another incident, in a show advertised as being in support of "human rights" (by which the producers meant gay rights, but they wouldn't say so), he invited the audience to kiss his Black ass and told them about how, when he was young, he had enjoyed sucking somebody or other's dick. This was at the Hollywood Bowl, with an audience of seventeen thousand. If people were offended by his remarks, he said, "I hope y'all get raped by Black folks with clap." Elsewhere, he boasted publicly of how much cocaine he had consumed: "I could have bought Peru for all the shit I snorted."

It's amazing, given this record, how many producers rehired him, and just took out more insurance. Not all of them, though. Notoriously, Pryor lost the role of Sheriff Bart, in *Blazing Saddles*, to Cleavon Little because, reportedly, the producers believed that Little was less likely than Pryor to destroy himself on drugs in the course of the shooting. Mel Brooks told Saul that he went down on his knees to the Warner Bros. bosses to get them to change their minds. They refused.

In 1980 came the famous self-immolation incident. Saul, braiding several strands of evidence (including Pryor's own account), claims that what happened was not an accident, as is so often said, but a sort of grotesque improvisation. Pryor's beloved grandmother Marie, the one who used to beat him to a pulp, died at the end of 1978, which, according to Saul, plunged him into a long, harrowing depression. One night, in June 1980, he was at home, in Los Angeles. Courtesy of his freebase pipe, he had not slept in five days. He was watching a television program that included footage of a Buddhist monk, in Vietnam, setting himself on fire. As Pryor later recalled, he was trying, at that moment, to talk to God. "What do you want me to do?" he asked his Maker. Receiving no answer, he poured a bottle of liquor over his head, soaking himself down through his shirt, and then set himself on fire with a cigarette lighter. His bodyguard and his aunt, who were present, tried to quench the flames, but he decided that they were trying to smother him. He ran out of the house, down its long, curving driveway, and onto the sidewalk, still expostulating with the Almighty: "Lord, give me another chance. . . . Haven't I brought happiness to anyone in this world?"

By this time, apparently, the fire was extinguished, and his polyester shirt had melted onto his chest. As he remembered it, he smelled like "a burned piece of meat." The police had been called, and an officer was now trotting along behind Pryor, asking him please to stop. He wouldn't. Finally, when he had got about a mile from his house, the fire department medics arrived. They grabbed him, put him in an ambulance, and took him to the burn unit of Sherman Oaks Community Hospital.

As you read of this event in Saul's telling, you may notice, to your surprise, that you are very few pages (thirteen) from the end of the book. Pryor was only thirty-nine years old when he set himself on fire, and his biggest commercial successes were still ahead of him. Does Saul really mean to conclude his narrative now? Yes. His book, he writes, "is about the shaping of a talent until it rose to the level of its full genius." For that reason, he says, the story ends with the film *Richard Pryor:*

Live in Concert (1979). Among the events surrounding that project were Marie's death, the terrible depression, and then the fire. In the process, Saul claims, Pryor cast away "a crucial part of his artistic self: the love of experiment."

Once he emerged from treatment, Pryor was a changed man, much tamer. In a way, he had gotten his wish: he was Cosby! (One barely needs to point out the ironies here. To many people today, Cosby looks like the criminal, and Pryor the honest citizen.) Of the movie *Brewster's Millions*, from 1985, the *New York Times* critic Vincent Canby, who had adored Pryor, said that he felt as though he were looking at "the extremely busy shadow of someone who has disappeared." Pryor acknowledged that he was now a different person, and he seemed to know that something had been lost. But, as he told a journalist, "at least . . . I'm not waking up saying, 'Oh, no, did I kill someone last night?'" If the fire slowed him down artistically, a larger impediment arose soon afterward. In 1986, Pryor was diagnosed with multiple sclerosis, and from then on he worked less and less, though it was not until 2005, when he was sixty-five, that he died, of a heart attack. Basically, he had one decade of greatness, the seventies.

One can sympathize with Pryor's relief at waking up in the morning without having to wonder if the police were coming, but one can also understand Saul's reluctance to take us through the artistic consequences of Pryor's new respectability. Consider just one thing: Pryor's constant use, in the sixties and seventies, of the word "nigger." Already, at the time, this was awkward for critics. Today, when we are more subject than ever to political language codes, it is a greater focus of dispute—for users and for disapprovers, Black and white. Saul points out that Pryor started saying "nigger" when he began making comedy out of character sketches, inspired by the world he had been born into. "You cannot represent that world without using that word," Saul says. Other commentators have offered more complicated explanations. But one should be careful not to rationalize the term, detoxify it, pat it on the head, and say, Don't worry, we know you didn't mean to be bad. No, Pryor used it partly because he liked to be bad, and to drive moralists nuts. Saul is true to that fact throughout the book, and so, in walking away from the post-immolation material, he is not being unfaithful to Pryor.

In the process, he does lose a few important things—for example, the 1982 concert album *Richard Pryor: Live on the Sunset Strip*, so full of wonderful material: the poetic monologue for Mudbone, Pryor's garrulous old know-it-all character; the story of Pryor's trip to Africa, with its superb animal imitations; the playlet about Italian mobsters, which I think is the funniest routine ever created about any ethnic group. What do these items have in common apart from their great artistry? Most of them back off from Pryor's usual overt concern with racism. Actually, they don't just back off; they declare that they're doing so. Pryor tells us that when he was in Africa, he decided that he wasn't going to say "nigger" anymore. He looked out his hotel window, he said, and saw all these lovely Black people and concluded that the word was demeaning. In *Sunset Strip* he also explains the self-immolation episode in a way that is, for him, notably self-accusatory. In other words, Pryor, in this album, is moving as far away from his bad-boy persona as he can without abandoning comedy. However artistic the resulting material, it might still have looked to Saul like self-betrayal. Pryor was clearly an exhausting subject, one who was constantly pushing Saul into the position of moralist or mental-health counselor, rather than what he clearly wanted to be: an arts critic.

He is an excellent critic, always willing to analyze and generalize and just plain do historical work. He is always supplying context. Whatever Pryor is involved with—brothels in postwar Peoria, high-school dropout rates for Black teenagers in that time and place, an African American GI's chance of getting a date in Germany in the late fifties, the coffeehouse scene in Berkeley in the sixties, the Black Power movement in Oakland in the seventies (and that's just the beginning—forget all the later and much more complicated business of working in nightclubs and TV and movies)—Saul has studied it. He knows Pryor's influences and he doesn't overestimate the specialness of the man's experience.

Saul also never seems to want to cover over Pryor's mixed feelings, what he calls the "pinballing" of the man's mind. "Once he settled on a truth, he was compelled to unsettle it," Saul writes. "Once the foundation seemed solid under his feet, his mind turned to thoughts of earthquakes, quicksand, dynamite." This could be very nerve-racking when the subject was race, as it often was. Pryor befriended Black Power militants and also made jokes about them. He deplored police brutality and also mocked the Black Power handshake, which he said you could never get right. "Niggers change their shit all the time," he complained. Without routines like this, we would have no Chris Rock, no Dave Chappelle. Larry Wilmore, in his debut as host of *The Nightly Show*, snickered over the complaints that *Selma* hadn't received enough Academy Award nominations, and he made a joke incorporating the words Eric Garner spoke as he died in a police choke hold last year: "I can't breathe." This is something Pryor might have done, and it was certainly not in good taste. But taste, even virtue, cannot be the criterion for what we are allowed to say. Pryor would not toe the line, any line, and we should honor him for this.

Not only does Saul never paper over Pryor's ambivalences; he never hides his own. In a recent interview with *Salon*, he said that he was never sure that he "came to grips" with Pryor's propensity for violence. He does what he can—he tells the truth—and then he talks about the art and doesn't disguise the fact that its beauty may be related to ugliness. In *Live in Concert*, Pryor describes the beatings he got from his father, which were different from Marie's punishments—sloppier, crazier:

> He hit me in the chest—hard.
> He hit me so hard my chest caved in and wrapped around his fist, and I held on to it with my chest.
> I would not let go so he could hit my ass again. And everywhere he moved his arm, I was hanging on.

What is so wonderful here is the fantasy of his chest's having ideas of its own, and refusing to let go of the father's fist. The scene is almost sexual. It's repulsive. It's hilarious. Early on, Pryor did an impression of "my sweater talking to my ass." Later, he had a skit about breaking up with a woman. "Take the TV," he says, "but leave the pussy, please." This is not realism or memoir or satire, but a very far-out-on-the-branch species of—what? Surrealism seems closest. The people Pryor should be compared to are not Cosby, or even the darker-minded comics of the period, such as Dick Gregory and Lenny Bruce, but artists such as Swift and Jarry and Lautréamont and even Hieronymus Bosch—people who entered a truly extreme territory, almost beyond comedy, but not beyond what the heart still recognizes as its own.

Hilton Als, in a 1999 profile of Pryor for *The New Yorker*, wrote of "the poignancy cradling his sharp wit." Saul writes of "his fragility, tenderness, and openness to emotional confusion." He describes how Pryor, after making a bad movie, *Adios Amigo*, told *Ebony* to give a message to his fans: "Tell them I apologize. Tell them I needed some money. Tell them I promise never to do it again." What other actor, having made a terrible movie, has said something so naked and sad and human to a national magazine?

In a way, I don't want to know about Pryor's fundamental good-ness. That's an argument often made for people who act badly, and I'd almost rather have Pryor bad. I want my *poète maudit*. But if you look at his face in the concert movies or even just on the DVD covers, you can see the real story, a double story. Sly, shifting, "pinballing": yes, he was those things. Life was harder for him than it is for you, and he's not going to let you forget that. Wait, though. Suddenly his shiny face rises to the light, and you see his beautiful smile. The crime of racism, which was his great subject, suddenly seems not just a subject but a plinth, a pedestal. He stands on it—"The funniest stand-up comic that ever lived," Mel Brooks said—and everything is lifted, irradiated, with him.

Originally published as "Richard Pryor, Flame-Thrower,"
The New Yorker, 2015

Two Italian girls, 1953

ART WINS

Elena Ferrante

A few paragraphs into Elena Ferrante's novel *The Story of the Lost Child*, the final volume of the writer's so-called Neapolitan quartet—the first three volumes are *My Brilliant Friend*, *The Story of a New Name*, and *Those Who Leave and Those Who Stay*—Lena, the narrator, says that now we're coming to "the most painful part of the story." Really? It's going to get worse? When we last saw Lena, she was walking out on a decent husband and two daughters to run off with a man who we know is going to betray her. The little girls scream and weep and hang on to her skirt, begging her not to go. "I couldn't bear it," she writes. "I knelt down, I held them around the waist, I said: All right, I won't go, you are my children, I'll stay with you." This calms them down. Then she goes to her bedroom and packs the suitcase she will take when, a few days later—as she already knows—she will drop the girls off with a neighbor, saying she'll be back shortly, and leave for the train station.

Ferrante's Neapolitan series, unlike other long historical novels we might compare it with (*Buddenbrooks*, *Remembrance of Things Past*), does not go to a lot of trouble to span generations or social classes. Most of its characters come from a single cluster of working-poor families living in a noisy, hot slum on the outskirts of Naples between 1950 and 2010. Ferrante supplies a dramatis personae at the beginning of the first volume—the shoemaker's family, the Cerullos, Fernando, Nunzia, Lila, and Rino; the mad widow's family, the Cappuccios, Melina, Ada, and Antonio; the grocer's family, the Carraccis, Don Achille, Maria, Stefano, Pinuccia, and Alfonso; and so on—and, apart from births and deaths, the cast hasn't changed much by the fourth volume. All these people are fantastically enmeshed. They practically can't walk to the corner without running into someone they've slept with or beaten up.

But no two characters are more bound together than Lila, the shoe-maker's daughter, and Lena, the porter's daughter. Both were born in 1944; they meet at the age of six, when they are entering first grade. Lena is blond and plump and inclined to do as she's told. Lila is dark and skinny and ferocious. "Her quickness of mind was like a hiss, a dart, a lethal bite." Everyone's afraid of Lila, and most of them are in love with her, too, but none more than Lena, and Lila loves Lena back, though "love" is too narrow a word for it. The two envy each other, compete with each other. They help and gravely harm each other. In *The Story of the Lost Child*, they get pregnant at the same time; they go to their doctor's appointments together, and each holds the other's hand during her pelvic examination. For much of that book, Lena's family lives upstairs from Lila's, and their children eat and sleep now at one apartment, now at the other. You could say that they are two halves of one complete woman, but actually each is complete in herself. And it is through their interaction that Ferrante says what she has to say about the world.

She has two subjects, basically. The first is women. This is the most thoroughgoing feminist novel I have ever read. (I will call the four books one novel. They are, though the first volume, at least, could be read without the others.) In the person of Lila, we have an embodiment of female beauty like something out of Titian. At the end of *My Brilliant Friend*, this girl, sixteen years old and due to get married, to Stefano, that afternoon, asks Lena to give her a bath. Lena speaks of her inner turmoil at being asked to rest her gaze

> on the childish shoulders, on the breasts and stiffly cold nipples, on the narrow hips and the tense buttocks, on the black sex, on the long legs, and on the tender knees, on the curved ankles, on the elegant feet; and to act as if it's nothing, when instead everything is there, present, in the poor dim room, amid the worn furniture, on the uneven, water-stained floor. . . . I washed her with slow, careful gestures, first letting her squat in the tub, then asking her to stand up: I still have in my ears the sound of the dripping water, and the impression that the copper of the tub had a consistency not different from Lila's flesh, which was smooth, solid, calm. I had a confusion of feelings and thoughts: embrace her, weep with her, kiss her, pull her hair, laugh, pretend to sexual experience and instruct her in a learned voice, distancing her with words just at the moment of greatest closeness. But in the end there was only the hostile thought that I was washing her, from her hair to the soles of her feet, early in the morning, just so that Stefano could sully her in the course of the night. I imagined her naked as she was at that moment, entwined with her husband, in the bed in the new house, while the train clattered under their windows and his violent flesh entered her with a sharp blow, like the cork pushed by the palm into the neck of a wine bottle.

As Ferrante makes clear here, a woman's sexual allure will not get her much. Lila never liked sex. (Her wedding night is a violent rape scene.) As for Lena, she does like sex, and in a touching passage she says to her old boyfriend Antonio—whose heart she broke for the sake of the no-good Nino she's running away with at the end of *Those Who Leave and*

Those Who Stay—that it was he who awakened her to it: "He was the discovery of excitement, he was the pit of the stomach that grew warm, that opened up, that turned liquid, releasing a burning indolence." But, as she goes on to tell him, nothing ever fulfilled that expectation. At the end of the book, Lena is alone, and Lila, no doubt, is, too.

Yet there is no repudiation of the trappings of femininity: the dolls, the bracelets, the buttons and bows. The book fairly teems with women's things, women's bodies, which, furthermore, are imagined as being in a state of constant flow, as if they were part of some piece of French *écriture féminine*. Lena again and again has visions that her mother, whom she mostly hates, has crawled inside her body and is kicking around in there. Lila has something worse, a condition she calls "dissolving boundaries": it seems to her that edges of things melt, and their innards squirt and slosh into each other. Do you remember, Lila asks Lena, that night on Ischia, when you all said how beautiful the sky was? To Lila, it wasn't beautiful: "I smelled an odor of rotten eggs, eggs with a greenish-yellow yolk inside the white and inside the shell, a hard-boiled egg cracked open. I had in my mouth poisoned egg stars, their light had a white, gummy consistency, it stuck to your teeth, along with the gelatinous black of the sky, I crushed it with disgust, I tasted a crackling of grit. Am I clear? Am I making myself clear?"

As most of her readers will know by now, "Elena Ferrante" is a pen name. Apart from the information in the jacket bio—that she is a woman and was born in Naples—we know nothing about the author. (There is an interview with her by Sandro and Sandra Ferri in the Spring 2015 issue of *The Paris Review*, but it gives no further biographical details.) It seems to me unquestionable, though, that these books were written not just by a female but by one who has been pregnant. Lila says that if she didn't stay alert, the world would undergo a huge inundation: "The waters would break through, a flood would rise, carrying everything off in clots of menstrual blood, in cancerous polyps, in bits of yellowish fiber." In fact, at this point in the novel waters might indeed be breaking. Lila and Lena are both heavily pregnant, and they are sitting in a car in the middle of Naples, where they have taken refuge from an earthquake, the Irpinia earthquake of 1980. (The book tracks world events closely. We hear about the Red Brigades, Chernobyl, the World Trade Center.) All around them, gas mains are exploding; buildings are collapsing; a cemetery is breaking off the mainland and falling into the sea.

Here, Ferrante has used a catastrophic real-life event to exemplify—indeed, culminate—her sense of women's undefended boundaries, but the matter comes up again and again, even in modest circumstances. At one point, Lena's daughter Dede, now a young woman, who for years has avoided any physical contact with her—she's another one who fears being invaded—breaks her rule and goes and sits in her mother's lap. Lena describes the feeling of her daughter's warm bottom, the "wide hips," against her thighs. To me, that was almost as unsettling as the earthquake.

Much of the thrill of the four books lies in just this elastic back-and-forth between realism and hallucination. No one is a more careful realist than Ferrante. When Lena's husband, in their kitchen, gets ready to punch her in the face, Ferrante takes time to tell us about the hum of the refrigerator and the drip of the faucet in the background. And her general faithfulness to reality encourages us to stay with her as she veers off into hallucination. Some scenes, just by their tone and pacing, and by what they omit as much as by what they include, seem to take place in slow motion or underwater or on another planet. It's not that things are askew. The very air is different. This, Ferrante seems to say, is what happens in the world of women, and though much of the book is devoted to women's more frequently discussed problems—such as how they are supposed to go out to work and raise the kids at the same time, and, if they do have work, work they care about, how come this still seems to them secondary to their relationship with a man?—it is the exploration of the women's mental underworld that makes the book so singular an achievement in feminist literature; indeed, in all literature.

Ferrante's other subject is language. Insofar as the book is realist, the critical thing in it is the neighborhood: the poverty, the ignorance, the unremitting violence. The only way to gain any power or happiness is to get out, and the only way to do that is via schooling, the learning of words, and not the words your parents speak—that's dialect—but standard Italian. Apart from femaleness, there is nothing in the book more important than this. From page to page, in passages of dialogue, Ferrante tells us (and then so does her excellent translator, Ann Goldstein) if someone is speaking standard Italian and the other is speaking dialect, so that we can understand what is going on between them, and then, if anyone switches, as they may do, what that means.

Basically, what the linguistic difference means is whether the person is going to remain in the neighborhood and—to put it in female terms, Ferrante's terms—get pregnant every two years, and get beaten up by her husband if dinner is late, or whether she's going to escape this. Both Lila and Lena understand the situation early. When they are twelve and have the chance to go to middle school—where you can perfect your Italian and even learn Latin, and also write essays and read books—both of them are desperate to go. But first you must pass an exam, and taking the exam costs money, and Lila's family is marginally poorer than Lena's. Also, Lila's father fails to see why a girl needs an education, as Lena's father, for some reason, does not. So Lila is told that she can't continue her schooling. This is the fork in the road for the two girls, and it is marked by the book's first serious moral crime. Lila, with all her powers of seduction, suggests to Lena that they play hooky one morning and walk across the city to the harbor, to the sea, which they have never seen. Lena agrees, as she always does to Lila's mad plans. But on the appointed morning, when they set out, Lila begins acting strange. She slows down; she keeps looking behind her, as if she's afraid they're being followed. Her hands start to sweat. Suddenly a storm breaks, and Lila insists that they go back. This baffles Lena— Lila is never afraid of anything—but they run back home, and Lena gets a beating. The next day, Lila inspects Lena's bruises:

> "All they did was beat you?"
> "What should they have done?"
> "They're still sending you to study Latin?"
> I looked at her in bewilderment.
> Was it possible? She had taken me with her hoping that as a punishment my parents would not send me to middle school?

Yes, presumably, and then she repented. For the rest of the novel, that ambivalence never lets up. From middle school, Lena keeps on going, through university. She becomes a writer—of feminist novels! Along the way, Lila helps her. She encourages her, praises her. Once she gets married and has some money, she buys Lena's schoolbooks, and not secondhand ones but new ones. "My brilliant friend," she calls her. She also mocks her and, for long periods, stops speaking to her. She knows that the more learning Lena has, the more this will separate them. But her feelings are also in accord with the old, primitivist formula whereby the less refined something is, the truer it is.

Lena works ceaselessly, in school and later. Her books make her famous. And sadly, in the dark of night, she too trusts the old formula. She feels she can never truly write well because she lacks Lila's wild, prodigal spirit. Lila, she thinks, "possessed intelligence and didn't put it to use but, rather, wasted it, like a great lady for whom all the riches in the world are merely a sign of vulgarity." If, on occasion, Lena thinks she has written well, that, in her opinion, is because she has somehow captured Lila's spirit, made "space for her in me." (This is why, in *The Story of the Lost Child*, Lena has moved back into her natal slum. She feels that she needs to be near Lila in order to do her work.) When she's not worried about whether she's been able to absorb Lila into her books, she worries that Lila will turn out books of her own.

Because she has had so little education, Lila can't produce a book, but she does write little things now and then. In the second volume of the series, when she gets married, she gives Lena a tin box tied with a piece of string—her writings, she says. She doesn't want her husband to find them. Neither must Lena ever read them. Of course, Lila is no sooner out of sight than Lena opens the box and begins poring over the eight notebooks it contains. They are poignant: Lila practicing Italian, penning descriptions of things (a leaf, a pot), recording what she thought of a movie she saw in the church hall. But halfway down a page, she will lose patience and fill the rest of the space with drawings: "twisted trees, humped, smoking mountains, grim faces." For weeks, Lena studies the notebooks, "learning by heart the passages I liked, the ones that thrilled me, . . . the ones that humiliated me." Finally, one night, she leaves the house with the box under her arm:

> I stopped on the Solferino bridge to look at the lights filtered through a cold mist. I placed the box on the parapet, and pushed it slowly, a little at a time, until it fell into the river, as if it were her, Lila in person, plummeting, with her thoughts, words, the malice with which she struck back at anyone, the way she appropriated me, as she did every person or thing or event or thought that touched her.

This person that Lena loves more than anything in the world: she is trying to kill her. And in keeping with the book's logic, she is doing it by killing her words.

In *The Story of the Lost Child*, something very terrible happens to Lila (see the book's title), and one day, after laboring for years under her sorrow, she simply disappears. Her son, Rino, calls Lena, now living in Turin. Everything Lila owns, he says, is gone from the apartment. As Lena understands, this is not because Lila needed those things but because she wanted to erase herself. She even scissored herself out of the photos of herself with Rino. Lena, who had been stalled in her work, now starts to write again, to prevent Lila's self-annihilation. To Lila's oppressive disorder—the things sloshing into other things, the things flying apart—she will oppose her own, once-despised instinct for order. Dispersal will meet containment; dialect, Italian. This is an old literary trick, or at least as old as Proust: to tell a story of pain and defeat and then, at the end, say that it will all be redeemed by art, by a book—indeed, the book you are reading. Lena will write for months and months, for as long as it takes, she says, to give Lila "a form whose boundaries won't dissolve." She will thus calm her friend, and herself— and, to reach beneath the metaphor, rescue life from grief, clarity from chaos, without denying the existence of grief and chaos. She pulls her chair up to her desk. "We'll see who wins this time," she says. Art wins. We win.

Originally published as "Elena Ferrante's New Book: Art Wins,"
The New Yorker, 2015

Elmore Leonard at his desk, 2010

ALL VILLAINS HAVE MOTHERS

Elmore Leonard

Elmore Leonard (1925–2013) became famous as a crime novelist, but he didn't like being grouped with most of the big names in that genre, people such as Raymond Chandler and Dashiell Hammett or, indeed, any of the noir writers. He disapproved of their melodrama, their pessimism, their psychos and nymphos and fancy writing. He saw in crime no glamour or sexiness but, on the contrary, long hours and sore feet. His criminals didn't become what they were out of any fondness for vice. They just needed work, and that's what was available. They are not serial killers (or only one is) but bank robbers, loan sharks, bookies.

Leonard's father worked for General Motors, and Leonard spent most of his early years in Detroit, his mind occupied mainly by sports and girls. He also liked to read: adventure books and, later, the novels that his sister received from the Book of the Month Club. (Hemingway became his idol.) After graduating from high school in 1943, he was drafted and went with the Seabees to New Guinea and the Admiralty

Islands, where, he said, he mostly handed out beers and emptied garbage. Once he got back from the war, he went to the University of Detroit on the GI Bill, majoring in English and philosophy. (His entire education was acquired in Roman Catholic institutions, to which, he later said, he was very grateful, since they taught him to write a proper English sentence.) After graduation, he got a job right away, working for Campbell-Ewald, the ad agency that handled Chevrolet. But he soon came to hate advertising, and he thought he might try writing stories for magazines.

Stories about what? During Leonard's youth, Wild West movies—*My Darling Clementine, Red River*—were immensely popular, and he adored them. In the 1940s and '50s, there was also a big market for western novels and, in the magazines, for western stories. Leonard made a schedule for himself. He would get up early, go down to his basement, and, from five to seven, write stories before going to work. The third one he sent out, "Trail of the Apache" (1951), got taken by *Argosy*, a popular men's magazine. In the decade that followed, Leonard sold many more stories and several novels. A couple of the stories were also made into Hollywood films. Riding high, he quit Campbell-Ewald in 1961, intending to become a full-time writer. But his family was growing—he and his wife eventually had five children—and he got sidetracked doing freelance jobs to make money.

Meanwhile, his market changed. In the 1960s, westerns were disappearing from both film and print. (The genre was being absorbed by TV.) Leonard's agent, a smart woman named Marguerite Harper, told him to get out of westerns. He tried. After writing his first non-western novel, *The Big Bounce* (1969), he backslid and wrote two more westerns. He really did love the genre. But then he finally made the break to crime fiction, and he stayed with it for forty-odd years.

Subject matter was only one of Leonard's commercial considerations. More important to him, probably, was his prose style. Not only his western tales, but fully twenty-seven of his novels and stories were

adapted for film or television. He said that a big reason his books sold
to makers of movies and TV was that, with their natural-seeming dialogue and their open-and-shut scenes, they looked easy to shoot. But
Hollywood didn't just discover those virtues in Leonard. He developed
them, at least in part, *for* Hollywood. After Marguerite Harper died, he
moved his business to a Hollywood agent, the famous H. N. Swanson,
and the Swanson Agency handled most of his work—novels, movies,
TV—from then on.

The only time Leonard got jitters about writing, he said, was
when, for some reason—a competing assignment, a delay in obtaining information—he couldn't get going on the job. Once he started,
he was fine. He went at it from nine to six, often skipping lunch. (He
ate peanuts out of a can.) In fifty-nine years, he produced forty-five
novels.

Many people would say that Leonard's greatest gift was his "ear,"
meaning, broadly, the ability to write English that, while it sounds
extremely natural, is also beautiful and musical. When critics speak
of a writer's ear, this often carries a political implication, of the democratic sort. They are talking about writers (Mark Twain, Willa Cather)
whose world, by virtue of being humble, would seem to exclude beauty
and music, so that when the writer manages to find in it those riches,
the world in question—and, by extension, the whole world—comes to
seem blessed. In *Glitz* (1985), one of Leonard's first truly distinguished
novels, the hero, Vincent Mora, a policeman, is about to go to Puerto
Rico on medical leave. He longs to make this trip. He wants to see
Roosevelt Roads Naval Station, where his father shipped out in World
War II:

> He had a picture of his dad . . . taken at El Yunque, up in the rain
> forest: the picture of a salty young guy, a coxswain, his white cover
> one finger over his eyebrows, grinning, nothing but clouds behind

him up there on the mountain: a young man Vincent had never known but who looked familiar. He was twenty years older than his dad now.

That's because his father was killed in the Battle of Anzio, in Italy, soon after the photograph was taken.

Leonard doesn't clobber us with this painful fact. Indeed, he tells us about the father's death before describing the photograph. And as Mora's mind turns to the photo, any sorrow is forgotten. It is then that we hear of the "salty young guy," "grinning, nothing but clouds behind him." That last phrase would seem the culmination of happiness. He is in the sky, this lucky boy! Then we come to the next clause—"a young man Vincent had never known"—and we remember. The reason Mora's father is in the sky is that he's dead.

There's another young man. The night before Mora has reason to think about his father, he is coming home from work, walking from his car to his front door, with a bag of groceries—"a half gallon of Gallo Hearty Burgundy, a bottle of prune juice and a jar of Ragú spaghetti sauce"—when he is accosted by a strung-out young mugger. Somehow he can't bring himself to drop his jug of Gallo on the sidewalk and reach for his gun, which would have been the safe, and also the professional, thing to do. Instead, he tries to reason with the boy:

He said, "You see that car? Standard Plymouth, nothing on it, not even wheel covers?" It was a pale gray. "You think I'd go out and buy a car like that?" The guy was wired or not paying attention. "It's a *police* car, asshole. Now gimme the gun and go lean against it."

The ploy doesn't work. The boy shoots Mora; the groceries fall; Mora, groping through the broken glass, finds his gun and fires it. He comes out okay; the mugger doesn't. Mora, the son of a dead boy, has given the world another dead boy.

In twenty years on the police force, this is the first time he has ever killed anyone. He cannot console himself. Lying in his hospital bed, he speaks to his closest friend on the Miami Beach police, Buck Torres:

> "I didn't scare him enough," Vincent said. . . .
>
> Torres said, "Scare him? That what you suppose to do?"
>
> Vincent said, "You know what I mean. I didn't handle it right, I let it go too far."
>
> Torres said, "What are you, a doctor? You want to talk to the asshole? You know how long the line would be, all the assholes out there? You didn't kill him somebody else would have to, sooner or later."

This is a sample of Leonard's "ear" in the narrow sense of the term: his feel for the spoken word. Asked, once, how he was able to tap into actual speech rhythms, Leonard answered, "I just listen." (He also tipped his hat to a few novelists he regarded as masters of dialogue, above all George V. Higgins, the author of *The Friends of Eddie Coyle*.) In the words he gives his characters, he often dispenses with verb-tense niceties and above all with subordinate conjunctions and the conditional and subjunctive verb forms that go with them. ("You didn't kill him somebody else would have to.")

In certain of his novels, these grammatical adjustments, combined with regional usage, produce something one could call dialect. Leonard's dialogue contains great tributes to the speech of Mexican Americans and Cuban Americans and old Jewish men who want to tell you how much better things were in Miami in the old days. But Leonard lived almost all his life in or around Detroit, a city where, in his time, more than half of the people, and well over half of the people involved in the criminal justice system, were African American. Consequently, a lot of his best characters are Black, and speak a language that many people, Black and white, would agree is classic African American, mid-twentieth century, northern. Early in his *Unknown Man No. 89* (1977) we encounter a situation commonly found in stories about crimes committed by people working in tandem: not all the collaborators know what the take was, and some of them suspect that they're not being given their fair share. In *Unknown Man* one bank robber asks another how much they got from the Wyandotte Savings job:

> "We didn't get nothing," Bobby said.
> Virgil nodded, very slowly. "That's what I was afraid you were going to say. Nothing from the cashier windows?"
> "Nothing," Bobby said. "No time."
> "I heard seventeen big big ones."
> "You heard shit."
> "Told to me by honest gentlemen work for the prosecuting attorney."
> "Told to you by your mama it still shit."

Virgil then excuses himself to go to the bathroom, emerges with a twelve-gauge shotgun, and blows Bobby away.

Even more masterful than Leonard's dialogue is his third-person point-of-view narrative, where events are narrated as if objectively but in fact are being related from a tight, though shifting, point of view. *Freaky Deaky* (1988), which may be the most beloved of Leonard's novels (it was his own favorite), is dominated by a superb odd couple, Donnell Lewis and Woody Ricks. In the novel's backstory, in the 1960s and '70s, Donnell was a Black Panther; Woody was a rich, radical-chic sympathizer. He gave money; he opened his house for parties, as long as he could take one or two of those girls who didn't shave their armpits upstairs to bed. Now in the 1980s, all that is over. Woody is a prostrate alcoholic—happy to be one—and Donnell, having managed to get rid of Woody's chauffeur, cleaning lady, gardener, lawyer, and everyone else, lives with him and sees to his every need while also trying to figure out a way to become his sole heir, soon.

In the morning, when it's time to get up, Donnell brings Woody two vodka and ginger ales on a tray. Woody drinks one, vomits, then drinks the other one and starts to feel okay. Breakfast is cornflakes and vodka; lunch seems to be some more vodka. Then nap. Though the nap is described in the third person, Donnell is clearly speaking, or thinking:

> What the man liked to do for his nap time, couple of hours before dinner: turn on the stereo way up loud enough to break windows, slide into the pool on his rubber raft naked to Ezio Pinza doing "Some Enchanted Evening" and float around a few minutes before he'd yell, "Donnell?" And Donnell, his hand ready on the button, would shut off the stereo. Like that, Ezio Pinza telling the man to make somebody his own or all through his lifetime he would dream all alone, and then dead silence. No sound at all in the dim swimming pool house, steam hanging over the water, steam rising from the pile of white flesh on the raft, like it was cooking.

Out of Donnell's combined fastidiousness ("steam rising from the pile of white flesh"), wonderment ("Ezio Pinza telling the man to make somebody his own"), and guile, Leonard creates this marvelous character. In the novel there are also two unsavory former radicals who are planning to extort money from Woody by threatening to blow up his house. And there is a police detective, Mankowski, from the bomb squad. (He's the hero, at least officially.) The point-of-view mike gets handed around among these people, each supplying his own accents, his own details, scores of them, every one of them perfect for that character, and also perfect just in itself, in its accuracy, its solidity, its wit.

In 1981 a fan of Leonard's, Gregg Sutter, began doing research for him; eventually he went to work for him full-time. Sutter is editing the Library of America's three-volume set of Leonard's work. The second volume was just published. Each volume ends with an invaluable twenty-eight-page chronology—almost a biography—and Sutter is at work on a full-scale biography. It is no doubt owing to him that I now know how to open a metal door locked by a dead bolt. Indeed, I believe I could steal a car.

Leonard had a taste for the grotesque, for an almost magical ugliness. Apart from Detroit, his favorite setting was South Florida (he had a condo in North Palm Beach), and that area offered him a lot of vivid material: a drug culture, a flavorful ethnic mix, shirts with hibiscus prints. In one Florida novel, *LaBrava* (1983), a Cuban immigrant named Cundo Rey—car thief by day, go-go dancer by night—tells a man who is trying to eat lunch how he once saw a snake digesting a bat. As he watched this, Cundo says, one of the bat's wings was still sticking out of the snake's jaws, and moving. I don't understand how that's possible, but I'll see it until I die: a bat's wing, or maybe just the tip, feebly moving for a few minutes more, while, as Cundo enthusiastically explains, the other end of the animal is "down in the snake turning to juice."

In another Florida tale, *Stick* (1983), we are told what it's like for a drug importer, Chucky, when his daily quaalude regimen is interrupted: "He felt exactly the way he had felt when he was twelve years old and had killed the dog with his hands." That sentence is all we hear about the dog until fifty pages later, when we get one more sentence, informing us that after Chucky choked the little thing—it was annoying him—he threw it against a brick wall.

But whatever his fondness for the elaborately horrible, Leonard's books are sometimes surprisingly short on ordinary violence. Chili Palmer, the loan shark hero of *Get Shorty* (1990)—he is probably Leonard's most beloved character (he was played by John Travolta in the movie, and that no doubt helped)—doesn't carry a weapon. Violence is bad for business, he says. When there is violence, even murder, it is often hedged in by so many confusing and ridiculous circumstances that it no longer feels violent. In *Maximum Bob* (1991), a Florida novel, we get the following: "When Roland was shot dead and Elvin sent to prison for killing a man he thought was the one had got the woman to kill Roland, nobody in the family seemed surprised." By the time you get to the end of that sentence, you're not surprised either. Makes sense.

This may have less to do with Leonard's ethics than with his aesthetics. He just wasn't that interested in his plots, and the reason, he explained, was that he was too interested in his characters, above all the bad guys. In his mind, he said, "I see convicts sitting around talking about a baseball game. I see them as kids. All villains have mothers." Indeed, he was their mother. He picked out their clothes; he chose their names. (He was a champion namer. This was part of his "ear": Mr. Woody, Jackie Garbo, Chili Palmer, Cundo Rey. One thug has a tiny little daughter named Farrah.) He gave them girlfriends, ways of speaking, things they liked to eat. And as they were flowering under the beam of his affection—riding around in their stolen cars, discussing their upcoming felonies—he tended to ignore the noncriminal element in his books: the police, the decent citizens, the people who might push the plot forward by preventing or solving the crimes. Regular people, he complained, "don't talk with any certain sound."

The resulting story lines may, in the words of Ben Yagoda of *The New York Times*, come to seem like "smoky improvisations." Eventually, Yagoda said, "the elements congeal into a taut climax, but for the first two-thirds or so of the book, the characters, the reader and, it turns out, the author simmer on the low burner . . . trying to figure out what's going on." This isn't true of all Leonard's novels—he created some masterful farce plots—but it's true of many of them, especially the better ones. Leonard thought writing was fun. (That's how he could do it from nine to six, five days a week.) And he kept it fun by not forcing himself to do what he didn't want to do, such as construct tidy plots. It should be added that his plots, however meandering, do not usually make him hard to read. *Glitz*, the book that inspired Yagoda's remarks above, spent sixteen weeks on the *Times* bestseller list, and from that point on every last one of Leonard's novels was a bestseller. He wasn't the only person having fun.

As for the quality of the writing, his career follows a neat bell curve. This is not usually the case with artists whom we consider first-rate. Very many of them have finished doing their best work by age sixty. Leonard *started* doing his best work at age sixty. You can see his earliest efforts in the just-published *Charlie Martz and Other Stories*, a file-cabinet-clean-out collection, with a foreword by Leonard's son Peter. These are the stories that Leonard pulled out of himself in the basement before going to work at the ad agency in the 1950s, and they are touching, because even though most of them didn't find publishers, they show you Leonard growing, page by page—getting over the need to be cool, breathing life into the dialogue, giving the characters little tweaks that make them singular, memorable.

The collection covers about ten years. Multiply that by three, and you have something like the first thirty years of Leonard's novel-writing career, consisting of twenty-two books. Some were duds, and he probably knew this, but he kept going. (For one thing, the duds still made money. Crime fiction sells.) Slowly, slowly, he got better, and even slow betterment, if it goes on for thirty years, adds up to serious improvement.

In the early 1980s, something changes. His plots, auspiciously, become messier, and his characters, as if electroshocked, come to full, breathing life. In the eleven years from 1985 to 1996, he produces his five best novels: *Glitz*, with Vincent Mora and the father in the sky; *Freaky Deaky*, with Mr. Woody on the raft; *Get Shorty*, with Chili Palmer; *Maximum Bob*, with Elvin killing the man he thought was the one had got the woman to kill Roland; and *Out of Sight* (1996), whose hero has robbed more than two hundred banks. Then, quite smoothly, Leonard passes the apex and begins to decline. Once more, he must have known; once more, this did not stop him.

Most of the critics said nothing, either out of deference to his age or because by then he was not just a writer but a symbol of that cluster of virtues—virility, stoicism, plainspokenness—that are supposedly central to American art, and constitute our bulwark against its takeover by the snobs and the fancy-pants. Such caricatures are routinely drawn of aging artists, partly in defense against anticipated criticisms of their now-weakening product. It is hard for an artist over seventy to get an honest review. Leonard was seventy when *Out of Sight* was published. He wrote thirteen more novels. All of them were overpraised.

But their predecessors weren't. Part of the reason genre art is held in lower esteem than other art is that it hews to a formula and thereby gives artist and audience less work to do—indeed, less work they *can* do. If, for example, a crime novelist takes on love or hope or the loss of hope, there is a limit to how subtle and fresh his thoughts about such things can be, because if he gets too interesting, he might violate the formula. But in *Out of Sight*, Leonard's masterpiece, he takes on exactly those three subjects, and gives them a tender new life. Jack Foley, the veteran bank robber, has no interest in changing his line of work. The day after he escapes from prison—the book begins, wonderfully, with the jail break—he holds up another bank. His old bank-robbing partner, Buddy, comes to the prison to pick him up. Buddy congratulates him: "Fell off your horse and got right back on."

But in the middle of the escape, something happens to him. Outside the prison yard, he runs into a good-looking twenty-nine-year-old deputy federal marshal, Karen Sisco, carrying a pump-action shotgun. She is there on some other business, but she immediately realizes what Foley is up to and tells him he's under arrest, whereupon he pushes her into the trunk of her car, climbs in after her, and pulls down the lid. Buddy gets behind the wheel, and off they go.

Foley and Karen spend about ten pages in the trunk together—after the initial awkwardness, they talk about movies ("Another one Faye Dunaway was in I liked, *Three Days of the Condor*")—and Foley falls in love. So, probably, does Karen, though soon afterward, when they are switching cars, she tries to shoot him. (She takes her job seriously.) Later, as Foley is mooning over her, Buddy tells him he's too old (forty-seven), and has too long a rap sheet, to think about having a woman like that: "The best either of us can do is look at nice pretty girls and think, well, if we had done it different . . ."

The remaining chapters are devoted to finding out whether that's true. At points, *Out of Sight* is throbbingly romantic. (Foley and Karen get a single night together, after having drinks in one of those glass-walled revolving cocktail lounges, in a snowstorm.) The book is also, for Leonard, extremely violent. At the same time, strangely, it is one of the author's funniest books. It ends as we knew it would. Not only does Foley not get the girl; she finally succeeds in arresting him. He asks her to kill him. He can't bear to go back to prison. She shoots him, but only in the leg, to prevent him from escaping. She then goes up the stairs to where he has fallen and lifts his ski mask:

> "I'm sorry, Jack, but I can't shoot you."
>
> "You just did, for Christ's sake."
>
> "You know what I mean." She said, "I want you to know . . . I never for a minute felt you were too old for me." She said, "I'm afraid, though, thirty years from now I'll feel different about it. I'm sorry, Jack, I really am."

It's a cold ending—Hollywood couldn't bear it; they changed it—but it's warmly cold. Before this, there was love, and comedy. They're still there, and so the sadness is greater: *lacrimae rerum*. Not all of Leonard's books are on this level, but five or six of them are, plus parts of many others. That's a lot.

Originally published as "The Elmore Leonard Story,"
The New York Review of Books, 2015

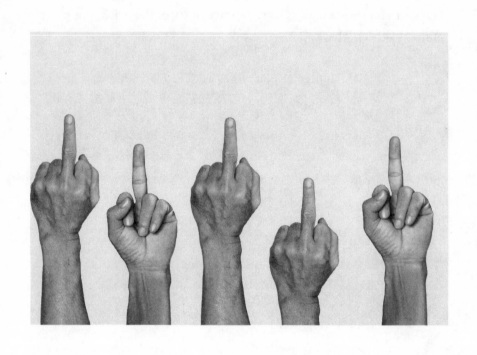

FUCKWAD

Dirty Words

Obscene language presents problems, the linguist Michael Adams writes in his new book, *In Praise of Profanity* (2016), "but no one seems to spend much time thinking about the good it does." Actually, a lot of people in the last few decades have been considering its benefits, together with its history, its neuroanatomy, and above all its fantastically large and colorful word list. Jesse Sheidlower's *F-Word*, an *OED*-style treatment of "fuck" that was first published in 1995, has gone into its third edition, ringing ever more changes—"artfuck," "bearfuck," "fuckbag," "fuckwad," "horsefuck," "sportfuck," "Dutch fuck," "unfuck"—on that venerable theme.

Meanwhile, Jonathon Green's *Green's Dictionary of Slang*, in three volumes (2010), lists 1,740 words for sexual intercourse, 1,351 for penis, 1,180 for vagina, 634 for anus or buttocks, and 540 for defecation and urination. In the last few months alone there have been two new books: *What the F* (2016), by Benjamin Bergen, a cognitive scientist at the University of California at San Diego; and Adams's *In Praise of Profanity*. So somebody is interested in profanity.

Many writers point out that there hasn't been enough research on the subject. As long as we haven't cured cancer, it's hard to get grants to study dirty words. Accordingly, there don't seem to have been a lot of recent discoveries in this field. Very many of Bergen's and Adams's points, as they acknowledge, have been made in earlier books, an especially rich source being Melissa Mohr's *Holy Shit: A Brief History of Swearing* (2013). Mohr even reads us the graffiti from the brothel in ancient Pompeii—disappointingly laconic (for example, "I came here and fucked, then went home"), but good to know all the same.

Of course one wants to know the history of the words, and all the books provide it, insofar as they can. "Fuck" did not get its start as an acronym, as has sometimes been jocosely proposed ("For Unlawful Carnal Knowledge," and so on). If it had, there wouldn't be so many obvious cognates in neighboring languages. Sheidlower lists, among others, the German *ficken* (to copulate), the Norwegian regional *fukka* (ditto), and the Middle Dutch *fokken* (to thrust, to beget children), all of them apparently descendants of a Germanic root meaning "to move back and forth." Sheidlower says "fuck" probably entered English in the fifteenth century, but Bergen, writing later, reports that the medievalist Paul Booth recently came across a legal document from 1310 identifying a man as Roger Fuckebythenavele. Booth conjectures that this might have been a metaphor for something like "dimwit." On the other hand, it could have been a nickname inflicted on an inexperienced young man who actually tried to do it that way, and whose partner could not resist telling her girlfriends.

Something to note here is that the word appeared in a legal document. For a long time "fuck" was not considered an especially nasty word. "Cunt," too, was once an ordinary word. A fourteenth-century surgery textbook calmly states that "in women the neck of the bladder is short and is made fast to the cunt." Until well after the Renaissance, the words that truly shocked people had to do not with sexual or excretory functions but with religion—words that took the Lord's name in vain. As late as 1866, Baudelaire, who had been rendered aphasic by a stroke, was expelled from a hospital for compulsively repeating the phrase *cré nom*, short for *sacré nom* (holy name).

Many exclamations that now seem to us merely quaint were once "minced oaths," or euphemisms. "Criminy," "crikey," "cripes," "gee," "jeez," "bejesus," "geez Louise," "gee willikers," "jiminy," and "jeepers creepers" are all to "Christ" and "Jesus" what "frigging" is to "fucking." The shock-shift from religion to sexual and bathroom matters was of course due primarily to the decline of religion, but Mohr points out that once domestic arrangements were changed so as to give people some privacy for sex and elimination, references to these matters became violations of privacy, and hence shocking.

Though research has not done much for profanity, the opposite is not true. Neurologists have learned a great deal about the brain from studying how brain-damaged people use swearwords—notably, that they *do* use them, heavily, even when they have lost all other speech. What this suggests is that profanity is encoded in the brain separately from most other language. While neutral words are processed in the cerebral cortex, the late-developing region that separates us from other animals, profanity seems to originate in the more primitive limbic system, which lies embedded below the cortex and controls emotions. As a result, we care about swearwords differently. Hearing them, people may sweat (this can be measured by a polygraph), and, tellingly, bilingual people sweat more when the taboo word is in their first language.

The very sound of obscenities—forget their sense—seems to ring a bell in us, as is clear from the fact that many of them sound alike. In English, at least, one-third of the so-called four-letter words are indeed made up of four letters, forming one syllable, and in nine out of ten cases, Bergen writes, the syllable is "closed"—that is, it ends in a consonant or two consonants. Why? Probably because consonants sound sharper, surer of themselves, than vowels do. (Compare "piss" with "pee," "cunt" with "pussy.") It may be this tough-talk quality that accounts for certain widely recognized benefits of swearwords. For example, they help us endure pain. In one widely cited experiment, subjects were instructed to plunge a hand into ice-cold water and keep it there as long as they could. Half were told that they could utter a swearword while doing this, if they wanted to; the other half were told to say some harmless word, such as "wood." The swearing subjects were able to keep their hands in the water significantly longer than the pure-mouthed group.

Related to this analgesic function is swearing's well-known cathartic power. When you drop your grocery bag into a puddle or close the window on your finger, "geez Louise" is not going to help you much. "Fuck" is what you need, the more so, Adams says, because it doesn't just express an emotion; it states a philosophical truth. By its very extremeness, it is saying that "one has found the end of language and can go no further. Profanity is no parochial gesture, then. It strikes a complaint against the human condition." And in allowing us to do so verbally, it prevents more serious damage. "Take away swearwords," writes Melissa Mohr, "and we are left with fists and guns." The same is no doubt true of obscene gestures. According to Bergen, people have been giving each other the finger for more than two thousand years, and that must certainly be due in part to its usefulness in forestalling stronger action.

But even when anger is not involved, obscenity seems to operate on the side of fellowship. The philosopher Noël Carroll told me once of an international conference in Hanoi in 2006. On the first day, to break the ice, the Vietnamese and the Western scholars, taking turns, had a joke-telling contest at lunch. The first two Vietnamese scholars told off-color jokes, but the Westerners, fearful of committing a social error, stuck to clean jokes. A stiff courtesy reigned. Finally, the third

Western contestant (Carroll, and he recounted this with pride) told a dirty joke, about a rooster, and everyone relaxed. The conference went on to be a great success.

This barrier-crossing function, together with other forces—boredom, machismo, the analgesic effect—helps to account for the notorious frequency of "fuck" and, perhaps more frequently, of "motherfucker" in speech exchanged by people in the military and by men in work crews, jazz groups, and similar situations. Adams proposes that the reason swearwords are good for human relations is that they depend on trust, our trust that the person we are talking to shares our values and therefore won't dislike us for using a taboo word. "If a relationship passes the profanity test," he writes, "the parties conclude a pact that whatever they say in their intimate relationship stays in their intimate relationship." I would conjecture, indeed, that they make a pact that they *have* an intimate relationship. (This is the place to add that many people find that "talking dirty" enhances sex.) But such considerations seem too tender to apply to the ubiquity of "fuck" and "motherfucker" among soldiers and workmen, to whose interchanges these words seem, rather, to apply a sort of hard, even glaze, a compound of irritation and stoicism, together with, yes, a sense of subjection to a common fate.

But situations vary. According to the largest surveys that Bergen could lay his hands on, the English, the Americans, and the New Zealanders all agree that of sexually related profanities, "cunt" is the dirtiest. Yet there is huge disagreement within these countries about how foul a word it is. (About one-third of New Zealanders thought "cunt" would be acceptable for use on television.) There is great variation in the investment that different societies have in religious profanity. In some, the taboo on blasphemy has survived considerable secularization. In Quebec, Bergen says, *tabarnack* (tabernacle) and *calisse* (chalice) are far stronger obscenities than *merde* (shit) and *foutre* (fuck). Germany is often cited as having a specialty in scatological obscenities: *Arschloch* (asshole), *Arschgesicht* (ass face), *Arschgeburt* (born from an asshole), et cetera.

Japan, curiously, does not have swearwords in the usual sense. You can insult a Japanese person by telling him that he has made a mistake or done something foolish, but the Japanese language does not have any of those blunt-instrument epithets—no "ass face," no "fuckwad"—that can take care of the job in a word or two. The Japanese baseball star Ichiro Suzuki told *The Wall Street Journal* that one of the things he liked best about playing ball in the United States was swearing, which he learned to do in both English and Spanish. "Western languages," he reported happily, "allow me to say things that I otherwise can't."

The West is moving toward further liberalization, a trend hastened by cable TV and the Internet. Melissa Mohr reports that in March 2011 three of the top-ten hit songs on the *Billboard* pop music chart had titles containing obscenities. Nevertheless, the Federal Communications Commission still imposes fines on broadcasters who use what it regards as profanity. Steven Pinker, in his *Stuff of Thought* (2007), reprints the excellent "FCC Song," by Eric Idle, of Monty Python:

> *Fuck you very much, the FCC.*
> *Fuck you very much for fining me.*
> *Five thousand bucks a fuck,*
> *So I'm really out of luck.*
> *That's more than Heidi Fleiss was charging me.*

But though the FCC levies fines, it has never published a list of the words that in its view merit this penalty, nor does the ratings board of the Motion Picture Association of America specify what material leads to what ratings. Bergen records that when Matt Stone and Trey Parker submitted their *South Park* feature to the MPAA board, it came back with an NC-17 rating, one level below R. No one under the age of seventeen, even if accompanied by an adult, may be admitted to a film rated NC-17. Therefore, in the filmmakers' view, this rating would have sunk the film financially. At the same time, they resented the meddling. And so, while they changed passages that the board singled out as problematic, they took advantage of its failure to explain exactly what the problem was. Stone told the *Los Angeles Times*, "If there was something they said couldn't stay in the movie, we'd make it 10 times worse and five times as long. And they'd come back and say, 'OK, that's better.'"

The act of writing a sober book, with charts and notes and bibliography, about dirty words is itself a species of comedy, and Bergen and Adams use this for all it's worth. While actually doing a serious job— Bergen offers useful information, and Adams supplies subtle, nuanced reflections (he is the most philosophical of the writers I have read on obscenity)—they are also, unmistakably, having a good time, and trying to give us one. Bergen publishes scholarly graphics full of filthy gestures, and on the stated assumption that we need to know how American Sign Language lines up with spoken English, he reproduces photos of an attractive woman signing "You bitch you" and worse.

Adams, in a long digression, pays tribute to a book on latrine-wall graffiti by the linguist Allen Walker Read. Ostensibly, he is trying to rescue Read's findings from oblivion (the book was privately printed in Paris in 1935 and is now unavailable), but the quotations, like Bergen's dirty pictures in ASL, are suspiciously numerous and entertaining. In an auto camp in Truckee, California, Read found the following:

> *Shit here shit clear*
> *Wipe your ass*
> *And disappear*
> *Shakespear*

Adams himself has made a long study of the walls of public bathrooms and adds his findings to Read's. The traditional offerings, he says, are reflections on the meaning of life, contact information for people who would like to make friends, specifications of the length and girth of one's penis ("My dick is so long it can turn corners"), teacher evaluations ("Mr. Radley is a cocksucker"), and art, of course, together with art criticism ("The man that drew this never saw a cunt"). The discussion goes on for twenty-five pages, all of them rewarding.

But while the subject of these books sends the writers off on enjoyable tangents, it also encourages some tediousness. Adams cannot avoid the temptation to set up straw men—for example, a book, *The No Cussing Club: How I Fought Against Peer Pressure and How You Can Too!*, brought out in 2009 by a fourteen-year-old boy, McKay Hatch. Hatch, disgusted by the amount of obscenity he heard in his school, founded this clean-speaking organization. According to publicity materials, the No Cussing Club now has twenty thousand members. "I was just a regular kid," Hatch writes. "Except, now, my dad, my teachers, even the mayor of my city and people from all different countries tell me that I've made a difference. Sometimes, they even say I changed the world."

This kind of thing is fun to read about for a paragraph or two, but Adams gives us five. Also, the implication that objections to obscenity are gaining ground seems to be just plain wrong. As noted, many signs point to increasing linguistic permissiveness in our country, a good example being the public reaction to the release of Donald Trump's 2005 "pussy tape." Many people (me too), seeing the tape when it was released, four weeks before last year's election, concluded that, after this, Trump could not possibly be elected. We have learned otherwise.

As for Benjamin Bergen, his problem is that he cannot get over his joy in being naughty. Often, very often, he reminded me of a little boy who runs into the kitchen, yells "Fuck, fuck, doody, doody" at his mother, bursts out laughing, and runs off, expecting her to come after

him with a rolling pin or something. There's not a dirty joke in the
world that he doesn't think is funny.

In 2014, Pope Francis, trying, in his weekly Vatican address, to say
"in questo caso" (in this case), ended up saying "in questo cazzo" (in
this fuck) instead. This was an understandable mistake—the two words
are close—and the pope corrected himself immediately. Nevertheless,
Bergen, in a chapter titled "The Day the Pope Dropped the *C*-Bomb,"
goes on and on about the supposed implications. Uttering a profane
word like *cazzo* places the pope "in an ideological double bind," he
writes. And what might that be? Well,

> if the curse word was accidental, then he's just as linguistically fal-
> lible as the next guy, which isn't necessarily the ideal public image for
> the professed terrestrial representative of God. Conversely, he might
> still be infallible, yet have intended to say *cazzo*. Again, likely not the
> image he means to project.

But clearly the substitution was accidental. Bergen just can't bear not to
have a good snigger over the pope's saying "fuck." Sometimes he seems
to have written this book for teenagers. He explains what a syllable is,
and a pronoun. He calls us "dude."

So great is Bergen's passion to liberate dirty words from censorship that
he includes racial slurs among them. He says he has a principle—he
calls it his "Holy, Fucking, Shit, Nigger Principle"—that almost all
obscenities in English have to do with religion, sex, excretion, or ethnic
difference, and he thinks that words in the fourth category deserve the
same safe-conduct as those in the other three. He summons several old
arguments, notably that people saying "nigger" are using not standard
English but a different language, AAE, or African American English
(which seems to be the same as the Ebonics so argued over in the late
1990s), and that suppressing "nigger" means punishing the very people

we are supposedly trying to protect, since users of AAE are primarily African American.

But I think that lurking behind these arguments is another circumstance, the so-called "I'm offended" veto, which is causing students at our universities, and many other people, to demand that they be shielded from any information they might find disagreeable. Bergen hates righteousness, which, to him, I believe, would include all those who, when under the necessity of saying "nigger," even to designate a word (for example, "He said 'nigger'"), not a thing (for example, "He's a nigger"), will substitute the phrase "the n-word"—a usage that seems designed not so much to avoid giving offense as to point to the speaker as a person who could never commit such a wrong. This maneuver now has a name: virtue signaling. And like other recent commentators—for example, Greg Lukianoff and Jonathan Haidt in their much-discussed essay "The Coddling of the American Mind" in *The Atlantic* of September 2015 and Timothy Garton Ash in his recent book *Free Speech: Ten Principles for a Connected World*—he is worried that our brains will become enfeebled if we avoid disagreement and debate.

I applaud his sentiment, but he should not have tried to make this controversy parallel to quarrels over obscenity. Calling someone a "fuck face" is not nice, but it is meant to insult only one person. By contrast, a white person calling a Black person "nigger," the word the slave owners used, is insulting 13 percent of the population of the United States and reinvoking, in a perversely casual tone—as if everything were okay now—the worst crime our country ever committed. (By the end of his discussion of slurs, Bergen seems to agree. I think his editor might have asked him to tone it down.)

As for "fuck" and its brothers, though, you can see Bergen's point. Sometimes they are simply the mot juste, and even if you could come up with an inoffensive substitute, chances are it would be a lot less satisfying. Swearwords, as he says, are "good dirty fun." Michael Adams, too, is fond of them and, more than that, feels that they emerge from a kind of shadowland in our minds and our lives—an intersection of anger and gaiety—that demands acknowledgment. Bergen is sometimes silly, and Adams sentimental, but both are on the right side.

Originally published as "'Fuck'-ing Around,"
The New York Review of Books, 2017

Postscript: Since this essay appeared, many writers have dealt with the imposition of race-based taboos on American English. I recommend John McWhorter's 2021 book *Woke Racism*.

Angela Carter, 1987

METAMORPHOSES

Angela Carter

The English novelist Angela Carter is best known for her 1979 book *The Bloody Chamber*, which is a kind of updating of the classic European fairy tales. This means not that Carter's Little Red Riding Hood chews gum or rides a motorcycle but that the strange things in those tales—the werewolves and snow maidens, the cobwebbed caves and liquefying mirrors—are made to live again by means of a prose informed by psychoanalysis and cinema and Symbolist poetry. In Carter's version of "Beauty and the Beast," retitled "The Tiger's Bride," the beast doesn't change into a beauty. The beauty is changed into a beast, a beautiful one, by means of one of the more memorable sex acts in twentieth-century fiction. At the end of the tale, the heroine is ushered, naked, into the beast's chamber. He paces back and forth:

> I squatted on the wet straw and stretched out my hand. I was now within the field of force of his golden eyes. He growled at the back of his throat, lowered his head, sank on to his forepaws, snarled, showed

me his red gullet, his yellow teeth. I never moved. He snuffed the air, as if to smell my fear; he could not.

Slowly, slowly he began to drag his heavy, gleaming weight across the floor towards me.

A tremendous throbbing, as of the engine that makes the earth turn, filled the little room; he had begun to purr. . . .

He dragged himself closer and closer to me, until I felt the harsh velvet of his head against my hand, then a tongue, abrasive as sandpaper. "He will lick the skin off me!"

And each stroke of his tongue ripped off skin after successive skin, all the skins of a life in the world, and left behind a nascent patina of shiny hairs. My earrings turned back to water and trickled down my shoulders; I shrugged the drops off my beautiful fur.

Imagine that: a great, warm, wet, abrasive tongue licking off skin after skin, down to the bottommost one, which then sprouts shiny little animal hairs.

Because Carter took on fairy tales, she was sometimes pigeonholed as a "white witch," the sort of person who reads tarot cards and believes that trees speak to her. It didn't help that she favored an outré look, with long, flowing skirts and, in her late years, a great, disorderly mane of white hair. (Andrew Motion said she looked like "someone who'd been left out in a hurricane.") So it's good to see that *The Invention of Angela Carter*, by Edmund Gordon, a lecturer in English at King's College London, is a levelheaded book. The first thorough account of Carter's life, it is an authorized biography. Gordon had the cooperation of Carter's intimates and access to her letters and diaries. The book shows the faults endemic to authorized biographies: too much detail, together with a curious vagueness about family members who are still alive. But it reclaims Carter from the fairy kingdom and places her within what sounds like a real life. Unsurprisingly, we find out that the white witch cared about her reviews and sales.

Carter was born Angela Olive Stalker in 1940 and grew up in a quiet, middle-class suburb of London, the second child of a straitlaced mother, Olive—she turned off the TV if a divorced actor came on the screen—and a father, Hugh, who was the night editor of London's Press Association. Both parents spoiled Angela outrageously. She was crammed with treats, smothered with kittens and storybooks. Her mother never put her to bed until after midnight, when Hugh got back from work—she wanted the child's company—and, even then, often let her stay up. Hugh brought home long rolls of white paper from the office for her, and as her parents chatted, she wrote stories in crayon.

She grew to be a tall, pudgy girl, with a stammer. Between those disadvantages and extreme shyness, which she covered with an aloof and frosty manner, she had few friends. Olive redoubled her attentions. Angela was not allowed to dress herself, or even to go to the bathroom alone. Finally, she rebelled, went on a diet, and changed from a fat, obliging girl to a skinny, badly behaved one. She slouched around in short skirts and fishnet stockings, smoking and saying rude things to her mother.

She was a good student, though, in a good school. The 1944 Butler Act, riding the same democratic wave as the American GI Bill, provided grants for gifted children from regular backgrounds to go to elite private schools. Carter, as an adult, had a theory that this created Britain's first real intelligentsia, a group of people who had no interest in using education to maintain the class system but who simply wanted to operate in a world of ideas. If so, she was one of them. Her teachers urged her to apply to Oxford. Olive, hearing this, pronounced it an excellent idea, and added that she and Hugh would take an apartment there, to be close to her. Angela thereupon dropped all thought of going to university. Marriage, she realized, would be the only way to get away from her parents.

Through her father's connections, she landed a job as a reporter.

She started writing record reviews and liner notes and getting involved in London's music scene. In an independent record store, she met a serious-minded young man, Paul Carter, an industrial chemist who moonlighted as a producer and seller of English folk-song records. Gordon thinks that Paul was the first man to take a romantic interest in Angela. Or, as Angela put it, "I finally bumped into somebody who would . . . have sexual intercourse with me." But Paul insisted that they get engaged first, and so Angela found herself, at twenty, a married woman.

They seem to have been happy at the beginning. Paul taught Angela to love English folk music, thereby giving her a great gift. The folk iconography, in time, offered her an escape hatch from the rather gray realism dominant in British fiction of the period. Folklore also presented her with a set of emotions that, while releasing her, eventually, from sixties truculence, nevertheless felt *true*, not genteel.

But soon the marriage was failing. Paul suffered engulfing depressions. Sometimes he and Angela barely spoke for days. She felt swollen with unexpressed emotion. "I want to touch him all the time, with my hands & my mouth," she wrote in her diary. "(Poor luv, it annoys him.)" The note of sarcasm here is interesting. Through some miracle, Angela, who had little sexual self-confidence—she once described herself as "a great, lumpy, butch cow . . . titless and broadbeamed"—did not allow Paul's withdrawal to demoralize her. She wanted to save herself. On her twenty-second birthday, her Uncle Cecil, knowing that she was unhappy, took her to lunch at an Italian restaurant and told her to apply to university. As she recalled, he said to her, "If you've got a degree, you can always get a job. You can leave your husband any time you want."

She took his advice. The couple had recently moved to Bristol for Paul's work, and she enrolled in the university there, studying English. Gordon, who is always good at contextualizing, says that Bristol's English department was not ideal for her; it was dominated by the principles of F. R. Leavis, who was intent on rescuing English fiction's "great tradition" from the showy, the sentimental, and the bizarre. Carter, who called this the "eat up your broccoli" school of criticism, managed to hide out in medieval studies, which she loved. She also encountered Freud, gaining, she thought, a scientific support for the world of shock, dream, and eros that she now saw as the realm of art. A little later, she discovered the Surrealists, and learned from them that the goal of art was not truth (as the Leavisites would have it) but the marvelous—indeed, that the marvelous *was* the truth.

All of this fed into her developing feminism. She became an ardent feminist, but not an orthodox one. Her concern was not with justice; she hated the idea of put-upon, suffering women, and implied that they had it coming, by being such weaklings. She wanted women to seize what they needed—power, freedom, sex—and she saw no fundamental difference between men and women that could prevent that. As she wrote to a friend, Carole Roffe,

> Somebody asked me who my favorite women writers were the other day, meaning, I guess, some kind of writers who expressed a specifically feminine sensibility—I said Emily Brontë, who's pure butch, and cursed myself afterwards because the greatest feminine writer who's ever lived is Dostoevsky, followed closely by Herman Melville, who has just the kind of relish of beautiful boys that emancipated ladies such as yourself express. And D. H. Lawrence is infinitely more feminine than Jane Austen, if one is talking about these qualities of sensitivity, vulnerability and perception traditionally ascribed by male critics to female novelists. . . . D. H. Lawrence's tragedy is that he thought he was a man.

I don't know what she means about Dostoevsky, but her general statement should sound familiar in our day of loose gender definitions.

Energized by her discoveries, she became a bustling presence in her department and the co-editor of its literary magazine. Gordon has gone through the stapled-together pages of this undergraduate publication, and reports that the best items were pseudonymous poems by Carter.

He quotes one called "Unicorn." In the Middle Ages, there was a belief that the only way to catch a unicorn was to send a virgin, alone, into the woods. The unicorn, spying the girl, would come and lay his head in her lap. Such a virgin is the speaker in Carter's poem, but she is not a tender little thing. She is naked, with breasts "like carrier bags" (shopping bags) and "curious plantations of pubic hair." The unicorn is drawn to her by "the fragrance of her moist / garden plot." He will be sorry. "I have sharp teeth inside my mouth," she says. "Inside my dark red lips."

At the same time, Carter was producing the first novels that she would be willing to publish. She wrote at a furious speed, turning out narratives of violence that were sometimes layered with comedy, sometimes not. In *Shadow Dance* (1966), her first novel, a man named Honeybuzzard carves up the face of an annoyingly virtuous girl, Ghislaine. (After she gets out of the hospital, he finishes the job, strangling her and leaving her naked corpse in an attic.) A year after that came *The Magic Toyshop*, in which the orphaned heroine is sent to live with her uncle, a sadistic puppeteer. In one scene, he forces her to play Leda to a mechanical swan. Her next two efforts were in a similar vein. There are excellent things in all these books, but there is also a strong suggestion that Carter is still trying to drive her mother crazy. Even when the material is not shocking, the treatment is often self-indulgent. An editor once forwarded to her a reader's report describing a novel of hers as "a queer little book." Carter, always lovably forthright, replied that the person who wrote that "put her finger on my weakest spot, which is a tendency to a batty kind of whimsicality." She said she was sure she would work out some satisfactory solution.

She did. In 1969, Carter received a Somerset Maugham Award, worth £500, to be used for foreign travel. She decided that she would grant herself an old wish, to go to Japan. She arrived in September of that year, without Paul.

"I arrived by air, in the dark," she wrote, two years later. "When night descended over the ocean, many unfamiliar stars sprang out in the sky; as we approached land, there began to blossom below me such an irregular confusion of small lights it was difficult to be certain if the starry sky lay above or below me. So the aeroplane ascended or descended into an electric city where nothing was what it seemed at first and I was absolutely confused." There she is—dizzy, suspended between two beds of light. It is like a painting of a conversion experience, and by the time she wrote it, she surely knew that.

Within a few weeks, at a Tokyo coffeehouse a Japanese man, Sozo Araki, twenty-four years old—six years her junior—stopped at her table. She described the scene in a later, unpublished story: "'Where are you from?' he asked her. 'England,' she said. 'That must be terribly boring,' he said & gave her the great international seducer's smile." They ended up, that evening, in a "pleasure hotel," the kind of hotel that rents rooms by the hour. The next morning, she went back to where she was staying, to take a shower, while he played pachinko, a Japanese version of pinball. Then they met again, had breakfast, and went to another hotel. Gordon tries hard to determine what Carter and Araki talked about when they weren't having sex. Araki had recently dropped out of a university program in political science, intending to write a novel, and they apparently did discuss fiction. He liked Faulkner and Dostoevsky. It seems, though, that he liked Elvis Presley and pachinko better.

But literary companionship was not what she was looking for. Nor, it appears, were her interests merely, or even primarily, sexual. Carter seems to have been seeking a sort of rapture, a sensation of being carried to a new place, or to an old, ideal one. "His face did not, when I first met him, seem to me the face of a stranger," she wrote of Araki. "His image was already present somewhere in my head, & I was seeking to discover him in reality, searching every face for the right face." She later said that in Japan she had "taken certain ideas (like living for love) as far as they will go." Gordon feels that she doesn't seem to mean love, exactly, but something *like* love—an idea, a Platonic idea.

As for the husband who was waiting for her in England, "I can't live with him anymore," she wrote to a friend, "or I'll kill myself & that's that." Two weeks after she met Araki, she had to go to Hong Kong briefly. In the airport's departure lounge, she took off her wedding ring and left it in an ashtray. (She wrote to Paul soon after, asking for a divorce. He took it badly. More than forty years later, he refused to speak to Gordon.) That was one captor disposed of. The other did the job herself. While Angela was back in England that winter, renewing her visa, Olive suffered a pulmonary embolism. Angela went to the hospital, but Olive, upon seeing her, turned her face to the wall. (She had always disliked Paul, but she disliked divorce more.) She died a few days later.

Carter returned to Tokyo, set up house with Araki, and soon found that she had to acquire an additional sort of freedom. Araki liked to go out with his friends at night, and Carter's joining them was not convenient. For one thing, she never learned to speak more than a few words of Japanese. Furthermore, as she soon realized, he was seeing other women—lots of them. (She came to describe him as an "ambulant penis.") One night, as they were undressing, Carter saw a smear of lipstick on Araki's underpants. She didn't wear lipstick. Describing the episode to a friend, she wrote that she burst out laughing.

Carter always said that the two years she spent in Japan were what radicalized her as a feminist. The young women of Tokyo, she wrote, acted as though they had "become their own dolls." Her rejection of that position, and of the enforced gender identity that lay behind it, meant, to her, that she could put up with Araki's infidelities. Gordon believes that she began to enjoy having the night to herself; she could write in quiet and then go to bed with Araki when he came home at five in the morning, once the trains started running again. But, if she could tolerate this routine, he couldn't. While he was out tomcatting, she was earning their daily bread, and, as he told Gordon, "I didn't want to be a gigolo anymore." He left her.

She was brokenhearted and furious. She had panic attacks. She couldn't eat. Finally, she comforted herself with a young Korean, Mansu

Kō. She relieved him of his virginity. In gratitude, he brought her a can of pineapple. He moved in with her almost immediately, and did all the cooking and cleaning. He was two inches shorter than she was, and nineteen years old, though she wrote that he looked fourteen: "Every time I pull down his underpants I feel more and more like Humbert Humbert." (She was thirty-one.) He spoke less English than Araki had and didn't have much to say, anyway. "Apart from the sheer delight, he *does* bore me," she wrote. The boredom didn't cancel out the delight: "the childlike delicacy and precision with which he stirs sugar into his coffee; his small sigh of content . . . the way he carries his head, like a bird." But, after five months with him, she went back to England.

"Apart from the sheer delight, he *does* bore me." That was what Carter discovered in Japan: the mixed, middle states of the heart. Having thrown pretty much everything else away, she had time to pay attention to this and, with the clarity she had gained, to present it in very stark imagery. In Japan, her best work went into short fiction—tales, she called them—which she later published in the collection *Fireworks* (1974). The finest of them, "A Souvenir of Japan," is a tribute to Araki. Here is the "pleasure hotel" they went to on their first night:

> We were shown into a room like a paper box. It contained nothing but a mattress spread on the floor. We lay down immediately and began to kiss one another. Then a maid soundlessly opened the sliding door and, stepping out of her slippers, crept in on stockinged feet, breathing apologies. She carried a tray which contained two cups of tea and a plate of candies. She put a tray down on the matted floor beside us and backed, bowing and apologizing, from the room whilst our uninterrupted kiss continued. He started to unfasten my shirt and then she came back again. This time, she carried an armful of towels. I was stripped stark naked when she returned for a third time to bring the receipt for his money.

There love is mixed with comedy. Three paragraphs later, it is mixed with death, a beautiful death: "I should have liked to have had him embalmed and been able to keep him beside me in a glass coffin, so that I could watch him all the time and he would not have been able to get away from me." A glass coffin: "Snow White." And that's where she was headed—to fairy tales.

In 1976, she accepted a commission to translate Charles Perrault's fairy tales. She had been back in England for four years, but she was still living off the psychological tank dive of her Japanese period. After the Perrault volume was published, she embarked on *The Bloody Chamber*, with her own, reconceived versions of Perrault and the Brothers Grimm. This is her great book, the one that only she could have written, the one in which everything that was good in her came to the fore and everything that had been bad became good. She was always best in the short form, as her friend Salman Rushdie noted. In her novels, he wrote, her voice, "that moonstone-and-rhinestone mix of opulence and flim-flam, can be exhausting. In her stories, she can dazzle and swoop, and quit while she's ahead."

The truth is that she never cared much about character development or plot, which are the meat of the novel. In a tale, she could dispense with them, and just go for emotion and image. We get Bluebeard smoking a cigar as "fat as a baby's arm," and the Erl-King gathering his dinner in the woods: "He knows which of the frilled, blotched, rotten fungi are fit to eat; he understands their eldritch ways, how they spring up overnight in lightless places and thrive on dead things." In "The Company of Wolves," Carter's famous version of "Little Red Riding Hood," the heroine doesn't struggle with the wolf. She goes to bed with him. Her grandmother's bones rattle beneath the bed. She doesn't hear them.

That was her peak, *Fireworks* and *The Bloody Chamber*. Strange to say, she wrote most of those unsettling stories in a period of relative contentment. Maybe she needed that in order to get past the aggressive luridness of her early work. In any case, she told an interviewer that she had a rather nice time in her thirties: "I started doing things like foreign travel and having a house, and you know, watching television and things like that." Soon she had someone steady to do those things with. One day, two years after her return from Japan, a water faucet in her kitchen burst. She had seen a construction worker in the house opposite, and she ran to get him. His name was Mark Pearce, another nineteen-year-old. (She was now thirty-four.) "He came in," Carter said, "and never left."

He was strikingly handsome. Friends said he looked like Jesus; tellingly, she claimed that he looked like a werewolf. He was silent most of the time, but she didn't mind, because she liked to do the talking, just as she liked being older. He went on doing construction work, she went on writing—and that was their life, except for one big change, in 1983: Carter, at the age of forty-three, gave birth to a son, Alexander. This made her very happy—repeatedly, she had had phantom pregnancies—but Mark was really the one who raised Alex. It was a bohemian household, with dirty dishes stacked in the sink, but they liked having people over. Carter was a good cook. Rushdie told Gordon that when he was in hiding, after the Ayatollah Khomeini issued the fatwa against him, his bodyguards always enjoyed it when he went to visit Carter, because she invariably had a nice meal for them to eat and they could watch TV.

A recurrent theme of Gordon's book is Carter's position as a woman in her profession. This is tiresome but unavoidable: in the 1980s, there was a much-trumpeted spurt of energy in English fiction, with the rise of a number of talented young men, notably Rushdie, Ian McEwan, Martin Amis, and Julian Barnes. In 1981, Rushdie's second novel, *Midnight's Children*, won the Booker Prize, and McEwan's second, *The Comfort of Strangers*, was short-listed. Barnes was short-listed in 1984. Carter was never short-listed, let alone given the prize, and she did feel that this was, in part, because she was a woman. In 1984, she told an interviewer,

> It would be whingeing to say that men who are no better than I are very much more famous and very much richer and also regarded as . . . the right stuff. It would ill become me. But it's amazing what the Old Boys' club does for itself. They list the "important British contemporary writers," and they'll list Malcolm Bradbury and Kingsley Amis, and they'll leave out Doris Lessing, who's the only one with a really huge international reputation.

There was a generational aspect, too. Carter was most of a decade older than the others, born a few months into the Second World War rather than after it, and her Freudian-influenced, "mythic" subject matter was out of step with their more postmodern concerns, their explorations of language, narrative, and representation. Still, there is no question that being female was part of the reason that Carter received less attention. Rushdie says that though she did wish for greater recognition, "she was not ever envious of other people's success." That must have been a comfort to them.

Soon after her son was born, Carter started to age quickly, as she recorded in her diary: "I catch myself in the mirror looking like my father." She resented this, and reacted defiantly, adopting, according to one friend, "a madwoman-in-the-attic look." Yet Gordon seems to think that, on balance, she got happier as she got older. This is certainly suggested by her final novel, *Wise Children*, in which a seventy-five-year-old woman, Dora Chance, tells of the life that she and her identical-twin sister had as music-hall artists. In a sense, *Wise Children* is about what happens to women when they're no longer salable, but it's hard to locate a note of regret, because the book contains so much life and fun—nice dresses and memorable fornications and wild parties and theater, theater, theater. ("We were *wet* for it," Dora recalls.) The sisters now live in a basement apartment with an ex-wife of their father's, drinking tea out of chipped mugs until six, when they switch to gin. The whole thing is as lovable and comfortable as an old shoe.

Early in 1991, just before *Wise Children* was published, Carter went to the doctor with a pain in her chest and was told that she had a cancerous tumor on her right lung which had spread to her lymph nodes, making it inoperable. Strong-minded woman that she was, she laid aside her plans for a new novel—*Adela*, about Jane Eyre's pupil, Mr. Rochester's daughter—and went to work, fast, with an assistant, on a collection of her nonfiction. (Over the years, needing the money, she had written many magazine articles.) She and Mark married, as they had neglected to do previously, and week after week she got dressed and sat up straight to have goodbye teas with her friends. In February 1992, she died at home, at the age of fifty-one. She was young, and she had had only a few years of absolutely first-rank work, but that is true of many writers, including some of the greatest. She had her time, and it was wonderful.

The New Yorker, 2017

Louisa May Alcott, age twenty-six

LADIES' CHOICE

Little Women

It is doubtful whether any novel has been more important to America's female writers than Louisa May Alcott's *Little Women*, the story of the four March sisters living in genteel poverty in Massachusetts in the 1860s. The eldest is Meg, beautiful, maternal, and mild. She is sixteen when the book opens. Then comes Meg's opposite, fifteen-year-old Jo: bookish and boyish, loud and wild. Jo writes plays that the girls perform, with false mustaches and paper swords, in the parlor. Next comes Beth, thirteen: recessive, kind, and doomed to die young. She collects cast-off dolls—dolls with no arms, dolls with their stuffing coming out—and cares for them in her doll hospital. Finally, there is Amy, who is vain and selfish but, at twelve, also the baby of the family, and cute, so everybody loves her anyway. The girls' father is away from home, serving as a chaplain in the Civil War. Their mother, whom they call Marmee, is with them, and the girls are always nuzzling up to her chair in order to draw on her bottomless fund of loving counsel. Next door lives a rich old man with his orphaned grandson, Laurie, who, when he is home from his Swiss boarding school, lurks behind the curtains to get a look at what the March sisters are up to. Jo catches him spying on them and befriends him. He soon falls in love with her.

These characters are not glamorous, and the events are mostly not of great moment. We witness one death, and it is a solemn matter, but otherwise the book is pretty much a business of how the cat had kittens and somebody went skating and fell through the ice. Yet *Little Women*, published in 1868–69, was a smash hit. Its first part, in an initial printing of two thousand copies, sold out in two weeks. Then, while the publisher rushed to produce more copies of that, he gave Alcott the go-ahead to write a second, concluding part. It, too, was promptly grabbed up. Since then, *Little Women* has never been out of print. Unsurprisingly, it has been most popular with women. "I read *Little Women* a thousand times," Cynthia Ozick has written. Many others have recorded how much the book meant to them: Nora and Delia Ephron, Barbara Kingsolver, Jane Smiley, Anne Tyler, Mary Gordon, Jhumpa Lahiri, Stephenie Meyer. As this list shows, the influence travels from the highbrow to the middlebrow to the lowbrow. And it extends far beyond our shores. Doris Lessing, Margaret Atwood, and A. S. Byatt have all paid tribute.

The book's fans didn't merely like it; it gave them a life, they said. Simone de Beauvoir, as a child, used to make up *Little Women* games that she played with her sister. Beauvoir always took the role of Jo. "I was able to tell myself that I too was like her," she recalled. "I too would be superior and find my place." Susan Sontag, in an interview, said she would never have become a writer without the example of Jo March. Ursula Le Guin said that Alcott's Jo, "as close as a sister and as common as grass," made writing seem like something even a girl could do. Writers also used *Little Women* to turn their characters into writers. In Elena Ferrante's *My Brilliant Friend*, the two child heroines have a shared copy of *Little Women* that finally crumbles from overuse. One of the girls becomes a famous writer, inspired, in part, by the other's childhood writing.

Long before she wrote *Little Women*, Alcott (1832–88) swore never to marry, a decision that was no doubt rooted in her observations of her parents' union. Her father, Bronson Alcott (1799–1888), was an intellectual, or, in any case, a man who had thoughts, a member of New England's Transcendental Club and a friend of its other members—Emerson, Thoreau. Bronson saw himself as a philosopher, but he is remembered primarily as a pioneer of "progressive education." He believed in self-expression and fresh air rather than times tables. But the schools and communities that he established quickly failed. His most famous project was Fruitlands, a utopian community that he founded with a friend in the town of Harvard, Massachusetts, in 1843. This was to be a new Eden, one that eschewed the sins that got humankind kicked out of the old one. The communards would till the soil without exploiting animal labor. Needless to say, they ate no animals, but they were vegetarians of a special kind: they ate only vegetables that grew upward, never those, like potatoes, that grew downward. They had no contact with alcohol, or even with milk. (It belonged to the cows.) They took only cold baths, never warm.

Understandably, people did not line up to join Fruitlands. The community folded after seven months. And that stands as a symbol for most of Bronson Alcott's projects. His ideas were interesting as ideas, but in action they came to little. Nor did he have any luck translating them into writing. Even his loyal friend Emerson said that when Bronson tried to put his ideas into words, he became helpless. And so Bronson, when he was still in his forties, basically gave up trying to make a living. "I have as yet no clear call to any work beyond myself," as he put it. Now and then, he staged a Socratic "conversation," or question-and-answer session, with an audience, and occasionally he was paid for this, but for the most part his household, consisting of his energetic wife, Abba, and his four daughters, the models for the March girls, had to fend for themselves. Sometimes—did he notice?—they were grievously poor, resorting to bread and water for dinner and accepting charity from relatives and friends. (Emerson was a steady donor.) By the time Louisa, the second-oldest girl, was in her mid-twenties, the family had moved more than thirty times. Eventually, Louisa decided that she might be able to help by writing stories for the popular press, and she soon discovered that the stories that sold most easily were thrillers. Only in 1950, when an enterprising scholar, Madeleine B. Stern, published the first comprehensive biography of Alcott, did the world discover that the author of *Little Women*, with its kittens and muffins, had once made a living producing "Pauline's Passion and Punishment," "The Abbot's Ghost, or Maurice Treherne's Temptation," and similar material, under a pen name, for various weeklies.

Soon, however, a publisher, Thomas Niles, sensed something about Louisa. Or maybe he just saw a market opportunity. If there were tales written specifically for boys—adventure tales—why shouldn't there also be stories about girls' concerns, written for them? Girls liked reading more than boys did. (This is still true.) So Niles suggested to Louisa that she write a "girls' story." She thought this was a stupid idea. "Never liked girls, or knew many, except my sisters," she wrote in her journal. But her family was terribly strapped, so what she did was write a novel about the few girls she knew, her sisters, and her life with them.

You can get the whole story from a new book, *Meg, Jo, Beth, Amy: The Story of "Little Women" and Why It Still Matters*, by Anne Boyd Rioux, an English professor at the University of New Orleans. This is a sort of collection of *Little Women* topics: the circumstances that brought Louisa to write the book and the difficult family on which the March family is based. It describes the book's thunderous success: its hundred-and-more editions, its translation into fifty-odd languages (reportedly, it is still the second most popular book among Japanese girls), its sequels, its spin-offs—the Hallmark cards, the Madame Alexander dolls—and, above all, its fabulous sales. Rioux can't give us a firm count, because in the early days the book was extensively pirated, and then it went into the public domain, but she estimates that ten million copies have been sold, and that's not including abridged editions. Perhaps worried about how a "girls' story" would fare in the marketplace, the publisher persuaded Alcott to take a royalty, of 6.6 percent, rather than a flat fee, which she might well have preferred. In consequence, the book and its sequels supported her and her relatives, plus some of her relatives' relatives, for the rest of their lives.

Rioux goes on from the book to the plays and the movies. The first *Little Women* play opened in New York, in 1912, and was a hit. It was soon followed by two silent movies, in 1917 and 1918. (Both are lost.) Then came the talkies, starting with George Cukor's 1933 version, which cast Katharine Hepburn, hitherto mainly a stage actress, as Jo and helped make her a movie star. Between 1935 and 1950, there were forty-eight radio dramatizations. Toward the end of that run came a second famous movie, Mervyn LeRoy's 1949 version, with June Allyson as Jo, Elizabeth Taylor as Amy, Janet Leigh as Meg, and Margaret O'Brien as Beth. In the past few decades, the most important version has been Gillian Armstrong's 1994 film, with Winona Ryder as Jo, Kirsten Dunst as Amy, and, as Marmee, Susan Sarandon, who had already been enshrined as a feminist icon by *Thelma and Louise*. Recently, it was announced that Greta Gerwig, who had such success last year with *Lady Bird*, her directorial debut, is at work on a new *Little Women* movie, with Saoirse Ronan, the star of *Lady Bird*, in the lead role. Ronan seems made to be Jo. And those are just the big-screen versions. By the time Rioux's book went to press, there had been twelve adaptations for American television, and plenty more elsewhere. In 1987, there was a *forty-eight*-episode anime version in Japan.

Rioux's chapter on the adaptations is a lot of fun. First, it teaches you the problems that face filmmakers adapting famous novels. In *Little Women* movies, the actors are almost always too old, because the directors need experienced people to play these interesting youngsters. June Allyson was thirty-one when she played the fifteen-year-old Jo. Then, partly because the actors are worried that they are too old, they accentuate everything to death. In the Cukor *Little Women*, Katharine Hepburn sometimes looks as though she were going to jump off the screen and sock you in the face, so eager is she to convince you that she is a tomboy. Amy's vanity is almost always overdone, never more so than by the teen actress Elizabeth Taylor, with a set of blond ringlets that look like a brace of bratwursts. Poor, sickly Beth is almost always sentimentalized; Marmee is often a bore. Whole hunks of the plot may be left out, because this is a twenty-seven-chapter book being squeezed into what is usually a movie of two to three hours.

Rioux apparently finished her book before she could see the most recent entry, a three-hour BBC miniseries directed by a newcomer, Vanessa Caswill. This version's Jo—Maya Hawke, who had had little acting experience but was blessed with good genes (her parents are Uma Thurman and Ethan Hawke)—manages to be Jo-like without being unsexy. Most moving, because the roles are so hard to play, are two other characters. Annes Elwy's freckle-faced Beth seems to carry her death within her, like an unborn child, from the moment we see her. The movie's other great standout is Emily Watson, whose features have sometimes seemed too childlike for the roles she has played. Here, as Marmee, she is perfect, both a girl and a mother, her waist a little thicker, her face redder, than what we saw in *Breaking the Waves*, in which, at twenty-eight, she became a star. Caswill can't take her eyes off her, and she gives her an amazing scene that is not in the book. When Meg gives birth—to twins—Marmee is the midwife. At the end of the ordeal, you can read in Watson's sweaty, exhausted face everything that Alcott hinted at but did not say about how her own mother was left to do everything. Another of Caswill's additions is a series of dazzling scenes from nature—light-dappled rivers, fat, furry bees circling pink flowers—that could turn you into a transcendentalist.

Alcott never swerved in her decision not to marry. "I'd rather be a free spinster and paddle my own canoe," as she put it. And yet she concluded the first volume of *Little Women* with a betrothal. Meg is proposed to by Laurie's tutor, John Brooke, a good man, and she accepts. Jo, who takes the same position as her creator on the subject of marriage—never!—is scandalized. How could Meg have done such a stupid and heartless thing, and created a breach in the March household? "I just wish I could marry Meg myself, and keep her safe in the family," she says. The first volume ends with the family adjourning to the parlor, where they all sit and gaze sentimentally at the newly promised couple—all of them, that is, except Jo, who is thinking that maybe something will go wrong and they'll break up. Now the curtain falls on the March girls. Alcott writes: "Whether it ever rises again, depends upon the reception given to the first act of the domestic drama called *Little Women*."

This sounds, now, as though she is teasing her readers, knowing full well that she will shortly receive huge bags of mail demanding that she get going on part 2. In any case, that's what happened, and the letter writers wanted to know one thing above all: Whom did the girls marry? Meg is taken, but what about Amy and Beth? Most important, what about Jo? Clearly, readers felt, Jo had to marry Laurie. Everyone was crazy about her, so she had to be given the best, and wasn't Laurie the best? He was handsome; he was rich; he spoke French; he loved her. In the final scene of part 1, as everyone is cooing over Meg and John, Laurie, leaning over Jo's chair, "smiled with his friendliest aspect, and nodded at her in the long glass which reflected them both." They're next, obviously.

Not so fast, Alcott wrote in a letter to a friend: "Jo should have remained a literary spinster but so many enthusiastic young ladies wrote to me clamorously demanding that she should marry Laurie, or somebody, that I didn't dare refuse & out of perversity went & made a funny match for her." Laurie, as Alcott has been telling us between the lines from the beginning, is a twit. Yes, he is handsome, and rich, but he is not a serious person. He does not, like Jo, think hard about things and fight his way through them in darkness.

So Jo does what she has long known she would have to do. She tells

Laurie that she can't love him other than as a friend. She breaks his heart, insofar as a heart like his can be broken. Then, perhaps to relieve herself of guilt, she takes to thinking that Beth, her favorite sister, is in love with him. Beth has told Jo she has a secret, which she cannot tell her just yet. That must be the secret! That Beth loves Laurie! The thing for Jo to do, then, is to get out of the way. So she takes a job as governess to two children of one of her mother's friends, who runs a boardinghouse in New York City.

On her second day there, she is doing her needlework when she hears someone singing in the next room. She pulls aside the curtain and discovers a man named Friedrich Bhaer, who, we are told, was a distinguished professor in his native Germany but is now a tutor of German, poor, and getting on in years (forty). He is stout; his hair sticks out every which way. His clothes are rumpled. He and Jo become friends, but there is a bump in their road. Jo, like her creator, writes lurid tales for the newspaper in order to make money. Bhaer sees some of this writing. "He did not say to himself, 'It is none of my business,'" Alcott writes. He remembered that Jo was young and poor, and "he moved to help her with an impulse as quick and natural as that which would prompt him to put out his hand to save a baby from a puddle." He tells her that it is wrong to write such trash. Jo has great respect for Professor Bhaer. She listens to what he has to say, goes back to her room, and consigns all her upcoming stories to the fire.

Soon, Jo gets the news that Beth is seriously ill. This was Beth's secret: not that she was in love with Laurie, but that she was dying. Jo rushes home and nurses her sister for the short time that remains to her. Beth dies without much protest, whereupon the book sinks for a while into a rather boring peacefulness. The world of the Marches becomes gentle, kind—beige, as it were—as if nothing could bring back the hour of real happiness, so we're all just going to get used to half measures. Amy is in Europe, where Laurie tracks her down, and the two fall quietly in love, or in like. They marry in Paris. Jo, at home with her parents, tries to content herself by doing the household chores that were once Beth's. She has nothing else.

Then the novel starts to build toward one of the most satisfying love scenes in our literature. Professor Bhaer suddenly arrives at the March house. He tells Jo that he has been offered a good teaching job in the West, and that he has come to say goodbye. But, strange to say, this formerly untidy man now seems quite soigné, in a new suit and with his hair smoothed down. "Dear old fellow!" Jo says to herself. "He couldn't have got himself up with more care if he'd been going a-wooing"—whereupon, oh, my God, she suddenly realizes what's going on. For two weeks, Bhaer calls on her every day. Then, abruptly, he vanishes. One day, two days, three days pass. Jo starts to go crazy. Finally, she runs to town to look for him. It turns out that Bhaer had come in order to find out whether Jo was promised to Laurie, and he overheard something that gave him the impression that she was. Now he finds her in some rough part of town—warehouses, countinghouses—where, as even he can figure out, she is searching for him. "I feel to know the strong-minded lady who goes so bravely under many horse noses," he says to her. I don't know if this is how German Americans spoke English in the 1860s, but the two innocents eventually make themselves understood to each other. Jo weeps; Bhaer weeps; the sky weeps. Great sheets of rain come down on them. They stand there in the road, completely drenched, looking into each other's eyes. "Ah," Bhaer says. "Thou gifest me such hope and courage, and I haf nothing to give back but a full heart and these empty hands." "Not empty now," Jo says, as she puts her hands in his. We then see what we have never seen before in this book, and won't see again: a serious kiss between a man and a woman.

Ravishing as this is, it still disappointed many of Alcott's contemporaries, because Jo didn't marry Laurie. And it has disappointed many of our contemporaries, too, because why did Jo, our hero, have to marry at all, not to speak of marrying a man who told her to stop writing? The problem is made worse by the fact that Alcott herself appeared to vacillate. It seems unlikely that anyone would honor her claim that she came up with a "funny match" for Jo in order to spite the fans who were demanding a marriage plot. But this might actually have been the case, because she goes back and forth about matrimony. On one page, Marmee, the font of all wisdom, tells Meg and Jo that to be loved by a good man is the best thing that can happen to a woman, but a few sentences later she says that it is better to be happy old maids than unhappy wives.

Which did Alcott believe? Was she just fooling around? If so, she left a lot of confused feminists in her wake. Even more displeased were the queer theorists. In an 1883 interview, Alcott said, "I am more than half-persuaded that I am a man's soul, put by some freak of nature into a woman's body . . . because I have fallen in love in my life with so many pretty girls and never once the least bit with a man." Hmm. And so we are not surprised that she herself did not marry, but then why did she have to force a husband on her most Louisa-like character, and one who had expressed similar sentiments? ("I can't get over my disappointment in not being a boy," Jo says, in the novel's first scene.) In recent *Little Women* scholarship, all this bewilderment was compounded by postmodern critics' emphasis on ambivalence, on conflict, on the dark truths lurking in what had once seemed clear, honest books.

Rioux tries to make everything okay by saying that if Jo married, at least she didn't make a would-be romantic match, the kind that women have been historically bamboozled by, but a "companionate union." Elizabeth Lennox Keyser, a children's literature scholar, has offered a more negative view: "Seeing no way to satisfy self, she adopts a policy of selflessness and, thus diminished, succumbs to the marriage proposal of fatherly Professor Bhaer." Both interpretations assume that Jo, by marrying someone old and fat—a foreigner, too!—doesn't so much take a husband as find a nice person to room with. I think that the situation is exactly the opposite, and that a "diminished" girl does not go running through the town, under so many horse noses, to find a booby prize. The heavens do not burst open when Meg says yes to John, or Amy to Laurie, but only when Jo and Bhaer, these two souls with no money or beauty or luck, come together.

There are other clues that Bhaer is a character very close to Alcott's heart. When Jo, on her second day in New York, hears the professor singing in the next room, Alcott tells us what the song is. It was first performed by a strange little character, Mignon, in Goethe's 1795 novel, *Wilhelm Meister's Apprenticeship*. Mignon is a girl dressed as a boy who, having been kidnapped in her native Italy by a gang of ruffians, is traveling with a troupe of actors. They treat her badly. She appeals to Wilhelm Meister, the novel's hero, to rescue her. Here, in Thomas Carlyle's translation, is the start of the song, "Kennst du das Land," that she sings to him:

> *Know'st thou the land where lemon-trees do bloom,*
> *And oranges like gold in leafy gloom;*
> *A gentle wind from deep blue heaven blows,*
> *The myrtle thick, and high the laurel grows?*
> *Know'st thou it, then?*
> * 'Tis there! 'tis there,*
> *O my belov'd one, I with thee would go!*

At first, it sounds as though Mignon is asking Wilhelm to take her back to Italy, but as the poem proceeds, it becomes clear that she means someplace farther away. (She dies at the end of the book.) The poem was set to music by dozens of composers in the nineteenth century. Alcott does not tell us which version Bhaer is singing. All we know is that he is speaking of some lost paradise—such as, for example, the Eden that Bronson Alcott tried to emulate at Fruitlands. Goethe was an idol of the members of the Transcendental Club, including Ralph Waldo Emerson, and Emerson, generous as ever, had given Louisa the run of his library when she was in her teens. There she found a translation of a book, *Goethe's Correspondence with a Child*, a collection of enraptured letters to the revered master from a young admirer, Bettina von Arnim. Louisa decided that she, likewise, would write a "heart-journal." She would take the part of Bettina, and her correspondent would be Emerson, whom she adored. Years later, in her diary, she recalled, "I wrote letters to him, but never sent them; sat in the tall cherry-tree at midnight, singing to the moon till the owls scared me to bed; left wild flowers on the doorstep of my 'Master,' and sang Mignon's song under his window in very bad German."

When Bhaer arrives to visit the Marches, Jo asks him to sing "Kennst du das Land" again. The first line, Alcott writes, was once Bhaer's favorite, because, before, "das Land" to him meant Germany, his homeland. "But now," Alcott writes, "he seemed to dwell, with peculiar warmth, and melody, upon the words 'There, there, might I go with thee / O, my beloved, go' and one listener was so thrilled by the tender invitation that she longed to say that she did know the land," and was ready to start packing. These, I believe, are the fragments still floating in the air of *Little Women* after the combustion that, in Alcott's brain, produced Professor Bhaer, a lover for her most cherished character. He is not a "funny match." He, together with Beth, is a sort of angel, like the souls in the *Divine Comedy*, beings who turn to us and say exactly who they are and what they stand for.

Behind these two angelic beings stands another, this one not a literary character but a real person: Bronson Alcott. It is hard to like Bronson, because he took so little care of his family. For a long time, Louisa appears to have despised him, or at least regarded him with irony. She once wrote to him that her goal in her work was to prove that "though an Alcott I can support myself." It would be hard to find an English-language work of fiction more autobiographical than *Little Women*. For almost every person in Louisa's immediate family, there is a corresponding character, an important one, in this book. The one exception is Bronson. Father March comes home from the war, stumbles into the back room, and thereafter mostly stays off-stage, reading books. Occasionally, he wanders in and says something or other. Then he wanders back out. In one sense, we could say that Louisa erased Bronson—a sort of revenge, perhaps. In another sense, this may just be an erasure of her feelings about him: she didn't want to talk about it.

Yet, while Bronson was more or less written out of the book, the ideals to which he held so stubbornly inform every page. Bronson's obsession was with the transcendence of the material world, with seeing through appearances to a moral and spiritual truth. He took this passion to extremes, and that is what made him eccentric, not to speak of irresponsible. But that is also the cast of mind that, with the addition of common sense and humor and an attachment to regular things—life, family, dinner—makes Alcott's most admirable characters admirable.

In addition to supplying the book's moral architecture, Bronson provided, by his neglect, the need for its creation. Louisa's one wish, as an adult, was to make her mother's life comfortable. With *Little Women* she did it, and then, with the work's two sequels—*Little Men* (1871) and *Jo's Boys* (1886), both having to do with a school that Jo and Bhaer eventually establish—she did it some more. When she was in the middle of a book, she wrote "in a vortex," as she put it, often remaining at her desk for fourteen hours a day. *Little Women* was written in less than six months. "Her health is by no means yet restored," Bronson wrote philosophically in his journal in 1869, soon after the book's publication. But it didn't bother him that she had just about killed herself to write it. In the words of his excellent biographer, John Matteson, Bronson regarded a physical person as "a lapsed soul, a debased descendant of pure being." A soul did not need to go to bed. A soul could work fourteen hours a day.

Louisa eventually developed chronic health problems, and her exhaustion showed in her work. *Little Men* is occasionally touching. You cry, and you wish you hadn't, because the book also feels like "The Three Bears," with the plumped-up beds all in a row. As for *Jo's Boys*, it is actually a chore to read. Alcott tries to whip up some excitement—there is a shipwreck, an explosion in a mine—but you can sense how bored she is, and how much she wants to go upstairs and take a nap.

In time, Louisa seems to have forgiven her father. At the age of fifty-five, she went to visit him one day at the convalescent home where he was then living (at her expense, no doubt). Kneeling at his bedside, she said, "Father, here is your Louy. What are you thinking of as you lie here so happily?" "I am going *up*," he said. "*Come with me*." She obliged him. Three days after their conversation, Bronson breathed his last. But Louisa never knew of this. Soon after her visit to her father, she had a stroke and fell into a coma. She died two days after him.

Of certain novelists it is said that they had only one book in them, or only one outstanding book. Such novels tend to have certain things in common. They are frequently autobiographical: *Look Homeward, Angel*, by Thomas Wolfe; *A Legacy*, by Sybille Bedford; *A Tree Grows in Brooklyn*, by Betty Smith. And they often have a force or a charisma, an ability to get under your skin and stay there, that other books, even many better-written books, don't have. Some people complain that university syllabi don't accord *Little Women* the status of *Huckleberry Finn*, which they see as its male counterpart. But no piece of literature is the counterpart of *Little Women*. The book is not so much a novel, in the Henry James sense of the term, as a sort of wad of themes and scenes and cultural wishes. It is more like the Mahabharata or the Old Testament than it is like a novel. And that makes it an extraordinary novel.

The New Yorker, 2018

Postscript: Greta Gerwig's film (2019) turned out to be interesting, if not exactly faithful to Alcott's novel. If Alcott sometimes dallied or even backtracked on her way to a wholehearted feminism, Gerwig picked her up and carried her over the finish line. In the movie, not just Jo but also Amy and even Beth are given considerable agency. As for Jo, the film's unwavering subject is how she became a writer. That is, Gerwig merged Jo's story with Alcott's—and probably, in some measure, with her own.

It joined them at breakfast and presently ate
All the syrup and toast, and a part of a plate.

FUNNY PECULIAR

Edward Gorey

The book artist Edward Gorey, when asked about his tastes in literature, would sometimes mention his mixed feelings about Thomas Mann: "I dutifully read *The Magic Mountain* and felt as if I had t.b. for a year afterward." As for Henry James: "Those endless sentences. I always pick up Henry James and I think, *Oooh!* This is *won*derful! And then I will hear a little sound. And it's the plug being pulled. . . . And the whole thing is going down the drain like the bathwater." Why? Because, Gorey said, James (like Mann) explained too much: "I'm beginning to feel that if you create something, you're killing a lot of other things. And the way I write, since I do leave out most of the connections, and very little is pinned down, I feel that I am doing a minimum of damage to other possibilities that might arise in a reader's mind." He thought that he might have adopted this way of working from Chinese and Japanese art, to which he was devoted, and which are famous for acts of brevity. Many Gorey books are little more than thirty pages long: a series of illustrations, one per page, accompanied, at the lower margin or on the facing page, by maybe two or three lines of text, sometimes verse, sometimes prose.

In the white space that remained, Gorey felt, wit had room to flower. A beautiful example is his early book *The Doubtful Guest* (1957). Here, members of a respectable Victorian family are standing around one night, looking bored, when their doorbell rings. They open the door and find no one. But they scout around the porch, and finally, on the top of an urn at the end of the balustrade, they see something peculiar. It sort of resembles a penguin. On the other hand, it has fur and wears white sneakers. In any case, by the next page it is standing in the family's foyer with its nose to the wallpaper, looking frightened but insistent, while they huddle in the next room, trying to figure out what to do. By the morning, the creature has made itself at home. An illustration (see page 228) shows us the family at the breakfast table, in their tight-fitting clothes, acting as though everything were perfectly fine, while the Guest, seated among them, and having finished what was on its plate, has begun eating the plate.

The next sixteen pages depict the unfolding of the creature's unfortunate habits: how it tears chapters out of the family's books and hides their bath towels and throws their pocket watches into the pond. At the end, we are told that the Guest has been with the family for seventeen years, and seems to have no intention of leaving. In the final drawing, we see the family, now gray-haired, staring at or away from this mysterious being as, still in its Keds, it sits on an elaborately tasseled ottoman, gazing straight ahead. It doesn't look happy; it doesn't look sad. It is just living its little life, as its hosts ceased to be able to do seventeen years ago. It wanted a home. It got one.

This is very funny, because, in the absence of any explanation, we are asked to imagine seventeen years of whispered conversations: "What shall we do?" "Should we call the constable?" "The vicar?" It's not entirely funny, though. It's poignant, too: a story of how something can suddenly appear in our lives—blood on the carpet, a letter without a return address—and after that nothing is ever the same. The novelist Alison Lurie, a friend of Gorey's from their college days, said that she thought the subject of *The Doubtful Guest* (which the author dedicated to her) was her decision—inexplicable to Gorey—to have a child. Others felt that the book was simply a species of Surrealism, something like Max Ernst's book *Une semaine de bonté* (*A Week of Kindness*), in which a collage of illustrations—harvested from Victorian encyclopedias, catalogs, and novels—hints at a mysterious narrative.

Gorey acknowledged his debt to the Surrealists:

> I sit reading André Breton and think, "Yes, yes, you're so right." What appeals to me most is an idea expressed by [Paul] Éluard. He has a line about there being another world, but it's in this one. And Raymond Queneau said the world is not what it seems—but it isn't anything else, either. These two ideas are the bedrock of my approach. If a book is only what it seems to be about, then somehow the author has failed.

But, however much Gorey owes to the Surrealists, I see in him, equally, their less fun-loving predecessors, the Symbolist poets and painters of the late nineteenth century: Baudelaire, Mallarmé, Khnopff, Munch, Puvis de Chavannes, Redon. That strange world of theirs, caught in a kind of syncope, or dead halt, of feeling: open a Gorey volume on a winter afternoon, and that's what you get.

There is a new book out on Gorey, the first biography, by the cultural critic Mark Dery, titled *Born to Be Posthumous: The Eccentric Life and Mysterious Genius of Edward Gorey*. Gorey was born in 1925, in Chicago, the only child of an unremarkable Irish American couple. The father was a newspaperman, among other things. The mother was a beauty and an oppression. Gorey recalled that as an adult he'd say to her, "Oh, Mother, let's face it. You dislike me sometimes as much as I dislike you." "Oh no, dear," she'd reply. "I've always loved you."

He was an extraordinarily precocious child. He was reading, he said, by the age of three. When the grown-ups decided it was time to teach him how, he'd already figured it out. He claimed to have read all the works of Victor Hugo by the age of eight: "I still remember Victor

Hugo being forcefully removed from my tiny hands . . . so I could eat my supper. They couldn't get me to put him down." On the city buses, he liked to simulate epileptic attacks. But don't get him wrong, he said: "I think that's a standard thing when you're about twelve or thirteen." When he was just entering his teens, his parents divorced. His father had run off with a nightclub singer, Corinna Mura. (Mura appears briefly in *Casablanca*, as a chanteuse in Rick's Café—the one who strums a guitar and sings "Tango delle Rose.") When Gorey was twenty-seven, the father returned, and the parents remarried.

Gorey had next to no art education. And, thanks to the Second World War, his college career was suspended soon after it began. He was drafted and, from 1944 to 1946, found himself in Utah, as a clerk in an army base set up to test chemical weapons. He later claimed that twelve thousand sheep mysteriously died there. Once the war ended, he went to Harvard, on the GI Bill. There he roomed for two years with the larky young poet Frank O'Hara, in a suite where, according to historians of the postwar arts in America, the two of them sat around on chaise longues, drinking cocktails and listening to Marlene Dietrich records. But they eventually drifted off into separate crowds, Gorey's less wild. He stayed at Harvard for the regulation four years, majoring in French and ping-ponging between dean's list and academic probation.

After graduation, he hung around Cambridge for a while, starting and abandoning novels, writing limericks and verse dramas, and doing illustrations for books and magazines. But he had no money and felt he was getting nowhere. Some of the experience of this time perhaps found its way into the first of his little books, *The Unstrung Harp* (1953), which tells the story of Mr. Earbrass, a novelist with a head shaped like a kielbasa, who starts writing a new book every other year, on November 18. He hates all of them, not to speak of the process of writing them. Looking at the one he's currently working on, he thinks,

Dreadful, *dreadful*, dreadful. He must be mad to go on enduring the unexquisite agony of writing when it all turns out drivel. Mad. Why

didn't he become a spy? How does one become one? He will burn
the MS. Why is there no fire? Why aren't there the makings of one?
How did he get in the unused room on the third floor?

While still casting about, Gorey received an invitation from an
editor at Doubleday, Barbara Zimmerman, whom he had known
during his college years. Zimmerman's soon-to-be husband, Jason
Epstein, also a Doubleday editor, was about to launch Anchor Books,
a line of quality literature in inexpensive paperback editions. Would
Gorey like to design covers for these books? He said yes and left for
New York.

He found a studio apartment in Murray Hill and installed himself,
his cats (he was devoted to cats all his life), and as many books as the
place could hold ("I can't go out without buying a book"). He hated
New York—he thought Manhattanites were a bunch of phonies—but
he carved out a life for himself there that he would have had a hard
time constructing elsewhere. From childhood, he had been addicted
to movies. New York in the 1950s probably had more revival and art-
movie houses than any other city in the United States. He also found
a screening society run by the film historian William K. Everson, who
showed rare treats—silents, early talkies, foreign films—in his apartment
on Saturday nights. Gorey glutted himself on cinema. He said that, some
years, he went to maybe a thousand movies. This is possible. Some were
two-reelers—in other words, twenty minutes long. Also, Gorey and his
friends would watch practically anything. Many of them hated Christmas, because it was a family holiday, and they had no family in New York
City, or none that they wanted to spend the evening with. "We used to
go to four or five movies on Christmas Day," Gorey recalled. "We'd have
breakfast at Howard Johnson's, and then we'd go to a movie—and then
we'd go back to the Howard Johnson's. Then we'd go to another movie,
and go back to Howard Johnson's—'til about midnight." This custom

survives today among people I know, though the Howard Johnson's that Gorey's crowd favored, in Times Square, is long gone.

Gorey's other haunt in Manhattan was New York City Ballet, which had been founded in 1948 by George Balanchine and Lincoln Kirstein at City Center, the midtown people's-art mecca. Gorey was just in time to witness the company's glory years, and started going not long after he arrived in the city. The next year, he went a little more; the following year, a bit more. Finally, he said, it was just less trouble to reserve a ticket to every performance. In other words, he was at City Ballet pretty much every night—and every Saturday and Sunday afternoon, too—for almost half the year, every year. He considered Balanchine, he said, "the great genius in the arts today," and it is not hard to see Balanchine's influence on him: the mixture of exultation with sorrow, the combination of abstraction with frank depiction, the indifference to psychology. "There is nothing underlying," Gorey said. Most important of all, it seems, was his high regard for Balanchine's self-editing. If you haven't got something good, Balanchine said, "better don't do." Gorey repeatedly quoted those words, and for his whole life as a book artist he followed Balanchine's rule. When he died, he left piles of uncompleted material behind.

Like many ballet lovers, he had strong opinions about the dancers. He worshipped Diana Adams, a very clean-lined, long-legged, unmannered ballerina. He loved Patricia McBride and Allegra Kent, of the next generation. He did not like Suzanne Farrell and Peter Martins, the gorgeous pair who were stars of City Ballet in the sixties and seventies. He called them "the world's tallest albino asparagus."

It is impossible to describe Gorey's projects without speaking of his self-presentation. Already at Harvard—indeed, earlier, as a faux epileptic on public transportation—he was a show. To start with, he grew to six feet two, and he lost his hair early, compensating with a nice, bushy beard. A friend said that he looked like a cross between Hemingway and Santa Claus. His clothes were widely celebrated. He had a shifting wardrobe of at least a dozen fur coats, some of them dyed electric colors—blue, green, yellow. Underneath, he tended to wear a turtleneck adorned with some sort of necklace—African beads, a lavaliere on a string—and he often sported half a dozen rings. The outfit would be completed by blue jeans and, in almost all weather, low-top white sneakers, classic Keds, like those of the Doubtful Guest. The sartorial display would be accompanied by a kind of gestural performance—a lot of "flapping around," in the words of one college friend—and a full-diapason vocal act: booming laughs, gut-drawn sighs. With this came some very camp speech. (Of Agatha Christie's death, "I thought: I can't go on.") To ears of today, such language may sound affected, but to Gorey it seems to have been just a way of playing, having a good time. His friend Arlene Croce, the dance critic for *The New Yorker*, said, "Ted! He's a big baby."

Dery's book is often fun, but that's mostly because Gorey was fun. As for Dery, he should have been wiser. His discussions of Gorey's work tend to be brief and shallow, and the writing is annoyingly matey. Bogart is Bogey; Philadelphia is Philly. Everything is goosed up—above all, what Dery regards as the dark, dark mystery of Gorey. Look at the book's title, *Born to Be Posthumous: The Eccentric Life and Mysterious Genius of Edward Gorey*. In what sense was Gorey born to be posthumous? To me, he seems to have done okay—found some happiness, created some admirable art—while still living. As regards eccentricity: funny how certain artists are that way. Don't let this biographer loose on Gogol!

In keeping with this slant, Dery is fond of psychoanalytic interpretation. When he gets to the bottom level—"a yearning for the absent phallus," and so on—he tends to quote others, as if they, not he, were fetching these bogeymen up out of the cellar, but by pointing to them, he is, of course, proposing them to us. And with lesser matters, such as the grandmother in the insane asylum (Gorey had one), he doesn't mind drawing a direct line from the art to the life. When, in a book Gorey contributed to, "we hear echoes of an unhappy childhood," Dery writes, "we know we're hearing Gorey." Really? Was your childhood unhappy? Did you then produce *The Doubtful Guest*?

A point heavily insisted upon is what Dery sees as Gorey's secrecy. He pushed people away, barricaded himself behind books. Is that so? I am told by those who knew him that he was just shy. Fussed over by a stranger, he might mumble or blush, but he wouldn't be rude. "Then, too, beards are masks," Dery informs us. That's what beards are for? Tolstoy's? Santa Claus's? This is all very cheesy.

The worst part is that the secret Dery assumes Gorey was most frantically hiding was that he was homosexual. Again, one must ask, *Really?* If so, then walking around in a green-dyed fur, with half a dozen rings on his fingers, was not a good cover. In 1980, an interviewer from *Boston* magazine, Lisa Solod, asked him, flat out, about his sexual orientation—gay or straight?—and he answered that, as far as he could tell, he was neither one thing nor the other, particularly: "I am fortunate in that I am reasonably undersexed or something. . . . I suppose I'm gay. But I don't really identify with it much."

So there it was, the "smoking gun," as Dery calls it. But, strangely, the avowal just seems to make Dery angrier, probably because this question, which he has tracked obsessively in his book—and which is the center of his claim that Gorey was an unfathomable mystery—is waved away by Gorey so casually. He *supposes* that he's gay?

Dery tries to solve the problem with a fancy straw-man argument. "From our historical vantage point," he writes, Gorey's idea that he can ignore the matter of sexual orientation seems "blithely entitled." He appears to be "wearing the blinkers of white male privilege." But wait, Dery says. Maybe Gorey is the one who's right, by refusing the "whole business of constructing identity . . . around sexuality." Dery quotes the choreographer Peter Anastos, a friend of Gorey's, who says that, starting in the 1960s and '70s, "people let their homosexuality become the absolute center of their lives and there was nothing else. I've known a lot of guys Ted's age and . . . they just see it in a whole different way. Being gay is not the center of their lives. . . . Ted never struck me as closeted; he was just who he was."

That's the correct answer, I think, but I'm not sure Dery really thinks so. If he did, he would have revised early sections of his book in which he makes Gorey look all kinds of wrong—afraid of sex, afraid of intimacy—because he did not confess his homosexuality. Well, never mind. Chalk it up to the culture wars, and maybe also a concern for the bottom line, plus our old friend bad taste. Anyway, it's nice to have a biography of Gorey, with whatever silliness. He's been dead for eighteen years.

Somehow, in between the moviegoing, the ballet attendance, and work on the Anchor covers, Gorey managed to go on creating art books of a singular quality. Most of them were set in the Victorian or Edwardian period, like *The Doubtful Guest*. How he loved the furniture and clothes of that era, their fanciness, their fussiness: the watch fobs, the quilted dressing gowns! He said that he filched most of this material from Dover books on nineteenth- and early twentieth-century design. He gave his overdecorated world a suitable graphic context. Gorey was famous for his hatching and crosshatching, endowing his figures with depth and tone by building them up out of thin parallel lines. See the drawing of breakfast time at the Doubtful Guest's adopted home: the carefully varied arrangement of thin lines in the wallpaper and the paintings. That is hatching. Crosshatching is the placing of one set of hatching, at an angle, over another, as in the tablecloth and the father's suit.

These dark territories give the book's overt themes a place in which to burrow and ripen. Alison Lurie wrote that in looking at such drawings of Gorey's, "one of the things you want to remember is what the 1950s were like. . . . All of a sudden everybody was sort of square and serious, and the whole idea was that America was this wonderful country and everybody was smiling and eating cornflakes and playing with puppies." Gorey's hatching and crosshatching were his answer to that—the shadows inside the sunny hedge.

In Gorey's mind, his mother seems to have epitomized America's mid-century attack of fake goodness. Well before the holidays, she would send him letters saying that she was busy making fruitcakes for her family and friends for Christmas. Gorey hated fruitcake. In Dery's words, "He insisted there was only one fruitcake in existence, endlessly regifted around the world. One of his Christmas cards depicts a festive scene: a Victorian family, bundled against the cold, disposing of unwanted fruitcakes . . . by heaving them into a hole in the ice." The big, brown, too-sweet pastry, which no one likes, being dumped into ice water: this sums up a lot of Gorey's early and middle books. Also prominent is heavy masonry, from which, sometimes, a large chunk will dislodge itself and clobber a passerby on the head, killing him instantly.

Gorey took great pains over these funny and melancholy books. He could go on drawing the fine little lines far into the night, and if one of his cats tipped over the inkpot—he let the cats sit on his desk and watch him work—he would patiently start over. In the thirty-odd years that he lived in New York, he published around seventy volumes, some of them real miracles of book art. Especially fine are the early ones. In 1958, right after *The Doubtful Guest*, came *The Object-Lesson*. Here are three pages of its text:

> *On the shore a bat, or possibly an umbrella,*
> *disengaged itself from the shrubbery,*
> *causing those nearby to recollect the miseries of childhood.*

And something that indeed looks like a cross between a bat and an umbrella does drift out of a patch of leafless trees as three expressionless figures look on.

In 1962, he published the marvelous *Willowdale Handcar*, in which three young people take off one day on a railroad handcar. They pass a burning house, a cemetery, a mansion on a bluff, a vinegar works, and a baked-bean supper at the Halfbath Methodist Church, among other things. After traversing a magnificently drawn railroad trestle, with a wrecked touring car at its base (Who was killed? Where's the body?), they enter a tunnel in the Iron Hills and do not come out the other side. That is the end of the book. In 1963, Gorey published *The West Wing*, which is mostly just drawings of rooms, one with torn wallpaper, another with a boulder on a table, another with a crack in the floor, another with what appears to be a dead man on the carpet. *The West Wing* is only drawings. It has no text. The volume was dedicated to Edmund Wilson, who had given Gorey's drawings their first truly enthusiastic review but had found fault with his texts.

These books, thrilling as they are, were nevertheless hard to sell. Book art generally is. Gorey did not feel that he could afford to give up his job at Anchor Books. But then Jason Epstein had a falling-out with the company and left. Gorey soon followed and basically went freelance, living in New York only about half the year, the half in which New York City Ballet was performing. As he said, "I leave New York to work at Cape Cod the day the [ballet] season closes and I arrive back the day it opens." During his months on the Cape, he lived at the home of cousins in Barnstable. They gave him the attic room.

Now, in the 1970s, he finally became famous—not, actually, because his work got better, but because it was marketed differently. First, in 1967, the Gotham Book Mart, a small, musty midtown bookstore that had been the main purveyor of Gorey literature, was bought by a book dealer, Andreas Brown, who believed in promotion and was good at it. By then, most of Gorey's books were out of print. Brown got them back on the market, with the publication, in 1972, of *Amphigorey*, an omnibus edition of fifteen of Gorey's earliest volumes. Those volumes, I believe, are the best things Gorey ever produced, and now people noticed. (With the book's three sequels—*Amphigorey Too*, in 1975; *Amphigorey Also*, in 1983; and *Amphigorey Again*, in 2006—they noticed some more.) Then, in 1977, a new production of the play *Dracula*, by Hamilton Deane and John L. Balderston, was mounted on Broadway, with Frank Langella as the Count, and Gorey designed the elegantly artificial sets and costumes. The show was a huge hit, and the producers knew why. What the posters advertised was not *Dracula* but "The Edward Gorey production of

Dracula." Gorey's contract gave him 10 percent of the profits, and this helped to support him for the rest of his life. In 1980, PBS launched *Mystery!*, a weekly telecast of British mysteries and crime dramas. Gorey created the animated introduction—gravestones crumbling, corpses sliding into fens—and it was almost as popular as the shows.

Gorey had always wondered what he would do when Balanchine died. City Ballet was the center of his New York existence. Finally, in 1983, it happened: the great old man expired, at the age of seventy-nine. Gorey now started spending much more of his time on Cape Cod, and in 1986, when he lost his rent-controlled apartment in Murray Hill, he moved into a big, old, falling-down house in Yarmouth Port that he'd bought with his *Dracula* earnings. There he was able to enlarge his collections of things—cats, rocks, beanbags, books. When he died, in 2000, his library came to approximately twenty-one thousand volumes.

In Yarmouth Port, he moved into a new stage in his art. Dery writes that at some point in his final years Gorey, with his accustomed unflinchingness, told a friend that around 1990 he had lost his talent. I would refine that statement. He lost his ability, or his wish, to draw, or to draw as he had done before. He spent less effort on crosshatching, and his figures became more cartoonish; a chubby cat, with a smug smile, appeared again and again in his pages, to tedious effect. The formats themselves became a little smug: flip books, pop-up books. Such changes had been coming for a long time, and not just in the books. Dery quotes the director Peter Sellars on why *Dracula* didn't feel like Gorey to him. Broadway, Sellars said, was "all about 'selling' everything . . . people coming right down to the middle stage and belting something. What I missed entirely in the Broadway shows was the mystery, the haunted quality, and the reserve and the secrecy, because Broadway is about showing it all."

Apparently this didn't bother Gorey, who now transferred his energies from books to theater. From 1985 almost to the end of his life, he put on vaudevillian musical revues up and down the Cape, using, for the most part, nonprofessional actors. Many of the shows were mystifying. Of one, *Useful Urns*, a spectator said, "There were these big stage pieces shaped like urns that would move about the stage with actors popping out saying various unconnected phrases." Reportedly, a lot of the audience walked out. Gorey, by contrast, had the time of his life. "He hooted, whooped," a witness recalled. "It was almost more entertaining watching him than the performance." Asked, once, exactly what he did on these shows, he answered, "I direct, I design, I do everything." He didn't do it too hard, though. His assistant director said that his idea of directing was "to keep the actors from running into the furniture."

He had often said that he did not wish to live forever—indeed, unnervingly, that he wasn't really sure he was alive. Once, in a letter to a friend, he signed off as "Ted (I think)." In 1994, he suffered a heart attack. His doctor suggested three possible remedies—a pacemaker, strong medication, or milder medication. Gorey went with the milder medication. Six years later, he was watching a friend install a battery in his (Gorey's) new cordless phone when the other man turned to him and said, "Edward, do you believe this battery cost *twenty-two* dollars?" Gorey threw his head back and groaned, which the friend thought was a comment on the price of the battery. In fact, it was a second heart attack. Gorey, at the age of seventy-five, died in the hospital three days later.

The will was read soon after. Gorey left $100,000 each to the painter Connie Joerns, whom he'd known since high school, and to Robert Greskovic, the dance critic for *The Wall Street Journal* and a friend of thirty years' standing. His art collection—photos by Atget, drawings by Balthus, lithographs by Bonnard, and much else—went to the Wadsworth Atheneum, in Hartford, Connecticut, where it was exhibited earlier this year. (In 1933, the director of the Atheneum, Chick Austin, had paid for Balanchine's passage to the United States.) Other bequests went to animal-welfare societies—one, for example, to Bat Conservation International, in Austin, Texas.

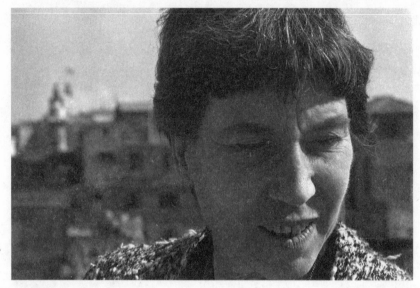
Natalia Ginzburg, 1970

BRAVE FACE

Natalia Ginzburg

In an early novella by the Italian writer Natalia Ginzburg—it has just been reissued by New Directions, as *The Dry Heart* (translated by Frances Frenaye)—the narrator walks into her husband's study and finds him sketching. He shows her his drawing: "a long, long train with a big cloud of black smoke swirling over it and himself leaning out of a window to wave a handkerchief." In other words, goodbye. He laughs. She doesn't. "I took the revolver out of his desk drawer and shot him between the eyes."

About time! For their entire marriage, four years, she has cowered before him: "I was always worried about my face and body, and when we made love I was afraid he might be bored. Every time I had something to say to him I thought it over to make sure it wasn't boring." Eventually, he takes to sleeping in his study, though he occasionally calls her in, to have sex, and then, presumably, sends her out again. "Why don't more wives kill their husbands?" the book's jacket copy asks.

Maybe they will, because there's a Natalia Ginzburg revival going on, abetted, perhaps, by the huge success of Elena Ferrante's Neapolitan quartet. Before that series was published in English (2012–15), who, among the people you know, was talking about modern Italian fiction? True, people talk about Primo Levi (a new, complete edition of his works came out in 2015, under the editorship of Ann Goldstein, who is also Ferrante's translator), but for reasons as much historical as they are literary. Levi was a prisoner of the Nazis and wrote our greatest book on that subject, *Survival in Auschwitz*. But the rest of Italy's stellar postwar generation—Carlo Levi, Alberto Moravia, Cesare Pavese, Elsa Morante, Giorgio Bassani, Leonardo Sciascia, Ginzburg—have been widely neglected in recent decades.

Now, at least for Ginzburg, the wheels are turning again. This year has seen not just the republication of *The Dry Heart* (originally *È stato così*, or "That's How It Was," 1947) but also a new translation, by Minna Zallman Proctor, of Ginzburg's more mature *Happiness, as Such* (*Caro Michele*, 1973). Another novel, *The Manzoni Family* (1983), will be reprinted in August. Most important, her masterpiece, *Family Lexicon* (*Lessico famigliare*, 1963), was brought out by New York Review Books in a fresh translation, by Jenny McPhee, two years ago. But several of Ginzburg's books remain out of print. The only English-language biography I've found, a translation of a German book by Maja Pflug, is not in print, either. And it amounts only to some two hundred pages—this for a woman who lived and wrote into her mid-seventies.

It's good to have *The Dry Heart* back, good to see what Ginzburg, whom few people encouraged to write, did at the beginning—something quite different from what she did later. Ginzburg became famous for her ability to conjure up a mixed emotional atmosphere, poignant yet unsentimental. (Chekhov was a favorite of hers.) *The Dry Heart* is not very mixed. Although it is not without comedy, it is a cold, angry book. The main reason, unquestionably, is that it was written in the shadow of Fascism, a matter that, for Ginzburg, cut very close to the bone.

Born in 1916, Ginzburg came from a large, fractious, high-IQ family based in Turin, the headquarters of Italy's automotive industry (the flagship Fiat plant is there) and of Olivetti business machines. The city is also an important center of learning. Ginzburg's father, Giuseppe Levi, was a professor of neuroanatomy at the University of Turin. (Three of his lab assistants went on to win Nobel Prizes.) Paola, Natalia's beautiful older sister, married a future president of Olivetti. Of her three brothers, Gino became Olivetti's technical director, Mario a journalist, and Alberto a doctor. Natalia, the youngest by seven years, didn't have much formal education. Her father wouldn't let her go to elementary school—he believed that children picked up germs there—and she dropped out of college.

In the 1930s and '40s, Turin was a hotbed of anti-Fascist activity, and almost everyone in the Levi family was part of it. Relatedly, they were Jews. (Or Giuseppe was Jewish; the mother, Lidia, was a Gentile.) They suffered for it. The Germans were not the only people in Europe who thought that opposition to Fascism was a Jewish plot. Natalia's brothers were in and out of jail for seditious acts. Giuseppe lost his job at the university and had to move to Belgium in order to go on teaching. Natalia's first novel appeared, in 1942, under a nom de plume, because Mussolini's racial laws forbade Jews to publish books.

Most of the family's friends were, like them, high achievers— publishers, writers, professors, scientists—and anti-Fascist and Jewish. Probably the most notorious Resistance fighter in this circle was the fearless Leone Ginzburg, an Odessa-born Jew who was a professor of Russian literature at the University of Turin. He was a leader of the Turin branch of the anti-Fascist organization Giustizia e Libertà (Justice and Liberty), to which the Levi men belonged. He, too, was dismissed from his university position. Eventually, he stopped visiting the Levis' house, because he felt that his presence there endangered them, but he obviously managed to see Natalia, because in 1938 she married him. They had three children, the eldest of whom is the eminent historian Carlo Ginzburg.

Leone, Natalia recalls, was arrested whenever an important politician came to town, and certainly whenever the king, Victor Emmanuel III, visited Turin. "Accursed king!" her mother would say. "If only he'd stay at home!" Finally, in 1940, Leone was sent into *confino*, or "internal exile," meaning confinement to a town so poor and isolated that, in the government's view, the accused could do no damage from there. But Leone, in *confino*, went on doing what harm he could to the fascist authorities. In 1943, when Mussolini was deposed, Leone decamped to Rome, to supervise an underground press. But after five months he disappeared.

Already when she was just beginning to write, Natalia learned that unhappiness, though it feels quite powerful, doesn't always help one write well. As she said in her essay "My Vocation" (1949),

> When we are happy our imagination is stronger; when we are unhappy our memory works with greater vitality. Suffering makes the imagination weak and lazy. . . . A particular sympathy grows up between us and the characters we invent—that our debilitated imagination is still just able to invent—a sympathy that is tender and almost maternal, warm and damp with tears, intimately physical and stifling. We are deeply, painfully rooted in every being and thing in the world, the world which has become filled with echoes and trembling and shadows, to which we are bound by a devout and passionate pity. Then we risk foundering on a dark lake of stagnant, dead water, and dragging our mind's creations down with us, so that they are left to perish among dead rats and rotting flowers in a dark, warm whirlpool.

Change the "we" to "women," and that's basically what Virginia Woolf said in *A Room of One's Own*, twenty years earlier: women, if they want to be artists, should stop sloshing around in their emotions. No doubt that statement disappointed many female writers at the time Woolf made it, and it is probably not popular even today. I wonder what the male-female ratio is among the students in those courses on writing "personal essays."

But Ginzburg learned the lesson early. In 1944, she wrote "Winter in the Abruzzi," an essay about the time she and her family spent in Pizzoli, the poor, chalky-soiled town that was the site of Leone's *confino*. Miraculously, she makes it a kind of happy tale. She talked to her children about life back in Turin:

> They had been very small when we left, and had no memories of it at all. I told them that there the houses had many storeys, that there were so many houses and so many streets, and so many big fine shops. "But here there is Giro's," the children said.
>
> Giro's shop was exactly opposite our house. Giro used to stand in the doorway like an old owl, gazing at the street with his round, indifferent eyes. He sold a bit of everything; groceries and candles, postcards, shoes and oranges. When the stock arrived and Giro unloaded the crates, boys ran to eat the rotten oranges that he threw away. . . . At Christmas the men returned from Terni, Sulmona and Rome, stayed for a few days, and set off again after they had slaughtered the pigs. For a few days people ate nothing but *sfrizzoli*, incredible sausages that made you drink the whole time; and then the squeal of the new piglets would fill the street.

The oranges the town's boys grab at are rotten, but they are probably pretty good all the same, or better than no oranges. The men of the town come home from the cities where they went to find work after the harvest was over. For days everyone eats sausages, and the streets are filled with the cries of newborn piglets, the makings of Christmas sausages to come. Crocetta, the Ginzburg family's fourteen-year-old maid, runs around town, trying to borrow a pan big enough for making dumplings. Crocetta also tells the children stories—for example, one that many people know as "The Juniper Tree," in which a woman cuts off her stepson's head and cooks it and feeds it to his father. The eight pages of "Winter in the Abruzzi" may be the most beautiful piece of work Ginzburg ever produced, full of oinks and smells, fellowship and cruelty.

It ends in sorrow. In the fall of 1943, after Germany began to occupy Italy and the Italian commanders fled to the south, Leone wrote to Natalia telling her to come to Rome, with the children, as quickly as possible. But how was she to get out of there, with three small children? In a hilarious episode, a friend in the village convinces the Nazis that Ginzburg is a poor, sad refugee who has no papers because they were lost in an air raid. She has to get to the capital. Can they help? And so this woman, the wife of a famously militant anti-Fascist, is driven to Rome, with her children, by a bunch of Nazis in a military vehicle. Presumably, she thanked them very much. She had three weeks with her husband before he was arrested again, for the last time. According to prison records, the cause of death was cardiac arrest combined with acute cholecystitis, a gallbladder infection that is often the product of trauma. That is, Leone probably died under torture. He was thirty-four. Natalia wrote:

> My husband died in Rome, in the prison of Regina Coeli, a few months after we left the Abruzzi. Faced with the horror of his solitary death, and faced with the anguish which preceded his death, I ask myself if this happened to us—to us, who bought oranges at Giro's and went for walks in the snow. At that time I believed in a simple and happy future, rich with hopes that were fulfilled, with experiences and plans that were shared. But that was the best time of my life, and only now that it has gone from me forever—only now do I realize it.

This, finally, is the grief that in her writing Ginzburg staved off with the oranges and the piglets.

Many of her readers, knowing what she had been through, wished she had shared her sorrows with them more often. But in her time Italian literature was still largely a men's club, and therefore Ginzburg had wanted, as she later flatly stated, to write like a man. Besides, emotionalism was not in her nature. As her granddaughter Lisa Ginzburg wrote, her ways were "always sober and austere."

You can get a sense of this from her appearance in her friend Pier Paolo Pasolini's film *The Gospel According to St. Matthew* (1964). For this movie Pasolini used mainly nonprofessional actors, people with plain faces, in dusty clothes. Ginzburg he cast as the woman who, in Matthew 26:6–13, intrudes on Jesus's dinner with Simon the leper and anoints Jesus's head. Anyone who can stream this film should do so. It is interesting to see Ginzburg's face: one critic said that she looked more Inca than Italian. Movingly, one can sense her embarrassment at being in a movie, and in a slightly naughty role. The woman with the jar of ointment has often been said to be a prostitute; the disciples object to her presence at their gathering. But Ginzburg's Mary is blunt, not seductive. She looks as though she were giving Jesus a shampoo.

In a radio interview in 1990, a year before she died, Ginzburg, likable and laconic—the interviewers probably talk more than she does—mentioned how much she admired her friend and fellow novelist Elsa Morante for being able, in her fiction, to use the third person confidently. She herself didn't have that ability, she said: she couldn't "climb up on mountains and see everything from above." But neither was she able to deploy the first person easily. Ginzburg was a moralist, which is a hard thing for a modern novelist to be, and, partly for that reason, she didn't like to declaim, or to let her characters do so. She needed to break up the voice. Two of her novels are epistolary, so that the characters take turns speaking in the first person. Another way that she avoided an overbearing "I" was simply with the terseness of her prose. (In some passages, she averaged perhaps twelve words per sentence.) When interviewers asked her about this, she would often reply that she was so much younger than her many siblings that as a child, if she had something to say, she had to say it quickly, before somebody interrupted her.

Whatever her sorrows, Ginzburg made a life for herself after Leone's death. In her earlier years, she had done some work for Einaudi Editore, the celebrated publishing company established in Turin, in 1933, by Giulio Einaudi (the son of a future president of Italy), together with Cesare Pavese and Leone Ginzburg. Now she went back to work there. In 1950, she got married again, to Gabriele Baldini, a professor of English at the University of Rome, and she moved to the capital to be with him. (She writes about Baldini in a tender essay, "He and I," collected in *The Little Virtues*, a book of beautiful short pieces that also includes "Winter in the Abruzzi.") In 1983, Ginzburg was even induced to run for a seat in the Italian parliament, as the candidate of the Independent Left. She won and was later reelected. All told, however, she had bad luck. Baldini died young (in 1969, at the age of forty-nine), and the two children they had together were both born severely disabled. The first, a boy, died within a year. The second, a girl, Susanna, lived, and Ginzburg kept her at home. I have read no description of how this was for her.

Nevertheless, it seems to me that critics overstress the theme of sorrow in Ginzburg's works. She always knew how to convert the griefs into some sort of beauty. In *Happiness, as Such*, she pulled off a wonderful act of virtuosity, an epistolary novel in which a young man, Michele, is the subject of a series of letters written to, by, and also about him, by his mother, his sisters, a friend, a former girlfriend, and assorted others. Most of these people are comically selfish; they want what they want from Michele. And where the hell is he, anyway? As it turns out, he has had to leave Italy, where he was involved in left-wing causes. He writes to his sister Angelica to please go get the machine gun out of the oven where he stored it, in his kitchen, and throw it into the river. In another letter, he tells his friend Osvaldo to go to the same apartment and get the white cashmere scarf with the blue stripes out of the bottom drawer of a bureau. It will remind Osvaldo, he says, of the walks they used to take along the Tiber. Osvaldo replies that he looked for the scarf but couldn't find it, so he went to the store and bought another scarf. It probably wasn't cashmere, and didn't have stripes, but it was white. Michele is later killed in a demonstration. By then, ironically, he seems to have given up politics. Everything in the book is a little sad and a little funny.

This tone, a kind of melancholy touched with poetry, is carried forward in Ginzburg's superb *Family Lexicon*, which she said was to be read as a novel even though everything in it really happened. The title means, sort of, "the way we used to refer to things," and most families probably have such a lexicon. If Natalia arrived at the dinner table in an adolescent funk, her mother would say, "Here comes Hurricane Maria." An uncle who was a doctor specializing in the treatment of the insane was referred to as "the Lunatic."

Ginzburg is best when writing about her parents. Her father, Giuseppe, a loud, choleric Triestine, always took a cold shower in the morning:

> Under the water's lash, he'd let out a long roar, then he'd get dressed and, after stirring in many spoonfuls of sugar, he'd gobble down great cupfuls of that cold *mezzorado* [yogurt]. By the time he left the apartment, the streets were still dark and mostly deserted. He'd set out into the cold fog of those Turin dawns wearing a large beret that formed a kind of visor over his brow and a great big raincoat full of pockets and with many leather buttons. He'd go out with his hands clasped behind his back, his pipe in his mouth, his stride lopsided because one shoulder was higher than the other. Almost no one was on the street yet but he still managed to bump into whoever happened to be out then.

The mother, Lidia, a Milanese, is the opposite: immovably serene, playing solitaire and chatting with the seamstress when she is not journeying happily here and there to bring clean clothes to the men in the family who are in jail. Lidia loved to tell stories:

She would turn to one of us at the dinner table and begin telling a story, and whether she was telling one about my father's family or about her own, she lit up with joy. It was as if she were telling the story for the first time, telling it to fresh ears. "I had an uncle," she would begin, "whom they called Barbison."

And if one of us said, "I know that story! I've already heard it a thousand times!" she would turn to another one of us and in a low-ered voice continue on with her story.

"I can't even begin to count how many times I've heard this story," my father would shout, overhearing a word or two as he passed by.

My mother, her voice lowered, would continue on with the story.

In 1934, Natalia's brother Mario was the star of a scandal in which he and an associate were caught at the Swiss border trying to bring anti-Fascist literature into Italy. The other man was arrested, but Mario jumped into the Tresa River and swam for the Swiss shore. "In the water with his overcoat on!" Lidia exclaimed when she was told. She regretted that her menfolk were always being locked up, but she was proud that they were often incarcerated with distinguished people. When her son Alberto was sent to prison with his friend Vittorio, she said of Vittorio, "He's just done very well on his law school exams." This theme, of the blindness of European Jewish families to the actual, mortal threat of the Fascists, has been sounded before, but rarely with such flair. "I wrote poems for Mussolini," a woman the Ginzburgs knew in Pizzoli says. "What a mistake!"

The dinner table was the scene of loud arguments. The small Natalia sat there, listening, and what people said she stored away. Her later life, too, was grist for this poet of remembrance. (She had translated Proust's *Swann's Way* for Einaudi.) I especially treasure her 1957 essay "Portrait of a Friend" (also collected in *The Little Virtues*), about Cesare Pavese, who took an overdose of barbiturates in Turin, in 1950, at the age of forty-one:

He died in the summer. In summer our city is deserted and seems very large, clear and echoing, like an empty city-square; the sky has a milky pallor, limpid but not luminous; the river flows as level as a street and gives off neither humidity nor freshness. Sudden clouds of dust rise from the streets; huge carts loaded with sand pass by on their way from the river; the asphalt of the main avenue is littered with pebbles that bake in the tar. Outside the cafés, beneath their fringed umbrellas, the little tables are deserted and red-hot.

None of us were there. He chose to die on an ordinary, stiflingly hot day in August, and he chose a room in a hotel near the station; he wanted to die like a stranger in the city to which he belonged.

Although Pavese was eight years older than Natalia—he went to school with her brothers—he became not only her colleague at Einaudi but also a close friend and, through his novels, a significant influence on her. His death was a terrible blow, and, as usual, one admires the restraint of her report. One must also admire the portrait of Turin. She makes the city absorb all the desolation that she is too delicate-minded to tell us was Pavese's. But the city is also beautiful, in an eerie way: "very large, clear and echoing, like an empty city-square." (It seems like a de Chirico.) And Pavese is not just a man who committed suicide. He is also a person who was young once. He loved cherries, Ginzburg says, and used to come over to the Levis' house in the evening with a pocket full of them, which he would then distribute. Usually, when Pavese is spoken of, he is the man of the bleak books and the death by Seconal. But, thanks to Ginzburg, I now see him, sometimes, dangling cherries in front of a young girl. Later, he was one of the few people who urged her to write. When she was living in the Abruzzi, he sent her a postcard: "Dear Natalia, stop having children and write a book." She had more children, but she also sat down and wrote more than a dozen books.

The New Yorker, 2019

Gilgamesh holding a captured lion. Assyrian, eighth century BC

BEYOND THE WATERS
OF DEATH

Gilgamesh

The mid-nineteenth century was a time when very many Western people began to doubt the historical truth of the Bible. Was it really the case that we were all descended from Adam and Eve, whom God created in his own image and placed in a beautiful garden and then, by reason of their sins, banished from there? Did their descendants compound their wickedness, to the point where God decided to drown them all, in a huge flood? And did he, afterward, seeing the destruction he had wrought, make a covenant with the one surviving family, that of Noah, promising that he would never again raise his hand against his creation? "While the earth remaineth," he decided, according to the King James Bible, "seedtime and harvest, and cold and heat, and summer and winter, and day and night shall not cease." For many centuries, this story comforted people. Though we might sin, we could hope for God's mercy, because that's what he had promised to Noah.

By the early nineteenth century, however, scholars from various young fields—geology, archaeology, paleontology—were producing evidence that the earth was much older than anyone had thought and that human societies had existed long before the dates assigned to the Creation and the Flood. In 1859, Charles Darwin, in his *On the Origin of Species*, put forth a theory suggesting that human beings might be descended not from Adam and Eve but from lower animals, things with fur. Not surprisingly, such ideas encountered vigorous opposition. Many scientists and scholars redoubled their efforts to find evidence of the truth of the Bible.

Around the time that Darwin was writing his book, a young Londoner, George Smith, who had left school at the age of fourteen and was employed as an engraver of banknotes, became fascinated by reports of artifacts that were being turned up by explorers in what is today Iraq and sent to England. As David Damrosch writes in *The Buried Book* (2007), Smith spent his lunch hours at the British Museum, studying its holdings. The staff eventually noticed him, and in 1866 the management hired him to help analyze the tens of thousands of clay shards that had been shipped there years earlier and had been sitting around in the museum's storage boxes.

The site they came from was Nineveh, an important city in ancient Mesopotamia, and the reason so many tablets had been found in one place was that they were the remains of a renowned library, that of Ashurbanipal, a king of the neo-Assyrian Empire in the seventh century BC. When the tablets were first dug up, no one could read the curious-looking script, later called cuneiform, in which they were written. Scholars worked on it for decades.

Now George Smith joined the hunt. He studied the shards for around ten years, and it was he who found the most famous passage inscribed on them, an account of a great flood wiping out almost all of humanity, with only one man's family surviving. When he read this, we are told, he became so excited that he jumped out of his chair and ran around the room, tearing off his clothes. This ancient document could support the truth of Genesis, or so it seemed to Smith.

And to others. In 1872, when Smith presented his findings to the Society of Biblical Archaeology, even William Gladstone, the prime minister, was in attendance. The discovery became front-page news across Europe and the United States. Soon, London's *Daily Telegraph* gave Smith a grant to go to the Middle East to see if he could add to his findings. Within days, he hit pay dirt—a shard that appeared to complete the flood story—and the British Museum financed two further trips for him. On the second of these, he died of dysentery in Aleppo, at the age of thirty-six. He never lived to understand that, in fact, he had not proved the truth of the Old Testament with his clay tablet. (Both flood narratives could have been descended from older sources, quite possibly fictional.) He had done something else, though. He had discovered what was then, and still is, the oldest long poem in the world, *Gilgamesh*.

The poet and scholar Michael Schmidt has just published a wonderful book, *"Gilgamesh": The Life of a Poem*, which is a kind of journey through the work, an account of its origins and discovery, of the state of the text, and of the many scholars and translators who have grappled with its meaning. Schmidt encourages us to see *Gilgamesh* not as a finished, polished composition—a literary epic, like the *Aeneid*, which is what many people would like it to be—but, rather, something more like life: untidy, ambiguous. Only by reading it that way, he thinks, will we get close to its hard, nubbly heart.

We meet Gilgamesh in the first line. He is the king of Uruk, a splendid, high-walled city in southern Mesopotamia. His mother was a goddess and his father a mortal. Accordingly, he is a fine specimen of a man, eleven cubits (seventeen feet) tall and four cubits from nipple to nipple. He is not an exemplary ruler, however. He wearies the young men of his city in athletic contests, and when they marry, he insists on the droit du seigneur: he, not the groom, spends the wedding night with the bride.

The people of Uruk complain to the gods about Gilgamesh's behavior, and in response the mother goddess, Aruru, pinches off a piece of clay and, from it, fashions a new person, Enkidu, to be a friend to Gilgamesh and distract him from his bad habits. Enkidu is a giant, too, though not as big as Gilgamesh. In the beginning, he is much like an animal. His body is covered with hair. He runs with the gazelles and drinks with them, on all fours, at the water hole. But he has human intelligence; he regularly releases his animal companions from traps. When one of the local trappers objects that Enkidu is interfering with his livelihood, he is instructed to bring a temple prostitute, Shamhat, to the water hole that Enkidu frequents and have her sit at the edge. (There were temple prostitutes, devotees of local fertility goddesses, in many ancient societies. This was a respected profession.) Enkidu arrives. Shamhat spreads her legs, and he instantly succumbs. With what must be the most robust erection in world literature, he engages Shamhat in an act of coitus lasting, uninterrupted, for six days and seven nights. Then he gets tired, and Shamhat takes him to a shepherds' encampment. For the first time in his life, he eats bread. He also drinks seven goblets of beer, and he starts to sing. But when, after this merrymaking, he tries to rejoin the gazelles, they shun him. Tragedy thus enters *Gilgamesh*. By making love with a human being and eating human food, Enkidu has become a man, and nothing will ever be the same for him.

For example, he now has morals. When he hears about Gilgamesh's exercise of the droit du seigneur, he becomes enraged. He goes to Uruk and draws Gilgamesh into a fight. The door jambs shake, the walls quake, but after a while the two men weary of the quarrel and decide to be friends. Gilgamesh introduces Enkidu to his mother, the goddess Ninsun. She doesn't like him. Who are his people? she asks. Thus snubbed, Enkidu weeps, and Gilgamesh, to cheer him up, proposes an adventure: the two of them will go to the Cedar Forest, kill its protector, the monster Humbaba, and harvest some cedarwood for building projects in Uruk.

Humbaba is no ordinary monster. He is like a miasma, or a nightmare. He has seven auras in which he can wrap himself, and which he can send out, as a means of defense. As Gilgamesh and Enkidu approach, he taunts them. "Spawn of a fish," he calls the fatherless Enkidu. He tells Gilgamesh that forest birds will soon be feasting on his body parts. Though shaking with fear, the two men seize him. Gilgamesh plunges a dirk into his neck. Enkidu rips out his lungs. The auras run away. Then the men cut down several giant cedars, build a raft, and, with Gilgamesh brandishing the head of Humbaba, sail back to Uruk.

Once home, Gilgamesh bathes, puts on clean clothes, and shakes out his long hair. Seeing him, Ishtar, the goddess of love and war, is dazzled, and calls out to him, proposing marriage: "Grant me your fruits, O grant me!" She will give him a chariot of lapis lazuli and gold, she says. His ewes will bear twins; his goats will bear triplets. In response, Gilgamesh asks Ishtar how he would profit from marrying her. You are a brazier that goes out in the cold, he tells her. You are a door that lets in the wind, a shoe that pinches the foot. The men that you loved: What became of them? One you turned into a frog, another into a wolf. No thank you, he says.

Ishtar, greatly insulted, runs up to heaven, to her father, Anu, and asks to be given the Bull of Heaven, to avenge these insults. Descending to Uruk with the goddess, the formidable beast does serious harm even as it lands. One snort, and the earth opens up; a hundred men fall into it. A second snort, and another pit opens; two hundred men are swallowed up. On the third snort, when the cleft opens, Enkidu falls into it, but only up to his waist (because he is a giant), and he grasps the bull by the horns. It slobbers on Enkidu's face. It defecates on him. But Gilgamesh stabs it in the neck, and it dies. When Ishtar protests, Enkidu tears off one of the bull's haunches and throws it at her, saying that he would happily have ripped off *her* limbs and thrown them at the bull. He and Gilgamesh then wash their hands in the Euphrates and, clasping each other, return in triumph to the palace. "Who is the finest among men?" Gilgamesh asks his serving maids. "Who the most glorious of fellows?"

The triumph is short-lived. That very night, Enkidu has a dream that to atone for the crime of murdering the Bull of Heaven, one of the two friends must die. No one needs to ask which. Enkidu sickens. He starts to complain. Why could he not have died in combat? That way, people would remember him. But then the tablets break off. As Michael Schmidt writes, Enkidu has "some thirty so far silent lines to bid his beloved Gilgamesh good-bye and perish."

There was a real king called Gilgamesh, it seems. Or, at least, his name appears in a list of kings compiled around 2000 BC, and he probably lived in the first half of the third millennium BC. For at least a thousand years after his death, poems were written about him, in various Mesopotamian languages. Then, sometime between 1300 and 1000 BC, one Sin-leqi-unninni (his name means "The moon god Sin hears my prayers") collected the stories. We might call Sin-leqi-unninni a scribe or an editor. According to one scholar, he was also a professional exorcist. What matters is that he pulled together the Gilgamesh poems that he had at hand and, adding this and deleting that, and attaching a beginning and an end, he made a unified literary work, in his language, Akkadian. This composition is what Assyriologists call the Standard Version of *Gilgamesh*. It was incised on eleven tablets, back and front, with roughly three hundred lines on each tablet.

We don't have a complete copy of Sin-leqi-unninni's tablets. Through the actions of time, wind, and, above all, war—Nineveh, with Ashurbanipal's library, was attacked and destroyed by neighboring forces in 612 BC—a great deal of the text was lost. Some of the holes can be plugged with material from other Gilgamesh poems, but even once that has been done, important sections are missing. Of an estimated thirty-six hundred lines, we have only thirty-two hundred,

whole or in part. (Translations often supply ellipses where text is missing, and use italics and brackets to mark varying degrees of conjecture.)

Furthermore, the thing that we are looking at, after the insertions,
is a patchwork of texts created at various times and places, in what are
often different, if related, languages. One highly respected translation,
by Andrew George, a professor of Babylonian at the University of London's School of Oriental and African Studies, gives what remains of
Sin-leqi-unninni's text and then appends the "Pennsylvania tablet"; the
"Yale tablet"; the "Nippur school tablet," in Baghdad; the "fragments
from Hattusa" (now Boğazköy, in central Turkey); and so on. Scholars
cannot afford to ignore these outliers, because the symbols that constitute cuneiform, up to a thousand of them, changed over the millennium
that produced Sin-leqi-unninni's materials. So the word for "goddess
of love and war" on a fragment in Baghdad may be different from its
analogue in the vitrines of the British Museum. Indeed, meanings may
change in the present as well, as additional discoveries are made. After a
new piece came to light in 2015, George wrote that the energetic Enkidu
and Shamhat had not one but two weeklong sex acts before repairing to
Uruk. The text has no stability. It shifts in your hands.

Also, the text was missing for so long that it is relatively new to us.
Schmidt estimates that the *Iliad* and the *Odyssey* have been studied by
scholars for about 150 generations; the *Aeneid*, for about a hundred; *Gilgamesh*, for only seven or eight. Translators of Homer and Virgil could
look back on the work of great predecessors such as Pope and Dryden.
Not so with *Gilgamesh*. The first sort-of-complete Western translation
was produced at the end of the nineteenth century. I was not taught the
poem in school, nor was anyone I know. There is no real tradition for
reading it. Modern translators are pretty much on their own.

And they have a special challenge. When, at the conclusion of tablet
7, Enkidu dies, *Gilgamesh* does not end. On the contrary, something

like a new poem begins, in a different key. Before, the two young men were killing monsters and having sex—not such a different plotline from that of a modern action movie. Now, with the death of Enkidu, everything changes. Gilgamesh sends up a great, torn-from-the-gut lament: "O my friend, wild ass on the run, donkey of the uplands, panther of the wild," may the Cedar Forest grieve for you, and the pure Euphrates. He calls for his craftsmen—"Forgemaster! [*Lapidary!*] Coppersmith! Goldsmith!"—and orders Enkidu's funerary monument: "Your *eyebrows* shall be of lapis lazuli, your chest of gold." For six days, Gilgamesh cannot bear to leave his watch over the body. Finally, a maggot falls out of one of Enkidu's nostrils. (That repulsive detail is recorded again and again. The poets knew its power.) Seeing it—and understanding, accordingly, that his friend has truly been turned into matter, dead meat—Gilgamesh is assailed by a new grief: he, too, must die. This frightens him to his very core, and it becomes the subject of the remainder of the poem. Can he find a way to avoid death?

He flees Uruk and clothes himself in animal skins. First he goes to the mountain where the sun rises and sets. It is guarded by two scorpions. Gilgamesh explains to them that he is seeking Uta-napishti, the one man, he has heard, who became immortal. The scorpions grant him entry into a tunnel that the sun passes through each night. But if he wants to get through it, they say, he must outpace the sun. He starts out and, in utter, enfolding darkness, he runs. He can see nothing behind him or ahead of him. This goes on for hours and hours. In the end, he beats the sun narrowly, emerging into a garden where the fruits on the trees are jewels:

> A carnelian tree was in fruit,
> hung with bunches of grapes, lovely to look on.
> A lapis lazuli tree bore foliage,
> in full fruit and gorgeous to gaze on.

To me, this is the most dazzling passage in the poem: the engulfing darkness, in which Gilgamesh can see nothing for hours—he is just an organism, in a hole—and then, suddenly, light, color, beautiful globes of purple and red hanging from the trees. God's world, made for us, or so we thought.

Gilgamesh does not linger in the garden. He at last finds Uta-napishti, the man who gazed on death and survived. Gilgamesh wants to know, How did you do this? Unhelpfully, Uta-napishti explains:

> *No one at all sees Death,*
> *no one at all sees the face [of*
> *Death,]*
> *no one at all [hears] the voice of*
> *Death,*
> *Death so savage, who hacks men*
> *down. . . .*
> *Ever the river has risen and*
> *brought us the flood,*
> *the mayfly floating on the water.*
> *On the face of the sun its*
> *countenance gazes,*
> *then all of a sudden nothing is*
> *there!*

Uta-napishti now tells Gilgamesh the story that made George Smith take off his clothes. We might have done the same, for Uta-napishti's tale is far more bloodcurdling than the one in the Old Testament. Like Noah, Uta-napishti was warned of the coming catastrophe, and he ordered an ark to be built. The bottom of the hull was one acre in area, with six decks raised on it. (And the vessel seems to have been cube shaped!) Once the ark was finished, Uta-napishti and his family and all the animals he could lay his hands on, plus whatever craftsmen he could summon, boarded the ark. Before he sailed, he gave his palace and all its goods to the shipwright—an ironic gift, since the palace and its goods, and presumably the shipwright, too, would be destroyed the next day. Uta-napishti continues:

> At the very first glimmer of
> brightening dawn,
> there rose from the horizon a dark
> cloud of black,
> and bellowing within it was Adad
> the Storm God.
> The gods Shullat and Hanish were
> going before him,
> bearing his throne over mountain
> and land.
>
> The god Errakal was uprooting
> the mooring-poles,
> Ninurta, passing by, made the
> weirs overflow.
> The Anunnaki gods carried
> torches of fire,
> scorching the country with
> brilliant flashes.
>
> The stillness of the Storm God
> passed over the sky,
> and all that was bright then turned
> into darkness.
> [He] charged the land like a bull
> [on the rampage,]
> he smashed [it] in pieces [like a
> vessel of clay.] . . .

Even the gods took fright at the
Deluge,
they left and went up to the
heaven of Anu,
lying like dogs curled up in the
open.
The goddess cried out like a
woman in childbirth.

These last lines are what everyone quotes. How thrilling they are, with the gods bent over, howling, in the skies and the storm shattering the earth like a clay pot. In the end, the rains stop, and Uta-napishti's ark, like Noah's, gets snagged on a mountaintop. He and his fellow survivors disembark and repeople the earth.

For suffering this ordeal, Uta-napishti and his wife are granted immortality, but, he suggests, no one but they can live forever. Then he relents and gives Gilgamesh some tests whereby he might cheat death. Gilgamesh fails. (They are silly tests, and he fails in silly ways. The poem is not perfect.) Uta-napishti's boatman takes Gilgamesh home. When they arrive in Uruk, Gilgamesh tells the boatman to climb Uruk's city wall:

Survey its foundations, examine
the brickwork!
Were its bricks not fired in an
oven?
Did the Seven Sages not lay its
foundations?

A square mile is city, a square mile
date grove, a square mile is clay-
pit, half a square mile the temple
of Ishtar:

three square miles and a half is
Uruk's expanse.

A few commentators interpret these words as a statement of consolation: we should take comfort in our achievements on earth and accept the inevitability of life's ending.

With the poem in its present state, however, such a case is hard to make. Having read the lines above, which form the conclusion of tablet 11 as translated by Andrew George, we turn the page and find not a tablet 12 but a brief note informing us that what is often presented as the ending of *Gilgamesh*—it describes the conditions of the underworld, where Gilgamesh, after his death, will reign—is not part of the epic at all. According to George, it is a fragment from an older poem, tacked on to supply an ending.

Twelve tablets would have been nice. That is the form of the *Aeneid*, and the *Iliad* and the *Odyssey* are each twenty-four books long—that is, twice twelve. But an eleven-tablet format doesn't bother Andrew George. He proposes that the structure of the poem is 5 + 1 + 5, and sees tablet 6, in which Gilgamesh and Enkidu return to Uruk after killing Humbaba, as a centerpiece—the manifestation of Gilgamesh at the height of his glory.

I wonder, though. It is surely in tablet 5, when he kills Humbaba, that Gilgamesh is shown at his most powerful. Whereas, in tablet 6, we get his crudely worded rejection of the infatuated Ishtar and then the slaughter of the Bull of Heaven, which so displeases the gods that they punish Gilgamesh by killing off his beloved Enkidu. The truth, I suspect, is that *Gilgamesh*, as befits something that was buried under a pile of sand for twenty-five hundred years, is simply missing some pieces.

Schmidt, in his book, sort of moseys through the poem, addressing topics as they arise. When the subject of war comes up, he nods at the wars in Iraq, which, beginning in 1990, were being waged when a number of translators of *Gilgamesh* were at work. When the characters are having sex, he discusses Assyrian sex. Did Gilgamesh and Enkidu have a homosexual relationship? He doesn't think so, but he gives the evidence for and against. He also makes the important point that their friendship is the most tender relationship in the poem. Each night, when the two men are traveling to the Cedar Forest, Enkidu makes a little house for Gilgamesh to sleep in, and, "like a net, lay himself in the doorway."

Again and again, Schmidt discusses the translations. You might think that a poem that exists in a pile of broken pieces, in an extremely dead language, would be something that translators would run from in a hurry. The very opposite is the case. Probably because it is, as Schmidt writes, such an "uncertain, porous" thing, translators are drawn to it. Often they are not, by profession, translators or Assyriologists but just poets. Others *are* Assyriologists, and, unsurprisingly, not all of them look kindly on people who publish versions of *Gilgamesh* without knowing the language in which it was written. Benjamin Foster, a professor of Assyriology and Babylonian literature at Yale, told an interviewer, "I have no patience with clueless folk who think that they can translate the epic without going to the trouble of mastering Babylonian, though of course they are welcome to retell it."

Since the mid-twentieth century, there have been, by my count, nearly a score of full-scale translations of *Gilgamesh* into English. The majority of the translators, not to speak of the commentators, have stepped forth from among Foster's clueless folk. What most of these people do is read a literal translation by an expert Assyriologist and then "poeticize" it, pushing it up into verse. Such a procedure should not scandalize anyone in our time. It is, basically, how Ezra Pound wrote his so-called translations of the Chinese poet Li Po, and Auden his versions of the Icelandic Eddas. But with a text so unknown as *Gilgamesh*, so hard for any of us to read, this method certainly raises some questions.

Schmidt doesn't linger over the questions. He is broad-minded. He is a poet, and the thing he is interested in is obtaining poetry, getting the grapes of carnelian truly red and round, getting Uta-napishti's deathless world appropriately wan and bloodless. Going through the poem tablet by tablet, he stops at his favorite parts and reads to us from various translations. How excited he gets when the men leave for the Cedar Forest! How ravished he is by the forest's richness!

> *A pigeon was cooing, a turtledove*
> *answering,*
> *The forest was joyous with the*
> *[cry] of the stork,*
> *The forest was lavishly joyous with*
> *the francolin's [lilt].*
> *Mother monkeys kept up their*
> *calls, baby monkeys chirruped.*

Sometimes Schmidt seems less a literary historian than just a friend who has come over to our house for the evening, with a bottle, to read us a terrific poem.

He recommends specific translations. He is acutely aware of the age of the poem, and its fragmentary condition, and its authorlessness—"a poem without a poet," he calls it. The translations he is most wary of are those that try to cover over that strangeness, de-"otherize" the poem, solve its riddles, and thus "free us to be contented literary consumers." He names names: in England, Nancy K. Sandars (1960); in the United States, Stephen Mitchell (2004). Both, he says, are "guilty as charged," guilty of producing a poem that tries to convince us that Gilgamesh is some guy we know, with problems like our own, and speaking the words that we would say. (Or not: in Mitchell's translation, Gilgamesh, rebuking Ishtar, claims that she implored her father's gardener, "Sweet Ishullanu, let me suck your rod." He's the one she eventually turned into a frog.)

All the same, Schmidt then goes on to suggest that if we haven't yet read *Gilgamesh*, we might as well start with Sandars, to get a sense of the poem. Next, we should move on to one of the Assyriologists,

Foster or George, and find out what the surviving inscriptions actually say. Finally, Schmidt sort of goes wild and sends us to *Dictator: A New Version of the Epic of Gilgamesh* (2018), in which the Belfast-born poet Philip Terry translates the poem into "Globish," a fifteen-hundred-word vocabulary put together by a former IBM executive, Jean-Paul Nerrière, and published in 2004 as a proposed language for international business, just as Akkadian, the language of *Gilgamesh*, was the lingua franca of Near Eastern commerce in its time. Here, in Globish—with plus signs indicating missing words that Terry apparently doesn't want to guess at and vertical lines demarcating metrical units—are the trapper's instructions to Shamhat for seducing Enkidu:

> *Here be | the man | party | girl*
> *get | ready | for a | kiss + + +*
> *Open | you leg | show WILD |*
> *MAN you | love box*
> *Hold no | thing back | make he |*
> *breathe hard . . .*
> *Then he | will come | close to |*
> *take a | look + + +*
> *Take off | you skirt | so he |*
> *can . . . | screw you.*

I think Schmidt is having a little fun with us here, and that he has read too many *Gilgamesh* translations. My own recommendation would be the same as his for the first two stops—Sandars, to get comfortable, and, after that, one of the Assyriologists, to get uncomfortable. Then I might go to *Gilgamesh Retold* (2018), by the Anglo-Welsh poet Jenny Lewis, who teaches at Oxford. Lewis's version is very musical, with rhymes and chimes and shifting meters. It can be blunt. Its account of the murder of Humbaba is the nastiest I know. Yet her translation is also the most tender, the most tragic. When Enkidu meets Shamhat at the water hole, there is no talk of love boxes. Enkidu strokes her thighs;

he sings to her. Likewise, when, as a result of his commerce with human beings, Enkidu loses his kinship with the animals, that melancholy fact is given its due:

> *Far away, under the forest's boughs*
> *A small gazelle still searched for*
> *him in vain*
> *And others sniffed the air to catch*
> *his scent*
> *But there was nothing carried on*
> *the wind*
> *And in his mind no thought of*
> *them was left.*

But I have a bizarre proposal: it would not be a bad idea, in approaching *Gilgamesh*, to start with Michael Schmidt's book. Yes, it is a commentary, not an end-to-end translation, but it includes a lot of translated passages—the best ones, no doubt. And Schmidt's argument for the poem as poetry, in the modern sense—concrete, unglazed, tough on the mind—is touching and persuasive. I read the book spellbound, in one sitting. (Like *Gilgamesh*, it is short, less than two hundred pages.)

Schmidt has emotions about these ancient tablets. When you handle one, he tells us, "especially the apprentice copyists' tablets that fit in the palm, almost as if we were shaking hands with the original scribe, the sensation of living contact can be intense. The fine-grained river mud was rolled and patted into shape, sliced, lifted to the eye and, in dazzling sunlight of a scribal courtyard, under supervision, the cuneiform figures were incised."

He sees the tablets again as, thousands of years later, various underpaid people sat in the British Museum, year after year, trying to figure out what they said. In George Smith's time, the museum lacked not only electrical light but gaslight as well. (The management was afraid of fire.)

Some of the higher-up staff had lanterns, but George Smith was not a higher-up. If it was a foggy day and the windows did not admit enough light to read by, he had to go home. On other days, though, he was at his post. "With devotion and patient application," Schmidt writes, these scholars "deciphered the languages, finding human voices in the clay, and a king terrified of dying came back to the long half-life of poetry."

The New Yorker, 2019

The casts of two bodies, probably a rich man and his slave, fleeing the eruption of Vesuvius. Pompeii, AD 79

THE DAY THE EARTH EXPLODED

Pliny the Elder and Pliny the Younger

If you were writing a biography of Gaius Plinius Caecilius Secundus—or Pliny the Younger, the author of one of the most famous collections of letters surviving from the early Roman Empire—it would be hard not to start with the eruption of Mount Vesuvius, on the Bay of Naples, in AD 79, for Pliny was the only writer to leave us an eyewitness account of the catastrophe. The English classicist Daisy Dunn, in her book *The Shadow of Vesuvius: A Life of Pliny*, wisely does not resist the temptation. For Westerners, that explosion is probably the paradigmatic natural disaster. When we think of the worst thing Mother Nature could do to us, we are likely to think of Vesuvius. Likewise, Pompeii, the hardest hit of the communities lying at the base of the volcano, is, for many people, the world's most compelling archaeological site. Although some two thousand of the town's inhabitants were killed, much of their world—the tools they gardened with, the paving stones they walked on, the graffiti they scratched on the walls of their brothels, the loaves of bread left baking in the oven, marked off into eight portions, just like a modern pizza—survived, however altered, under the layers of ash and pumice and rock that the volcano dumped on it.

Today, these things stand as a kind of textbook of how the citizens of Campania, the region over which Vesuvius loomed, lived in the late first century. Who, before the excavations of Pompeii, knew that many ordinary Romans, having only small, rudimentary kitchens, seem to have eaten takeout for dinner most nights? But if you go to Pompeii, as millions of tourists do each year, you can view the storefront food shops with the pots, sunk in their counters, that once contained fish stews, boiled lentils, and so on, ready to be bought and carried home.

And who, apart from those who have survived a war, knew what a person dying from thermal shock looks like? Archaeologists examining Pompeii and neighboring cities eventually came upon rooms full of skeletons, many of them surrounded by a bubble of empty space, which marked the outline of the victims' flesh. In a town just south of Vesuvius, known in ancient times as Oplontis, you can see the so-called Resin Lady, a facsimile created by pumping transparent epoxy resin into such a void. The Resin Lady is lying face down and spread-eagled, just as she was when she was found. Around her are the objects she was carrying when she died: some jewelry, an iron key (to what?), the traces of a cloth bag holding a small collection of coins, five silver and seven bronze. Apparently she thought that, wherever she was going, she might need money. Her mouth is open, in a silent scream. In front of this, one turns away, ashamed of having looked.

There is more, at least quantitatively. Herculaneum, on the coast, lay upwind of Vesuvius, giving the inhabitants time to seek shelter from the blast. Hundreds of people, Dunn writes, "made their way to the shore, where a series of arched vaults, probably boat stores, was set back from the coast." Each vault was barely ten feet wide by thirteen feet deep. The people who could not fit inside one of the vaults—many men ceded their places to women and children—remained exposed on the shore. A recent study suggests that those in the shelters might in fact have met slower and more agonizing deaths, perhaps by asphyxiation, than those outside, who were probably killed instantly by the heat. Other researchers have identified some glassy black material found in Herculaneum as the brain matter of one of the victims, vitrified by the eruption's pyroclastic flow—burning clouds of gas and ash. As this avalanche poured down on the coast at a speed of at least sixty miles an hour, the temperature on the ground rose to about 750 degrees Fahrenheit. Lead melts at 621 degrees Fahrenheit.

The terrible day dawned prettily. Pliny the Younger, seventeen years old, was staying at a villa in Misenum, across the Bay of Naples from Vesuvius, with his mother, Plinia, and her brother, Gaius Plinius Secundus, usually known as Pliny the Elder. (I will call the nephew Pliny, and the uncle the Elder.) Plinia was the first to notice that something strange was going on across the bay. Atop Vesuvius, there was a cloud that looked like an umbrella pine, Dunn says, "for it was raised high on a kind of very tall trunk and spread out into branches."

Plinia went into the house and spoke to her brother. The Elder was the admiral of Rome's navy, which, at that time, was docked at Misenum. He put down his book and called for his shoes so that he could climb to a higher vantage point and see what was happening.

The Elder, who was fifty-five, was not just a military man. He was also a naturalist—the greatest, perhaps, that the ancient world produced. He proudly claimed that his thirty-seven-volume *Natural History* contained facts gleaned not just from observation but from as many as two thousand volumes by Greek and Roman geographers, botanists, physicians, artists, and philosophers. In the book, he described his homeland, Campania, as a blessed spot, with

> plains so fertile, hills so sunny, glades so safe, woods so rich in shade, so many bountiful kinds of forest, so many mountain breezes, such fertility of crops and vines and olives, fleeces of sheep so handsome, bulls with such excellent necks, so many lakes, and rivers and springs

which are so abundant in their flow, so many seas and ports, the bosom of its lands open to commerce on all sides and running out into the sea with such eagerness to help mankind!

The fertility of the region's vineyards was famous. Some said that this was because of soil enriched by volcanic explosions, but Vesuvius had been dormant for around seven hundred years. Who remembered? There were frequent earthquakes in the area, but people were used to this. They didn't suspect that it was owing to anything going on inside their noble mountain.

When the Elder saw the strange cloud over Vesuvius, he decided to set sail across the bay to see what was going on. Although he gave the appearance of being unworried, he launched several quadriremes—large warships with four banks of oars on each side—presumably with the thought of evacuating as many people as possible. He asked his nephew to come with him, but Pliny said he had some writing to do and would rather stay home. The Elder's boats aimed straight for Vesuvius but couldn't land there, because the debris from the eruption was falling so fast that it formed islands in the shallows. So the fleet turned toward Stabiae, a port nine miles south, and there the Elder went ashore, to the house of a friend, Pomponianus. Thinking (so Pliny conjectures) to set an example of calm, he asked for a bath and dinner. Even as flames began leaping from the mountain, he told his companions that these were surely just burning houses abandoned by frightened peasants, and he went off to take a nap. But, during the night, Pomponianus's family, feeling the house sway above them, decided it was time to leave and woke their guest. The party strapped pillows over their heads to protect themselves and made a run for it. The Elder headed to the shore, hoping that he might find some way to escape by sea.

Back in Misenum, meanwhile, Pliny and his mother decided that they, too, had to escape. They tried to go by carriage, but the roads were clogged with other people fleeing, so they got out and ran. The darkness was complete: "Not so much a moonless or cloudy night, but as if the lamp had gone out in a locked room," Pliny wrote. Plinia begged her son to leave her and go on alone, but he refused. The two eventually found their way to safety. The Elder, on the opposite shore, did not. When the darkness lifted, his body was found on the beach. He was heavyset and had a weak windpipe. He probably died of asphyxiation from the ash. Dust from the explosion reached all the way to Africa, Pliny writes.

Of the two Plinys, Dunn focuses on the younger. Clearly, she would rather have done otherwise. The Elder was more famous, rightfully so. As his nephew said, the older man did things that deserved to be written about and wrote things that deserved to be read. His *Natural History*—Penguin Classics has a good abridged translation, by John F. Healy—is not merely huge but piquant and readable. Of bees, for example, he writes,

> The bees have a wonderful way of supervising their work-load: they note the idleness of slackers, reprove them and later even punish them with death. Their hygiene is amazing: everything is moved out of the way and no refuse is left in their work areas. Indeed the droppings of those working in the hive are heaped up in one place so that the bees do not have to go too far away. They carry out the droppings on stormy days when they have to interrupt work.
>
> As evening draws in, the buzzing inside the hive diminishes until one bee flies round, as though giving the order for "lights out," and makes the same loud buzzing with which reveille was sounded, just as if the hive were a military camp. Then suddenly all becomes silent.

How wonderfully, punctiliously factual that is, but also with a subtle moral. Reading the Elder's work, you come to feel that you know him. In fact, however, he told us almost nothing about himself.

That, no doubt, is the reason that Dunn chose to concentrate not on him but on his nephew. Pliny's letters, as published in his lifetime, ran to nine volumes, and a tenth was added after his death. (Here, too, there's a Penguin Classics abridged edition, this one translated by Betty Radice.) In them, we learn pretty much everything about this man's public life, and also a lot about the other well-placed Romans he corresponded with, such as the historians Tacitus and Suetonius, not to speak of the emperors he served, Domitian and Trajan. Pliny went to work as a lawyer at the age of eighteen, and he had other vocations as well. He was a poet, a senator, a public official. But in all his jobs he seems to have landed in the second- or third-best spot. The law court he worked in was the one that handled civil cases—wills, inheritance, fraud—not the juicy murders and other foul deeds for which the Roman Empire is famous. Later, he was appointed to a public office, but as the curator of the bed and banks of the river Tiber and of the city's sewers. Is that the job you would have wanted in imperial Rome? Later still, he was sent, as Trajan's imperial legate, to Bithynia (northern Turkey), where his main responsibility was to inspect the colony's finances. He wrote long letters to Trajan, asking whether he should do this or that. The letters took two months to arrive in Rome, and the answers took two months to get back. Reading them, you sense that Trajan often wished Pliny would just go ahead and make whatever decision seemed reasonable.

We do hear about some celebrated crimes: Agrippina, the emperor Claudius's wife, poisoning him in order to secure the succession for her son, Nero; Nero then killing Agrippina and also kicking his pregnant wife, Poppaea, to death. (That's after he arranged for the poisoning of his stepbrother, Britannicus.) Then there's Domitian, going off with, they say, whatever implement he had at hand, to terminate his niece Julia's pregnancy, engendered by him. This, Dunn writes, inspired a locally popular ditty: "Julia freed her fertile uterus by many / an abortion and shed clots which resembled their uncle." (Julia died from the procedure.) Next to such reports, the regular rubouts, as in the notorious Year of the Four Emperors, in AD 69—Nero, to avoid execution, stabbed himself in the throat and was replaced by Galba, who was assassinated after seven months by the Praetorian Guard and succeeded by Otho, who ruled for three months before, faced with a rebellion, he committed suicide, yielding his place to Vitellius (soon murdered by the soldiers of Vespasian, but let's stop there)—look like business as usual. Or they would seem so if they didn't involve those special little Cosa Nostra touches, such as a victim's being found with his penis cut off and stuffed in his mouth.

Of course, many of the most appalling episodes are well known from more famous accounts, in Tacitus's *Annals of Imperial Rome* and Suetonius's *Lives of the Twelve Caesars*. Dunn has no scoops, and she knows it. Furthermore, she is trying to be faithful to Pliny's account, but, as she notes, he made a point, when he published his correspondence, of excising all the dates and arranging the letters, as he put it, "however they came to hand." She thinks that he was trying, by this means, to show "a life of ups and downs, uncertainties, and questions rather than certain progress."

If so, he achieved his goal. The letters have a weirdly drifting quality, as if these people woke up, went to the law courts, sentenced some people to death, burned a few Christians, and then went home to dinner. With such a source, it is no surprise that Dunn's book contains a number of challenges to our understanding. One is the treatment of the widely hated Emperor Domitian. Dunn quotes Suetonius to the effect that Domitian amused himself at night by stabbing the flies on his desk with a stylus, and she repeats the stories of his alleged dealings with his niece. Pliny, she says, pictured Domitian as "a monster from Hades, hiding in his lair and licking his lips with the blood of relatives." But later she writes that the emperor was said to have been "a man of justice." Really? What do we do, then, with the jokes about the aborted fetuses that supposedly looked like their uncle Domitian? No matter how distant you feel from the morals of imperial Rome, you can't quite figure this out, and Dunn doesn't help us much.

At the risk, in such a context, of seeming sentimental, I must say that the most striking thing about Pliny's letters is the lack of tender feeling. Dunn makes much of Pliny's affection for his third wife, Calpurnia, and of his sorrow when she had a miscarriage. (In the end, she died childless.) Dunn points out, too, that Pliny took Calpurnia to Bithynia with him. Somehow, though, these seem small tributes. When the two were apart, he wrote begging her to send him a letter once or even twice a day—"to delight and to torture me." She wrote back that her consolation, when they were separated, was to take his books to bed with her and hold them in the place where he usually lay. Why does her tribute sound so much more serious than his?

Pliny knew the art of fine words. In AD 100, he gave a speech—the *Panegyricus*, famous in its day—in praise of Rome's recently installed emperor, Trajan, who had to sit in front of him, in the Senate house, the whole time. He then revised and expanded it for publication. Scholars disagree about how long the speech would have lasted, but no one seems to think that the running time was less than three hours. Elsewhere, Pliny proudly mentions giving a speech that lasted seven. Describing the *Panegyricus*, Dunn comes close to mocking Pliny. "To modern ears his chosen style is somewhat grating and turgid," she says. With such statements, however, she does succeed in making Pliny, whom she clearly considers a sort of dry stick, a poignant character, the kind of person who has to do the dirty jobs of an empire and, having done them, gets no compliments.

Pliny's deepest feeling seems to have been his love of nature. By my count, he had at least five villas, and many of the most ardent passages in his letters are devoted to agricultural matters. Dunn writes that at his Tuscan estate he grew so many grapevines that they threatened to invade the villa:

> One of the bedrooms was constructed almost entirely from marble and contained a cabinet-like alcove for a bed. There were windows on every facet, but in summer the vines shrouded them in shade. Being

in bed then, as flickers of light fought through the foliage, was "like lying in a wood, but without feeling the rain."

Here one feels the Romans' love of the world, and of that especially beautiful piece of it that is the Italian peninsula. In this sentiment, at least, Pliny was truly his uncle's nephew, which may go some way toward explaining the curious fact that after the fall of Rome anyone who still knew the name Pliny assumed that he was just one person. It was not until the early fourteenth century that a cleric at the cathedral of Verona figured out that there were two Plinys. And it was only in the fifteenth century that their books made it back into circulation. The Elder's *Natural History* had its first printed edition in 1469; his nephew's letters returned to publication in 1471. "The release of books by two Plinys," Dunn writes, "was met with considerable emotion across Italy."

Neither Pliny knew that his homeland's great mountain, Vesuvius, was nourishing in her bosom the extermination of so many of her people. This somehow makes the two men's kinship closer. In my mind's eye, I see Pliny, on the terrace of his mother's villa, watching the Roman quadriremes, under the Elder's direction, make for the opposite shore. Should he have gone with them? Perhaps, but it is typical of this cautious young person that he stayed back. In any case, his decision joined the two men permanently, at least in Roman history. Not only did Pliny live to tell the tale, but the next day, when his childless uncle died on the beach of Stabiae, he became, by the directives of the will, the Elder's adoptive son and the inheritor of his property. And so he spent his later life gathering grapes on the hillsides that had been the old man's joy.

The New Yorker, 2020

Andy Warhol, 1965

BIGGER THINGS TO HIDE BEHIND

Andy Warhol

Andy Warhol's life may be better documented than that of any other artist in the history of the world. That is because, every few days or so, he would sweep all the stuff on his desk into a storage box, date it, label it "TC"—short for "time capsule"—and then store it, with all the preceding TCs, in a special place in his studio. As a result, we have his movie-ticket stubs, his newspaper clippings, his cowboy boots, his wigs, his collection of dental molds, his collection of pornography, the countless Polaroids he took of the people at the countless parties he went to—you name it. We have copies of bills he sent and also of bills he received, from increasingly exasperated creditors, including one ("pay up you blowhard") from Giuseppe Rossi, the doctor who, in 1968, saved his life after a woman who felt she had been insufficiently featured in his movies came to his studio one day and shot him. In one box, I've heard, there is also a slice of cake, on a plate, with a fork. It wasn't just material objects he kept. When possible, he taped his phone conversations, and sometimes had an assistant transcribe them. He believed in the power of the banal. This faith was the wellspring of the Pop

Art paintings—the Campbell's soup cans, the Brillo cartons—that made him famous in the 1960s and changed America's taste in art.

After Warhol's death, in 1987, a museum dedicated to his work was established in his hometown, Pittsburgh. The time capsules—610 of them—were shipped there and lined up on banks of metal shelving, ready for the person who would work their contents into a fittingly rich biography. Seven years ago, the person arrived: Blake Gopnik, formerly the lead art critic of *The Washington Post*. Gopnik is fantastically thorough; his *Warhol* is nine hundred pages long—not counting the seven thousand endnotes, available in the e-book edition or online. But you don't lose heart, because Gopnik is a vivid chronicler. Here is a small clip from his description of the repair job Dr. Rossi did on Warhol's innards after the 1968 shooting. The surgeon found

> two holes in the arc of the diaphragm muscle, pierced both right and left as the bullet crossed through Warhol's body; an esophagus severed from the stomach, so that food and gastric acid were spilling out from below; a liver whose left lobe was mashed and bleeding and a spleen utterly destroyed and spilling more blood than any of the other organs. [The] bullet had also cut a ragged hole in Warhol's intestines, releasing feces and upping the chances of fatal infection.

Reading this, I felt as though I were having the operation myself.

Warhol was born in Pittsburgh in 1928, the youngest of the three sons of Andrej and Julia Warhola, who had immigrated to the United States from a small village in what is now Slovakia. The townsfolk were Carpatho-Rusyns, a Slavic people, and the family was Byzantine Catholic. (Warhol, as an adult, went to Mass sporadically. "Church is a fun place to go," he said.) Slavs were much in demand in Pittsburgh, with its steel mills, because they were reputedly willing to do any kind of work, at any wage. As a result, they were also the most looked-down-upon ethnic group in the city. Andrej was a manual laborer; Julia a domestic. When she didn't have enough work, she went door to door, often with her sons in tow, selling decorative flowers made from cut-up peach cans. Andrej died in 1942. The two older boys quit school and took full-time jobs. Andy stayed in school. For most of his youth, he was cosseted by his family. When the Warhols acquired a new Baby Brownie Special camera ($1.25), he immediately laid hands on it, and never let it go. His brothers built him a darkroom in the basement. Also, he fell in love with the movies; he said that he wanted to make his living showing films. This was an unusual life plan for a boy of his background, but Julia saved $9—nine days' wages from her housecleaning—to buy him a projector. He showed Mickey Mouse cartoons on a wall in the apartment.

Warhol liked to describe himself as self-educated, a widely accepted claim. In fact, he went to an excellent art college, the Carnegie Institute of Technology, where a number of his teachers recognized his gifts and kept the work that he turned in to them, a rare tribute. The minute he got out of school, in 1949, he packed his belongings in a paper bag and got on an overnight Greyhound bound for New York City. He was twenty.

In New York, Warhol lived in a series of roach-ridden sublets, usually shares, while trying to break into commercial illustration. Once, when he was showing samples of his work to the editor in chief of *Harper's Bazaar*, an insect crawled out of his portfolio, to his mortification. The editor felt so sorry for him that she gave him an assignment. Warhol was not shy. In the Museum of Modern Art, he went up to a staffer and proposed that he design Christmas cards for the gift shop. (He got the job.) A friend remembered seeing him in a bookstore, flipping through the record bins to see which labels were doing the most interesting jackets. Then he went home and cold-called the art directors. "He was like a little Czech tank," another friend said.

Many people who met him in those years, and later, found him strange—a "weird little creep," in the words of one. He was unabashedly homosexual, and in the early fifties that was weird enough. He liked to do drawings of nude boys, their nipples and crotches dotted with little hearts, like soft kisses. If he met a man who appealed to him, he might say that he liked to photograph penises, and would this man mind? "No, of course not," one self-possessed British curator replied. "What are you going to use them for?" "Oh, I don't know yet," Warhol said. "I'm just taking the pictures." The man unzipped.

Three years after Warhol arrived in New York, his mother turned up on his doorstep. She explained to one of his friends, "I come here to take care of my Andy, and when he's okay I go home." She stayed for almost twenty years. The household had a large, smelly collection of Siamese cats. At one point, there were reportedly seventeen of them, mostly named Sam. (But Julia, pointing, could introduce them separately: "That's the good Sam, that's the bad Sam, that's the dumb Sam . . .") Between the cats and Julia's late-life drinking problem, Warhol seems to have been hesitant to introduce her to his friends. On the other hand, one boyfriend said he thought Warhol was grateful for her presence, because it gave him an excuse not to have sex. He would explain to his guest that he didn't want to make any bedroom noises as long as his mother was within earshot.

Warhol claimed that he was a virgin until he was twenty-five, and some people would say that that was no surprise. All his life, he was pained by his looks. He was cursed with terrible skin, not just acne, but what seems to have been a disorder of pigment distribution so that his complexion was lighter here, darker there. He also had a bulbous nose, or so he thought, and he got a nose job. By the time he was in his thirties, he had lost much of his hair. Thereafter, he glued a toupee to his scalp every morning. His most celebrated wig was a silver one, which he usually wore with a fringe of his brown hair peeping out at the back of the neck. These difficulties boded ill for his sex life, and he was widely said to be lousy in bed. He thought sex was "messy and distasteful," a friend reported. He'd do it with you once or twice, and that was it. Gopnik, as is his practice, also gives competing evidence: "Within a few years Warhol was having surgery for anal warts and a tear, and a decade later he was taking penicillin for a venereal disease." Warhol's friend and collaborator Taylor Mead said that Warhol "blows like crazy."

Warhol lied constantly, almost recreationally. He lied about his age even to his doctor. He told *Who's Who* that he was born in Cleveland, to the "von Warhol" family. (He had traded in Warhola for Warhol soon after arriving in New York.) He adopted a gentle, whispery voice, into which, often, he would then drop a little grenade. If someone asked how he was, he might say, "I'm okay," and then, coming closer, he would add, "But I have diarrhea." Some people thought he was stupid. Not those who knew him well. "Warhol only plays dumb," a friend said. "He's incredibly analytical, intellectual, and perceptive."

His commercial specialty was drawings for women's-wear ads— above all, shoes. In 1955, the high-end women's shoemaker I. Miller gave him a contract for a minimum of $12,000 worth of work per year, a lot of money at the time. He also did window dressing, notably for Bonwit Teller. But already he was looking beyond this. He wanted to be a gallery artist. Teachers and classmates from Carnegie Tech provided some con- nections, and Manhattan's gay community supplied more. He also had a few special godfathers, attracted to him, it seems, by his charm (not everybody thought he was creepy) and by his drive. Perhaps his most important guide was Emile de Antonio, an artists' agent, who introduced him all around; he knew John Cage, whom Warhol revered, and lots of collectors. ("I gave a little party for a terribly rich woman I knew," de Antonio recalled, "and I served just marijuana and Dom Perignon, and Andy did a beautiful menu in French.") Another useful person was Ivan Karp, the director of the Leo Castelli Gallery, Manhattan's most presti- gious art mart. Through Karp, Warhol eventually met Henry Geldzahler, a curatorial assistant at the Metropolitan Museum, whose job there was to find out who the hot new artists were and tell the curators.

In the fifties, the United States already had a pocket of conceptual art, but the star painters were the Abstract Expressionists, above all Jackson Pollock and Willem de Kooning, with their effortful drips and impastos. At the Ab Exes' heels were the young Robert Rauschenberg and Jasper

Johns, part conceptual, part painterly, and edging into Pop, a style that used imagery from mass culture—comic strips, movies, advertising—and adopted a light, playful tone, the very opposite of the Abstract Expressionists' heavy lifting. Warhol, too, was interested in this popular matter and manner, and he was annoyed that other people were, as he saw it, stealing a march on him. According to a famous story, he was complaining about this to friends one night and asked if anyone could think of pop-culture images that no one else had used. A decorator named Muriel Latow said she had a suggestion, but she wanted $50, up front, before she would reveal it. The unembarrassable Warhol sat down and wrote a check. Then Latow said, "You've got to find something that's recognizable to almost everybody . . . something like a can of Campbell's Soup."

Gopnik calls this Warhol's "eureka moment," and it is typical of the book's sophistication that the crucial, seedling idea of Warhol's Pop Art should be attributed, without apology, to someone other than Warhol. Often, artists who are praised for birthing a new trend are not the actual originators but the ones who made the trend appealing to a large public. Warhol had as much of the latter gift as of the former; Gopnik calls him "the Great Sponge." In any case, the day after Latow shared with him her little brain bomb, Warhol (or his mother, in another version of the story) went to the Finast supermarket across the street and came home with one can of every kind of Campbell's soup on sale there. By the following year, 1962, he had produced *Campbell's Soup Cans*, a montage of all thirty-two varieties. Today, this painting hangs in the Museum of Modern Art—"the *Nude Descending a Staircase* of the Pop movement," in the words of Henry Geldzahler. It is both a slap in the face and a great joy: so fresh, so brash, so red and white, so certain that it has covered every kind of soup in the world, from Pepper Pot to Scotch Broth.

In rapid succession, the Campbell's soup cans were followed by Warhol's other now famous Pop paintings: *Green Coca-Cola Bottles* (1962), *200 One Dollar Bills* (1962), *Brillo Box (Soap Pads)* (1964), the Marilyn Monroes and Elizabeth Taylors and Marlon Brandos and Elvises. For some, you can easily construct a background narrative. The *Marilyn Diptych*, comprising fifty silk screens of Monroe, fading from garish color to spectral black and white, was exhibited just after her death. But I see no story lurking behind the Liz Taylors or the Elvises or, for that matter, the panels of twenty-four Statues of Liberty (1962) or thirty Mona Lisas (1963). All of these ladies, not to speak of Elvis and Brando, were stars, and Warhol, from his childhood until the day he died, was enthralled by celebrity.

He soon became a celebrity himself, if an unusual one. In his thirties, he was famous, in TV interviews, for putting two fingers over his lips and saying things like "er" and "um," but not much more, as the cameras rolled. (You can see this on YouTube. It is discomforting to watch.) For live interviews, he would often bring along Gerard Malanga, who worked with him, and say, "Why don't you ask my assistant Gerry Malanga some questions? He did a lot of my paintings." There was some truth to this. Of the works listed above, all but the 1962 *Campbell's Soup Cans* were silk screens, usually based on photographs that someone else had taken, and were made with Malanga wielding the squeegee. From 1963 to 1972—the period during which he created most of his Pop Art—Warhol produced no hand-drawn work.

Running parallel to Warhol's iconoclasm about authorship was a certain coolness toward his subjects. "For an artist with a lifelong reputation for sucking up to stars," Gopnik writes, "Warhol also had a lifelong knack for making art that underlined their shortcomings and hollowness." Probably the most important discussions of Warhol's work are the books and essays that the philosopher Arthur Danto wrote on him from the mid-sixties onward. These are not exactly art criticism. Their scope is broader. Danto says that Warhol's work, by disposing of modernism's assertions that painting should be about the nature of painting, liberated it to go its own way, while the art critics stayed back in the schoolroom, arguing. Danto doesn't say he loved Warhol's work, but I think he did. I'm sorry that he liked the Brillo carton—it supplied the title of his book *Beyond the Brillo Box*—better than the Campbell's soup cans, but he probably enjoyed the irony that the Brillo box Warhol immortalized was designed by an Abstract Expressionist painter, James Harvey, doing a money job on the side. The Ab Exes looked upon Warhol with hatred. At a party in the late sixties, a drunken de Kooning said to Warhol, "You're a killer of art, you're a killer of beauty, you're even a killer of laughter."

Warhol didn't kill laughter—he would have been less famous if he had done so—but his humor is muted, deadpan. In 1964, he produced a series of nine silk screens of Jacqueline Kennedy's face, based on press photos: one that showed her in the famous pillbox hat, just before JFK was shot; the second as Lyndon Johnson was being sworn in, on the airplane back to Washington; the third at Kennedy's funeral. There was nothing overtly mocking about these works. But in 1964, when, in the public mind, Kennedy's body was not yet cold, they raised a question: What was Warhol saying? Viewers might have asked the same of his earlier *Death and Disaster* series (1962–65), worked up from photographs of bloodied corpses hanging out of wrecked cars, mangled bodies of people who had jumped to their deaths, the electric chair in which Ethel and Julius Rosenberg, convicted of spying for the Soviet Union, were executed, and so on. Like the soup cans, the silk screens were often cheerfully multiplied and, like the Marilyns and the Liz Taylors, covered with washes of bright color: blue, red, violet, yellow.

In the same year as the *Nine Jackies*, Warhol unveiled silk screens of his *Flowers*, big, blobby hibiscus blossoms against a grassy field. They looked like wallpaper or, as Gopnik suggests, Marimekko dress fabrics. In any case, they were something that, unlike a picture of an electric chair, you might be willing to hang over your living-room sofa. This was what they were apparently designed for, because Warhol (or Malanga) turned out more than 450 of them, in different versions—different sizes, different colorways, to use Gopnik's inspired word—and they sold like hotcakes. Warhol claimed to be proud of them. If I'm not mistaken, Gopnik doesn't believe him. He quotes Warhol announcing, the following year, that he has retired as an artist. The *Flowers*, Gopnik writes, were "pretty much his last notable Pop paintings." But, as the author does not flat out say but repeatedly implies, they were also pretty much Warhol's last notable paintings, period. "I hate paintings," he told a reporter in 1966, adding, "That's why I started making movies."

He had made his first film in 1963. Titled *Sleep*, it was five and a half hours long, and all it showed was his boyfriend, John Giorno, sleeping. The next year, he followed this up with *Empire*, eight hours, overnight, of the Empire State Building, shot from a window in the nearby Time-Life Building. Thereafter, until the mid-seventies, he made scores of movies, some of them pure and severe, like *Sleep* and *Empire*, and others, such as *Chelsea Girls* and *Lonesome Cowboys*, shambling and funny and dirty, with drag queens sitting around licking bananas or people having dilatory conversations about sex, or having sex.

But the movies were not just movies. They were the motion-picture wing of what was by now a whole "scene." In 1964, Warhol moved his professional headquarters into a vast space he came to call the Factory—it had housed a hat factory before he took possession—on East Forty-Seventh Street, just west of the United Nations. The place was filthy, but Warhol's friend Billy Name (né Billy Linich, but Linich was a name, right? So why not just go by Name?) moved in with a pack of fellow speed freaks and transformed the space with tinfoil and spray paint so that in the end every surface was silver.

Just as Warhol's movies were not merely movies, the Factory was not merely a place where things were made. It was also a showcase for a certain group of people who clustered around Warhol. Billy Name was one; Gerard Malanga another. Also important was Ondine (Robert Olivo), wild and vicious. Best known to outsiders was Edie Sedgwick, a sweet-faced and rather hapless rich girl who, in black tights and expensive sweaters, often went along on Warhol's outings, as his "date," and paid the tab. These and a few others were Warhol's superstars, as he called them.

In 1966, he also became the manager of a proto-punk-rock band, the Velvet Underground, hatchery of Lou Reed, John Cale, and others, all

pretty much unknown at that point. One of its members described a typical show: "Some sailors or something were in the audience of five, and we
played something and they said, 'You play that again and we'll fuck the
shit out of you.' So we played it again." "Our aim was to upset people,"
one of the band's founders said, "make them vomit." Warhol knew little
about music, and he and the Velvets broke up in less than a year. ("Always
leave them wanting less," Warhol said.) But for a while Warhol's film
showings and performances—notably, the *Exploding Plastic Inevitable*
and ★ ★ ★ ★—were multimedia events, featuring the superstars bopping
around in a desultory fashion to the Velvets' discordant strains while two
or more films were projected side by side or, indeed, in superimposition.

It hardly needs to be said that drugs were involved here, and this fact,
augmented with reminiscences of Warhol's associates, has contributed to
a portrait of him as a sort of Mephistopheles, luring his young friends to
their ruin. A key story is that of Freddie Herko, part of the West Village
postmodern-dance scene in the sixties. One day, a while after he had
stopped hanging around the Factory, Herko took a bubble bath, and
some LSD, at a friend's apartment, danced naked for a while, and then,
to the strains of Mozart's Coronation Mass, threw himself out a window.
When informed of Herko's death, Warhol is said to have commented that
he was sorry not to have been there to film the fall.

This story won him an enduring reputation, with those so minded, as
an emotionless person, a sort of freak—an image reinforced by his paintings of soup cans and electric chairs. Cold heart, cold art. Gopnik doesn't
say whether he believes that Warhol spoke those words about Herko's
death, but he concludes that if the report was true, it says as much about
Warhol's desire to shock as about his supposed lack of feeling. He also
points out that whether or not Warhol used the joke on Herko, he used
it on others too. When his relationship with Edie Sedgwick was coming
to an end—she ran off with Bob Dylan—he said to a friend, "When do
you think Edie will commit suicide? I hope she lets us know, so we can
film it." If this was nasty, it was also clear-eyed: six years later, Sedgwick
died of a barbiturate overdose. Warhol also applied the joke to himself,

saying that he always regretted that no one had been there, in 1968, to film him being gunned down.

On June 3, 1968, a woman named Valerie Solanas emerged from the elevator at the Factory. She was a local eccentric, the founder and sole member of a feminist organization she called SCUM, the Society for Cutting Up Men. She was also, apparently, suffering from an acute mental disorder. She had previously drifted into Warhol's studio a few times, and he had put her in a sexploitation film, *I, a Man*, in 1967. She felt he should have used her more, and this was the reason for her visit that day. Entering the studio, she fired several times at Warhol and also put a bullet in a friend of his who was visiting. Then she turned around and stepped back into the elevator. A few hours later, in Times Square, she told a bewildered cop, "The police are looking for me. I am a flower child. He had too much control over my life." (She was sentenced to three years in prison. "You get more for stealing a car," Lou Reed said.) Meanwhile, an ambulance had taken Warhol to Columbus Hospital, where he was laid out on a table for Dr. Rossi's ministrations. His mother, summoned by one of his associates, stood in the lobby, praying for him. The doctors had her sedated and taken home. After the surgery, Warhol stayed in the hospital for two months, eating candy, talking on the phone, and trying to manage the studio from afar.

Gopnik describes the assault by Solanas as the dividing line between Warhol's "before" and his "after." He slowly got rid of his disreputable entourage, or they, feeling less valued, left him. He acquired fancier friends, like Lee Radziwill and Mick Jagger. He bought an estate in Montauk, and a chocolate-brown Rolls to go with it. In 1969, he founded *Interview*, a publication that was advertised as being devoted to movies (the original title was *inter/VIEW: A Monthly Film Journal*) but soon became a magazine about celebrities. Apparently, he did not often work on it—one of the early editors said he never read it until the printer delivered it—but it helped to snag clients for another department of his activities, the manufacture of silk-screen portraits of friends, patrons, and assorted big names: Dennis Hopper, Dominique de Menil, Gianni Versace, the shah of Iran, Chris Evert, Dolly Parton, Imelda Marcos.

Seeing Warhol's brush with death as a watershed has obvious narrative appeal, but on the evidence of Gopnik's chronicle the "after" had been coming for a while. Like most of Warhol's Pop paintings, the great majority of his films were made in less than five years. Then, it seems, he got bored. He fielded a few works in the I-dare-you-to-say-this-isn't-art manner of his hero and friend Marcel Duchamp, who, by exhibiting a signed urinal, in 1917, more or less invented conceptual art. In 1972, at Finch College, in New York, Warhol did his "vacuum-cleaner piece," which involved his vacuuming a patch of carpet in the college's art gallery, signing the dust bag, propping it on a pedestal, and going home. But as Gopnik points out, "Where Duchamp's urinal had involved a transformation of the banal into art, if only by the artist's say-so, Warhol's update involved jettisoning transformation altogether so that banality itself, left to do its banal thing, could count as high art."

Some years before, Warhol had placed an ad in *The Village Voice*: "I'll endorse with my name any of the following; clothing AC-DC, cigarettes small, tapes, sound equipment, rock n' roll records, anything, film, and film equipment, Food, Helium, Whips, money!! love and kisses Andy Warhol, EL 5–9941." This comically blatant announcement—the phone number was Warhol's real office number—can't seriously have been intended to bring in cash. Rather, it proclaimed that henceforward "selling out" would be, for Warhol, an aesthetic move.

But gradually the mask melted onto the face. When, two years later, Warhol told a reporter that his artistic medium was "business," he meant it. In Gopnik's words, this declaration "launched a new approach to his life and his art that would mold both for the following two decades, and then shape his reputation for all the years afterward." Reverting to his I. Miller days, he began designing ads: a sundae for Schrafft's, a limited-edition bottle for Absolut vodka, and the like. He also had an idea for a chain of Andy-Mat diners. "They're for people who eat alone," he explained. "You sit at a little table, order up any sort of frozen food you want, and watch TV at the same time. Everyone has his own TV set."

Warhol's new enterprises didn't take up much of his time. Gopnik says that the artist gave maybe two days each to the later silk-screen portraits—and that it showed. "Ever more vacant," Gopnik calls these paintings. Unsurprisingly, Warhol's star fell. By the time, in the early eighties, that he began doing collaborative paintings with Jean-Michel Basquiat—Gopnik guesses that the young prodigy reminded the older man of his earlier self—the association was enough to damage Basquiat's reputation. A critic for *The Times* wrote that their work together looked "like one of Warhol's manipulations, which increasingly seem based on the Mencken theory about nobody going broke underestimating the public's intelligence. Basquiat, meanwhile, comes across as the all too willing accessory." Basquiat soon distanced himself, which hurt Warhol. Gopnik feels, too, that Warhol was not as indifferent to artistic quality as he made himself out to be. Soon after the Centre Pompidou, in Paris, opened, Warhol spent a day looking at its modern-art masterworks and wrote in his diary, "I wanted to just rush home and paint and stop doing society portraits."

Still, many rich people were happy to have him do portraits of them. This third arm of his empire fell into a neat synergy with the others—the fancy Montauk house, the celebrity magazine—and made him a lot of money. He enjoyed spending it. He liked to buy loose diamonds and walk around jiggling them in his pocket. In his later years, he went antiques shopping most mornings and eventually bought around a million dollars' worth of heirloom furniture. He had no space for most of it in his living quarters and therefore had to stash it in empty rooms upstairs.

Warhol once tried to give an old friend one of his Marilyn Monroe silk screens, and the man, who disliked Pop, said, "Just tell me in your heart of hearts that you know it isn't art." Warhol, imperturbable, answered, "Wrap it up in brown paper, put it in the back of a closet—one day it will be worth a million dollars." He was right, Gopnik says, but off by two orders of magnitude: in 2008, a Warhol silk screen sold for $100 million. There was no huger reputation than Warhol's in the art of the sixties, and in late twentieth-century art there was no more important decade than the sixties. Much of the art that has followed, in the United States, is unthinkable without him, without his joining of high culture and low, without his love of sizzle and flash, without his combination of tenderness and sarcasm, without the use of photography and silk-screening and advertising.

If any artist of the past half century deserves a biography as detailed as this one, then, it is Warhol. Still, the long tail end of Warhol's career forces Gopnik into some tight corners as a critic. He acknowledges that even by the end of the sixties Warhol was treading water as an artist. Yet elsewhere, and often, he tries to defend the artist against the charge of having made inferior work in the seventies and eighties. Most frustrating are the instances when he excuses mediocre paintings by saying that mediocrity was what Warhol was going for and that we should congratulate him for having achieved his goal.

At times, the defenses reminded me of the philosopher Karl Popper's famous objection to Freudian analysis, on the ground that it was "unfalsifiable." (If you said that you'd never wanted to have sex with your mother, this was instantly interpretable, via the theory of repression, as an admission that you wanted to have sex with your mother. If, on the other hand, you said that you wanted to have sex with your mother, voilà: you wanted to have sex with your mother.) Gopnik writes that in the sixties and seventies "'Andy Warhol' may have promoted some banal popular culture. Andy Warhol, the brilliant artist inside those quotes, could be counted on to turn it into art." Really? How can you tell the difference between the two? "Anything bad is right," Warhol declared, and Gopnik calls this "as close as he ever came to a guiding aesthetic principle." But is it a good principle—not just for Warhol, but for us? Better, surely, just to acknowledge that the bad stuff was bad than to try to turn its badness into a postmodern triumph.

If special pleading for the late period is the book's one real weakness, its great strength is its tone. In his time, Warhol was very controversial.

Some people thought he was a genius; others, that he should be arrested. Gopnik, though he does believe that his subject is a genius, treats him fairly, calmly, and fondly. If Warhol tells a good joke, Gopnik relays it. In the hospital, soon after he was shot, Warhol said to a friend, "You know, we gotta get some bigger things to hide behind." When the artist stuffs a photograph of Brando down the front of his pants, we hear about it. As for Warhol's love life, Gopnik manages to convince us, without sentimentality, that, however many cute guys Warhol went through, he always just wanted to fall in love with somebody and settle down. He did fall in love, often—usually with someone who loved him less—but it never worked out for long. The last boyfriend, Jon Gould, a young vice president at Paramount, declined to sleep in Warhol's room with him, saying that the artist's dachshunds farted on him in bed. Gould died of AIDS within a few years.

Then there is Warhol's mother, with whom he lived for most of his life. By the time he was courting Jon Gould, Julia, now in her late seventies, was downstairs, going bats, hiding food in secret places around the house. In 1971, she moved back to Pittsburgh, living first with one of Warhol's brothers and then in a nursing home. A cousin repeatedly wrote to Warhol, telling him that Julia survived only in the hope that Andy would visit her before she died. He didn't visit, nor, eventually, did he attend her funeral, though he paid for it. One day soon afterward, a reporter asked him what was on his mind. He answered, "I think about my bird that died. If it went to bird heaven. But I really can't think about that. It just took a walk."

Fifteen years after his mother died, Warhol, fifty-eight, followed her. It's a wonder that he lasted that long. All his later life, he suffered from an infected gallbladder. He wore a girdle—there's a collection of them, dyed in pretty colors, in the time capsules—just to hold his guts in. He was in constant pain. Finally, one day in February 1987, he checked himself into New York Hospital. When the surgeons pulled out his gallbladder, they found it falling apart with gangrene. He died the next morning.

The New Yorker, 2020

The climax of Gianni Rodari's "The War of the Bells." Illustration by Valerio Vidali, 2020

A THEORY OF THE FANTASTIC

Gianni Rodari

Telephone Tales, a collection of stories by the Italian writer Gianni
Rodari (1920–80), contains a piece called "The War of the Bells" that
begins, "Once upon a time, there was a war—a great and terrible war—
in which vast numbers of soldiers died on both sides. We were on this
side and our enemies were on the other, and we shot at each other day
and night, but the war went on so long that finally, there was no more
bronze to make cannons." That didn't stop "our" general. He ordered
the army to melt down all the church bells in the land and recast them,
together, to make a single cannon:

> Just one, but one big enough to win the whole war with a single shot.
>
> It took a hundred thousand cranes to lift that cannon; it took
> ninety-seven trains to transport it to the front. The Mega General
> rubbed his hands together in delight and said, "When my cannon
> fires, our enemies will run away all the way to the moon."
>
> The great moment arrived. The super cannon was aimed at the
> enemy. We'd all stuffed cotton wads into our ears. . . .

An artilleryman pushed a button. Suddenly, from one end of the front to the other, came the gigantic sound of pealing bells: Ding! Dong! Bong!

We took the cotton out of our ears to be able to hear it more clearly.

Yes, it was true. No cannon blast, just chimes. The opposing general, who had adopted the same strategy, got the same result. Whereupon the two commanders, greatly embarrassed, jumped into their jeeps and drove away. The soldiers, left with no means of killing one another, crawled out of the trenches and embraced. "Peace has broken out!" they cried.

In Italy, everyone knows who Gianni Rodari was: one of the country's most cherished writers of children's books. In the United States, practically nobody knows his name. Of his thirty books, not one was published here during his lifetime. A few came out in the U.K., and you can still get a copy of one of these translations, if, for example, you are willing to mortgage your house. The other day, I tried to buy *Tales Told by a Machine*, from 1976. Amazon had a hardcover copy, for $967, plus shipping. This is a crime against art.

Things may be changing, though. In honor of the centenary, this year, of Rodari's birth, a small, enterprising publisher in Brooklyn, Enchanted Lion, has brought out the first full English-language edition of *Telephone Tales*, in a spirited translation by Antony Shugaar. Now, albeit decades late, Anglophone readers can find out why Italians love this writer.

Gianni (Giovanni) Rodari was born in 1920 in Omegna, a quiet little town on the edge of Lake Orta, in northern Italy. His father was a baker. Gianni loved his father. Every day, he said, the man would make a dozen rolls out of white flour for him and his younger brother. "These rolls were very crisp, and we devoured them like gluttons," he recalled. Another memory he recorded of his father was that one night, during a rainstorm, the family looked out the window and saw a cat marooned between two huge puddles, unable to move forward or back. The father went out, in the storm, and carried the cat to safety. When he returned, he was drenched. Rodari remembered him trembling, with his back pressed against the big oven, trying to get warm. Seven days later, he died, of pneumonia. Gianni was nine.

His mother moved the family back to her hometown, Gavirate, near Milan. As Vanessa Roghi narrates in her new biography of Rodari—*Lezioni di fantastica*, not yet translated—Gianni, in his teens, dreamed of going somewhere else, doing something interesting. (Maybe music? He had studied violin, and he played at weddings and such.) But the family needed money, and so he went to work as a teacher in local primary schools. He discovered that he was good at making up children's stories, not so much because he wanted to, he said, but as a way of getting his students to sit down and pay attention. In his free time, he read hungrily, especially books on philosophy and politics. In 1940, Italy entered the Second World War. Rodari, who was in delicate health all his life, was excused from military service on medical grounds. Late in the war, after two of his friends had died in action and his brother Cesare, the one he had shared the rolls with, had been interned in a German prison camp, he joined the Resistance and enrolled in the Italian Communist Party.

After the war, the party got in touch with him. Would he like to do some writing for its newspapers? In the next few years, Rodari produced copy—on sports, crime, the arts, everything—for Communist papers, one of which, *L'Unità*, finally asked him to write some pieces for children. In 1950, the party transferred him to Rome, to edit a children's weekly. And now he began publishing books, not just stories.

The Communist context of his writing is evident in the book that soon made his name, *The Adventures of Cipollino* (1951), in which a small onion-boy, Cipollino (the word means "little onion" in Italian), leads an uprising of aggrieved vegetables—Potato, Leek, Radish, and so on—against the tyranny of Prince Lemon and his brutal enforcer, Signor Tomato. Given the Cold War, it is no surprise that this book did not appear in English (Enchanted Lion hopes to publish a translation in 2022), or, conversely, that Rodari acquired a huge following in the Soviet Union, where *Cipollino* was adapted into an animated film, a live-action film, and even a ballet. Its hero's sweet, bland face adorned a Russian postage stamp, and when the Soviet astronomer Nikolai Chernykh discovered a new minor planet, between Mars and Jupiter, he named it 2703 Rodari.

Gradually, Rodari's reputation spread beyond leftist circles, and he acquired some literary friends. Italo Calvino, tiller of the same fields (folktales, new tales), admired him and stumped for him. But, like many autodidacts, Rodari was wary of the in-crowd, and he socialized mostly with newspapermen. In 1960, after being picked up by Giulio Einaudi, a politically unaffiliated and highly respected publisher (he published Primo Levi, Cesare Pavese, Natalia Ginzburg, Calvino), Rodari began to attract a mainstream audience. Eventually, he received the Hans Christian Andersen Award for Writing, a sort of children's-literature equivalent of the Booker Prize.

Telephone Tales is from this period. The book has a frame story. Once upon a time, there was a man, Signor Bianchi, who worked as a traveling salesman of pharmaceutical goods, a job that kept him on the road six days a week. He had one child, a daughter (as did Rodari, who married in 1953), and she missed him when he was away. But they had a deal. Every night, before she went to sleep, he would call her and tell her a story. Long-distance calls were expensive, so the stories were always very short, but they were wonderful. When Signor Bianchi was on the line, Rodari wrote, "all the young ladies who worked the telephone switchboard simply stopped putting calls through, so they could listen."

The sixty-seven tales in the collection show us where Rodari came from, and where he was going. A few are frank agitprop. Rodari had spent twenty-three years of his life under Fascism, and as the book's translator, Antony Shugaar, has pointed out, the subject of a number of the stories is simply how not to be a Fascist. That's what they say: don't kill one another, and don't listen to bullies who tell you to do so. But in other tales we can see agitprop morphing into something more bizarre. In "The Unlucky Hunter," a boy, Giuseppe, whose sister is getting married the next day, is told by his mother to go hunting and bring back a rabbit to accompany the polenta at the nuptial feast. He goes off and soon spies a rabbit. But, when he shoots his rifle, what issues from the gun is not a bullet but a "cheerful, fresh little voice," saying, "Boom!" almost as if it were making fun of him. Next thing, "the same rabbit as before strolled by, right in front of Giuseppe, only this time it had a white veil over its head dotted with orange blossoms." "'Well, what do you know,' said Giuseppe. 'The rabbit is getting married too.'" This is like a Surrealist painting, half-funny, half-unsettling. A rabbit bride, a talking gun—what's going on?

Part of what makes this story genuinely weird is that, unlike the chimes in "The War of the Bells," which employs the same comic device, the unexpected sound is human. This sort of transfer, from one mode of expression to another, starts to become common in Rodari's tales. In "A Distractible Child Goes for a Walk," the child in question, Giovanni, taking a stroll, loses his body parts along the way. He is looking at this and that—the cars, the clouds—and, oops, his hand falls off. Then he gets interested in a dog with a limp, and as he follows the animal, one of his arms detaches itself and vanishes. By the time he gets home, he's missing both arms, both ears, and a leg. "His mother shakes her head, puts him back together." (The neighbors have thoughtfully collected Giovanni's body parts and brought them to her.) She kisses him. "'Is anything missing, Mama? Have I been a good boy?' 'Yes, Giovanni, you've been a very good boy.'" This is sweet, and also appalling. When we leave the house, young readers might ask, do we have to be careful that our feet won't fall off?

From the moment he began teaching, Rodari never stopped thinking about the education of children. He wrote about it, delivered lectures on it, gave interviews on it, to the end of his life. In 1972, to his great satisfaction, he was invited to confer for four days with a group of fifty teachers in the city of Reggio Emilia, a hot spot of postwar Italy's vigorous early-education movement. The following year, he published a book, *The*

Grammar of Fantasy, based on the talks he had given there. Here are the opening lines of chapter 1, translated by the fairy-tale scholar Jack Zipes:

> A stone thrown into a pond sets in motion concentric waves that spread out on the surface of the water, and their reverberation has an effect on the water lilies and reeds, the paper boat, and the buoys of the fishermen at various distances. All these objects are just there for themselves, enjoying their tranquility, when they are wakened to life, as it were, and are compelled to react and to enter into contact with one another. Other invisible vibrations spread into the depths, in all directions, as the stone falls and brushes the algae, scaring the fish and continually causing new molecular movements. When it then touches the bottom, it stirs up the mud and bumps into things that have rested there forgotten, some of which are dislodged, others buried once again in the sand.

How I love this image, with its dark, wet, secret transactions, its mud and molecules. This is Rodari's metaphor for cognition. In his view, children learned not by having something inserted into their brains—the multiplication tables, the sonnets of Petrarch—but by responding, almost involuntarily, to a sight, an idea, or often just a word, absorbing it, moving other mental contents around to make room for it, and thereby creating something new.

There seems to be no question that Rodari's concern for education was related to the poverty of his youth. A modest man, he spoke not of his own difficulties but of other people's—his mother's, for example. She went to work at the age of eight, he wrote, first in a paper factory, then in a textile works, then as a domestic. When he began teaching, his pupils, too, were poor. In the winter, some could not come to school, because they had no shoes. Many of them also spoke a nonstandard Italian, and he worried lest people make them feel embarrassed.

Gianni Rodari

Apart from his students' ability to get to school, what most concerned Rodari was the development of their imaginations. He said that a line of Novalis's, which he read as a young man, always stuck in his mind: "If there were a theory of the fantastic such as there is in the case of logic, then we would be able to discover the art of inventing stories." This he connected with fantasist art of his own time, above all Surrealism. Surrealism is a brew of many ideas, but the one most important to Rodari, it seems, was the simplest, the pairing of opposites—particularly the joining of a dreamworld to a punctilious realism. A hardy movement, Surrealism lasted from the 1920s until well after the Second World War, because it fitted those wild and disastrous years. A locus classicus is Vittorio De Sica's film *Miracle in Milan* (1951), which ends with a collection of homeless people—they have just seen their shantytown razed by the authorities—taking off, on broomsticks, into the sky. Italy, after the war, was very, very poor. De Sica's other early films—*Shoeshine, Bicycle Thieves, Umberto D.*—give a sense of this, as do Rossellini's *Paisan* and *Rome, Open City*. The country was also humiliated. Many Italian artists were glad to move into new territory. Surrealism provided a picture of the truth they now faced—ugliness, violence, ruin—combined, however, with the memory of a happier past: trees, pocket watches, town squares, pretty women.

Many of the early Surrealists were committed Marxists. In *The Grammar of Fantasy*, Rodari writes of a day that he spent drinking wine with friends in a village outside Kazan, near the Volga. The group visited a local landmark, a wooden house whose furniture, he noticed, was curiously arranged. Sturdy benches were set under the windowsills so that the erstwhile owners' children, who liked to come in and out by the windows rather than by the door, could do so without breaking their necks. This, Rodari later decided, was a lesson of Communism. As it turned out, the house had once been the property of Lenin's grandfather. Whether or not Lenin adapted his political philosophy from his grandparent's furniture arrangements, Rodari learned critical thinking from Marxist doctrine. Whatever he writes about, he subjects to questioning, scrutiny, a mild irradiation of irony, or just wit. (Rodari inherited this approach in part, he said, from Russian formalist critics of the early twentieth century such as Viktor Shklovsky, who called it *ostranenie*, defamiliarization.) People in the West tend to associate Marxism with thought control. It is hard to convince them that in the late nineteenth century Marxism was considered by its adherents the standard-bearer of thought liberation.

In keeping with Rodari's concern for children's imaginations, some stories in *Telephone Tales*, like the stone in the pond in *The Grammar of Fantasy*, journey into distant realms of strangeness. Two of them feature a little girl named Alice Tumbledown. Alice falls a lot, into places where we wouldn't think to look for a missing child. Her favorite landing place is the silverware drawer in the kitchen. She loves it there, in the spoon section. One time, her grandfather finds her inside the alarm clock. Later, he has to fish her out of a bottle. "I was thirsty and fell in," she explains. Elsewhere, Alice wanders into the ocean. She'd like to become a starfish, she thinks:

> But instead she fell into the shell of a giant mollusk just as it was yawning, and it immediately snapped shut its valves, imprisoning Alice and all her dreams. Here I am, in trouble again, thought Alice. But she also felt what silence—what fresh, cool peace—was there inside the giant mollusk. It would have been wonderful to stay there forever.

Who would want to live inside a clamshell, in that cold, pungent fluid, next to that blob of a clam? Alice. But then she thinks of her parents, how they love her and would miss her. Regretfully, she pries the shell open, swims out, and goes home. I don't know of any writer, before Rodari, who would have explored such an experience.

There is worse, or better. In the tale called "Pulcinella's Escape," a Pulcinella marionette (Punch, from Punch and Judy) manages to cut the strings that attach him to his control bar. He escapes from the puppet theater and hides in a nearby garden, where he survives by eating flowers. When winter comes, there are no more flowers, but he's not afraid. "Oh, well," he says, "I'll just die here." And he does. In the spring, a carnation grows on the spot where his body lies. Under the ground, he says to himself, "Who could be happier than me?" Here, and in "Alice Falls into the Sea," two realities sit side by side, looking rather surprised, but not actually annoyed, to see each other. Yes, it would be rather dark and lonely under the ground or inside a clamshell. But how peaceful!

In keeping with his leftist sympathies, there is a rich vein of utopianism in Rodari's work. "When they are little, children must stock up on optimism," he wrote, "for the challenge of life." In one story, Jordan almonds rain down from a cloud in the sky. In a later tale, a Russian astronaut reports that on Planet X213 people who don't want to get up in the morning just grab the alarm clock and eat it and go back to sleep. Another planet, called Mun, has a machine that manufactures lies:

> For one token, you could hear fourteen thousand lies. The machine contained all the lies in the world—the lies that had already been told, the lies that people were thinking of at that very moment, and all the others that would be invented in the future. Once the machine had recited all the possible lies, people were forced to always tell the truth. That's why the planet Mun is also known as the Planet of Truth.

But there's always a hitch. Even a child could tell you that Mun is not a good name for a planet, nor should anyone try to eat an alarm clock. As for the rain of Jordan almonds, Rodari says that people always waited for it to come back, but it never did. The humor is not as daffy as in Edward Lear, and not as elaborate as in Lewis Carroll. (Rodari loved both writers.) And sweet as it sometimes is, *Telephone Tales* also carries a heavy load of sarcasm. In one story, a man's nose runs away. (Rodari credits Gogol.) It is finally chased down, brought back, and reattached to the man's face. The man remonstrates with it: "'But why did you ever run away in the first place? What did I ever do to you?' The nose glared at him . . . and said, 'Listen, just never pick me again as long as you live.'" Rodari was also fond of bathroom jokes. King Midas, when his touch-of-gold magic is revoked, does not immediately revert to normal. For a brief time, everything he touches turns to shit. These narratives were probably very popular with listeners young enough to remember their toilet training, but adults, too, might have enjoyed such talk.

It would be hard for anyone, of any age, not to love the illustrations, most of them in Magic Marker, that Enchanted Lion commissioned for *Telephone Tales*, from the Italian artist Valerio Vidali. The book design itself harbors surprises. Some pages have extra little inner pages glued to them. Others are gatefold pages, where you pull the inner edge and another page folds out. In the drawings, you are shown entire worlds of semiabstract figures: giant noses, a palace made of ice cream, birds eating cookies, plus, of course, kings and queens and a princess in a tower. The pages are sewn with stitches worthy of a Balenciaga gown. It is astonishing that the book costs only $27.95.

Politics accompanied Rodari all the days of his life. He first visited the Soviet Union in 1951 and went back every few years thereafter, to accept prizes, judge competitions, and, as he no doubt felt, just to do his part. Communism, in some measure, gave him his morals, without laying its heavy hand on his blithe spirit. But in the end, according to Vanessa Roghi's biography, it let him down. He wasn't the only one. Events in the Soviet Union—the show trials of the thirties, Khrushchev's famous speech three years after Stalin's death, enumerating the man's crimes—caused leftists across the Western world to abandon their loyalty to the U.S.S.R. If those developments didn't discourage them, later ones did: the bloody suppression of the Hungarian Revolution of 1956, the quelling of the Prague Spring in 1968.

Many Western Marxists openly disavowed the Soviet system, but not Rodari. He had been a Communist practically from his teenage years, and he would not abandon the party now, or not publicly. He stood by it even after Italy's so-called years of lead, beginning in the late sixties, when the country was shocked almost daily, it seemed, by acts of political terrorism. (An especially horrifying episode was the 1978 kidnapping and murder of Aldo Moro, a centrist who had served five terms as the nation's prime minister, by the Red Brigades, a neo-Marxist organization. Italians who lived through those years still speak of them with emotion.) In 1979, when Rodari made his last trip to the Soviet Union, he found little to praise about the country in which he had once placed so much hope. Roghi quotes his travel diary, in which he deplores the venality of the Soviet Union and the hypocrisy of its young people. "One thing is certain," he wrote. "They aren't Communists."

Rodari fans, however, should thank the U.S.S.R. By inspiring him and then disappointing him, it set him free, to work in a genre, the so-called children's tale, where he would not have to confront his bitterness. And, in the end, it drove him beyond bitterness, into a wonderful wildness. The year before that last trip to the Soviet Union, Einaudi brought out Rodari's final novel, a brilliant satire of both capitalists and revolutionaries. (It was published in English in 2011 with the title *Lamberto, Lamberto, Lamberto.*) In the book, a certain Baron Lamberto, who is ninety-three and fears that he may die, hears that the Egyptian pharaohs believed that if your name was endlessly repeated, you could live forever. He decides to give it a try. He has his servants speak his name continuously into microphones placed in the attic of his castle. By the end—despite the best efforts of a gang of terrorists, who take him hostage and cut off his ear (this is actually funny)—he survives.

Rodari didn't. Not long after *Lamberto* was published, an aneurysm was discovered in his leg. This necessitated a seven-hour operation, which seemed at first to have been successful. But then, three days later, he died suddenly, of heart failure. He was only fifty-nine. I hope that his soul is at rest on the Planet of Truth.

Originally published as "A Theory of Fantasy," *The New Yorker*, 2020

Graham Greene, 1954

ORIGINAL SINNER

Graham Greene

"The first thing I remember is sitting in a pram at the top of a hill with a dead dog lying at my feet." So opens an early chapter of a memoir by Graham Greene, who is viewed by some—including Richard Greene (no relation), the author of a new biography of Graham, *The Unquiet Englishman*—as one of the most important British novelists of his already remarkable generation. (It included George Orwell, Evelyn Waugh, Anthony Powell, Elizabeth Bowen.) The dog, Graham's sister's pug, had just been run over, and the nanny couldn't think of how to get the carcass home other than to stow it in the carriage with the baby. If that doesn't suffice to set the tone for the rather lurid events of Greene's life, one need only turn the page, to find him, at five or so, watching a man run into a local almshouse to slit his own throat. Around that time, Greene taught himself to read, and he always remembered the cover illustration of the first book to which he gained admission. It showed, he said, "a boy, bound and gagged, dangling at the end of a rope inside a well with water rising above his waist."

Greene was born in 1904, the fourth of six children. His family was comfortable and, by and large, accomplished. An older brother, Raymond, grew up to be an important endocrinologist; a younger brother, Hugh, became the director general of the BBC; the youngest child, Elisabeth, went to work for MI6, England's foreign-intelligence operation. As was usual with prosperous people of that period, the children were raised by servants, but they were brought downstairs to play with their mother every day for an hour after tea.

The family lived in Berkhamsted, a small, pleasant satellite town of London. It had a respectable boys' school, of which Greene's father was the headmaster. Greene was sent there at age seven, and thanks to his position as the director's son he was relentlessly persecuted by his classmates. They then suspected him of telling on them and therefore, it seems, went after him harder.

As an adolescent, he began attempting suicide—or seeming to—always with almost comic ineptness. Once, according to his mother, he tried to kill himself by ingesting eye drops. He also appears to have experimented, at different times, with allergy drops, deadly nightshade, and fistfuls of aspirin. Most often remarked on was his fondness for Russian roulette, although his brother Raymond, whose gun he borrowed for this purpose, said there were no bullets in the cabinet where the weapon was kept. Greene must have been shooting with empty chambers.

When he was in high school, his parents sent him to his first psychotherapist. Others followed. Eventually, he was declared to be suffering from manic depression, or bipolar disorder, as it is now called, and the diagnosis stuck. But the scientific-sounding label makes it easy to overlook other factors that might have been at work. Greene once recalled to his friend Evelyn Waugh that, at university (Balliol College, Oxford), he had spent much of his time in a "general haze of drink." In his writing years, he often lived on a regimen of Benzedrine in the morning, to wake himself up, and Nembutal at night, to put himself to sleep, supplemented, each day, with great vats of alcohol and, depending on what country he was in, other drugs as well. On his many trips to Vietnam, he smoked opium almost daily—sometimes as many as eight pipes a day. That's a lot.

The essential point about the manic-depressive diagnosis, however, is that Greene accepted it—indeed, saw it as key to his personality and his work. Richard Greene writes that his biography is intended, in part, as a corrective to prior biographers' excessive interest in the novelist's sex life. But, considering how much time and energy Graham Greene put into his sex life, one wonders how any biographer could look the other way for long. Greene got married when he was twenty-three, to a devout Catholic woman, Vivien Dayrell-Browning, and he stayed married to her until he died, in 1991, but only because Vivien, for religious reasons, would not give him a divorce. After about ten years, the marriage was effectively over, and he spent the remainder of his life having protracted, passionate affairs, plus, tucked into those main events, shorter adventures, not to mention many afternoons with prostitutes. Richard Greene, despite his objections to biographical prurience, does give us some piquant details. Of Graham and one of his mistresses, he writes, "This relationship was reckless and exuberant, involving on one occasion intercourse in the first-class carriage of a train from Southend, observable to those on each platform where the train stopped."

Meanwhile, when Greene felt he had to explain such matters to his wife, he summoned his bipolar disorder. As he wrote to her,

> The fact that has to be faced, dear, is that by my nature, my selfishness, even in some degree my profession, I should always, & with anyone, have been a bad husband. I think, you see, my restlessness, moods, melancholia, even my outside relationships, are symptoms of a disease & not the disease itself, & the disease, which has been going on ever since my childhood & was only temporarily alleviated by psychoanalysis, lies in a character profoundly antagonistic to ordinary domestic life.

So, you see, it wasn't his fault.

Greene did not, of course, feel like sticking around to dry Vivien's tears or help raise the son and daughter they had had together. (He didn't like children; he found them noisy.) So he took an apartment of his own, and Vivien stayed home, carving dollhouse furniture. In time, she became a great expert on dollhouses, and established a private museum for her collection.

What Greene wanted to do with his life was write novels, and after a rocky start he turned them out regularly, at least twenty-four (depending on how you count them) in six decades. He also did a fantastic amount of journalism, mostly for *The Spectator*. Richard Greene estimates that, in time, Graham produced about five hundred book reviews and six hundred movie reviews. One of the latter created his first little scandal. Of Twentieth Century Fox's *Wee Willie Winkie* (1937), starring Shirley Temple, he wrote that Temple, with her high-on-the-thigh dresses and "well-developed rump," was basically being pimped out by Fox to lonely middle-aged gentlemen in the cinema audience. Fox promptly sued and was awarded £3,500 in damages. Ever after, Greene was known to part of his audience as a dirty-minded man. (Not to Temple, though. In her 1988 memoir, she treated the whole thing as a tempest in a teapot. She also made it clear that at the movie studios many child actors were subject to unwelcome attentions.)

In Richard Greene's telling, Graham's bipolar disorder afflicted him not just, or even mostly, with overexcitement and depression but above all with a terrible boredom, which he could alleviate only by constant thrill-seeking. That's what caused him to play with guns; that's what made him defame Shirley Temple; that's what sent him to bed with every other woman he came across.

Finally, and crucially, this tedium is what made him spend much of his life outside England, not just away from home—from roasts and Bovril and damp woolens—but in the distant, hot, poor, war-torn countries whose efforts to throw off colonial rule formed so large and painful a part of twentieth-century history. He went to West Africa (Liberia, Sierra

Leone), Southeast Asia, the Caribbean, and Mexico. He spent years, on and off, in Central America. And he saw what the locals saw; at times, he experienced what they did. Bullets whizzed past his head. In Malaya, he had to have leeches pried off his neck. In Liberia, he was warned that he might contract any of a large number of diseases, which Richard Greene catalogs with a nasty glee: "Yaws, malaria, hookworm, schistosomiasis, dysentery, lassa fever, yellow fever, or an especially cruel thing, the Guinea worm, which grows under the skin and must be gradually spooled out onto a stick or pencil—if it breaks in the process, the remnant may mortify inside the host, causing infection or death." Unwilling to miss the Mau Mau rebellion, Graham Greene spent four weeks in Kenya. In Congo, he stayed at a leper colony, where he saw a man with thighs like tree trunks, and one with testes the size of footballs.

How, and why, did he end up in these places? Very often, he had an assignment from a newspaper or a magazine. As a sideline, he also did some information-gathering for MI6. (Nothing serious—he might merely send back a report on which political faction was gaining power and who the leader was.) Basically, anytime an organization needed someone to go, expenses paid, to a country that had civil unrest and crocodiles, he was interested. He was collecting material for his novels, most of which would be set in these faraway places.

Greene got out of town in another way as well. The family he was born into was Anglican, but they didn't make a fuss about it. As he told it, he had a vision of God on a croquet lawn around the age of seventeen, but he let this pass until four years later, when he fell in love with Vivien, a Catholic who wasn't at all sure she wanted to marry him, what with his being a Protestant and also, as he seemed to her, a rather strange person.

Leaving a note in the collection box at a nearby Catholic church, he asked for religious instruction, and was assigned to one Father George Trollope, whom he liked, as he wrote to Vivien, for "his careful avoidance of the slightest emotion or sentiment in his instruction." Some might have taken the wording of that endorsement as a bad sign, but what Greene wanted, apart from Vivien, was just, as he told her, "something firm & hard & certain, however uncomfortable, to catch hold of in the general flux."

So did others. There was a minor fashion for conversion to Catholicism among British artists and intellectuals in the years between the two world wars. Evelyn Waugh converted around the same time as Greene. (Later, Edith Sitwell and Muriel Spark also "poped.") This was part of the backwash from the rising secularism of the late nineteenth and early twentieth centuries. After the Second World War, the Catholic Church would provide a suitably august arena for the transition to another sort of religion: doubt, anxiety, existentialism.

Greene didn't wait for that. He converted when he was twenty-two, and was observant for a few years. As he pulled away from Vivien, though, he also let go of the things he had acquired with her, for her—above all, religious practice. Later, he said that after he saw a dead woman lying in a ditch, with her dead baby by her side, in North Vietnam, in 1951, he did not take Communion again for thirty years. But neither, ever, did he achieve a confident atheism. "Many of us," he said, "abandon Confession and Communion to join the Foreign Legion of the Church and fight for a city of which we are no longer full citizens."

Although Greene might have turned religion down to a low simmer in his life, in his novels he raised it to a rolling boil. In *Brighton Rock* (1938), his first big hit, the hero is a seventeen-year-old hoodlum named Pinkie. (Wonderful name, so wrong.) Pinkie would be an ordinary little sociopath were it not for the fact that he is a Roman Catholic and obsessed by sin. Again and again, he recalls the noise that, as a child, he heard across the room every Saturday night, when his parents engaged in their weekly sex act. Pinkie forces himself to marry a naive girl, Rose, because she is a potential witness in a murder that he has engineered.

The wedding night is pretty awful, as is much else in the novel, once it gets going. Actually, the book raises our neck hair in the opening sentence: "Hale knew, before he had been in Brighton three hours, that they meant to murder him." At that point, we don't even know who Hale is.

"They" are the gang of thugs that Pinkie leads, and before the day is out, they do indeed eliminate Hale, after which they kill several other people too. This violence is mixed with sex, in a hot stew, which Greene makes more repellent with the setting of Brighton—a tacky seaside resort, full of weekend pleasure seekers down from London, shooting ducks and throwing candy wrappers on the pavement. In Greene's Brighton, even the sky is dirty: "The huge darkness pressed a wet mouth against the panes." Sin ultimately crushes Pinkie, and, we are led to assume, Rose, too. As Greene himself pointed out, he was, if not a good Catholic, at least a good Gnostic, a person who believed that good and evil were equal powers, warring against each other.

The book that fixed him in the public mind as a Catholic writer, *The Power and the Glory*, came two years later. Its unnamed hero is a Mexican "whisky priest" in hiding in the south of the country in the 1930s, during a Marxist campaign against the Catholic Church. There is no end, almost, to the horrors the priest endures—heat, hunger, DTs. He finds dead babies, their eyes rolled back in their heads. Eventually, he is arrested and put in prison, among a close, dark, sweaty mob, including a couple fornicating loudly in a corner. You are sure he will survive, this holy man. He doesn't. You don't so much read this book as suffer it, climb it, like Calvary.

Greene's procedure—marrying torments of the soul to frenzies of the flesh—reaches a kind of apogee in *The End of the Affair* (1951). Maurice Bendrix, a novelist, is consumed with rage over the fact that his lover, Sarah, has left him, and he hires a private detective to find out whom she chose over him. On and on, in fevered remembrance, he calls up details of their love affair: the time they had sex on the parquet in her parlor, while her husband was nursing a cold upstairs; the secret words they had ("onions" was their code name for sex); the secret signs.

But eventually, after Sarah dies, Bendrix discovers that the new lover she left him for was God, at which point the novel goes from steamy to blasphemous. "I hate You," Bendrix tells God. "I hate You as though You existed." Finally, he's reduced to conducting a kind of virility contest with his Maker: "It was I who penetrated her, not You." Ugh.

Some of Greene's colleagues, not to speak of the Church, began to find his combining of religion and sex unseemly. George Orwell delivered a more withering critique. Greene, he wrote, seemed to believe

> that there is something rather *distingué* in being damned; Hell is a sort of high-class night club, entry to which is reserved for Catholics only, since the others, the non-Catholics, are too ignorant to be held guilty, like the beasts that perish. We are carefully informed that Catholics are no better than anybody else; they even, perhaps, have a tendency to be worse, since their temptations are greater. . . . But all the while—drunken, lecherous, criminal, or damned outright—the Catholics retain their superiority since they alone know the meaning of good and evil.

This cult of the sanctified sinner, Orwell thought, probably reflected a decline of belief, "for when people really believed in Hell, they were not so fond of striking graceful attitudes on its brink."

Still, plenty of readers found the mix of the spiritual and the carnal rather a thrill. When *The End of the Affair* was published, *Time* put Greene on its cover, with the tagline "Adultery can lead to sainthood."

One readership that found all this good and evil and sex and murder quite alluring was Hollywood. Bad behavior was fun, after all, and Greene's narratives, thanks to those hundreds of films he had reviewed, were already cinematic. Has any novelist been better at plotting than Greene? He can shuttle with ease back and forth among three plotlines at a time, and none of them ever stops charging forward. The suspense is huge. You think, "No, they can't shoot the priest," or "No, Pinkie can't assault Rose from beyond the grave," and, surprise, you're wrong. As for the camera action, the story is often told, or filmed, from separate points of view; big scenes are likely to end in wide shots; and so on.

Of Western "art" novelists, Greene may well be the one whose works have been most often adapted to film. Several of his novels were dramatized not once but twice or three times, and some of the films are better than the novels. It is hard to read *Brighton Rock* and not see, in your mind's eye, Richard Attenborough, who played Pinkie in the first cinematic version. What a piece of work is man, you think, as you look at Attenborough's beautiful young face. And Pinkie is rotten to the core. This paradox makes both the film and the book more textured, knotted. The book–movie relationship becomes even more interesting in the case of *The Third Man*. That book was actually a by-product of a film whose script Greene had agreed to write—something he produced to get a feel for atmosphere before applying himself to the script—and it will never be entirely free from the shadow, both literal and figurative, cast by Orson Welles in his indelible performance as the villain.

The colossal popularity of Greene's more down-market novels and their cinematic adaptations made him rich—for the movie rights to his 1966 novel, *The Comedians*, he was paid $250,000, the equivalent of almost $2 million today—but, apparently, it also embarrassed him. Like many people of his time, he didn't respect films as much as he did literature. Plus, the film studios wanted changes, big changes. Greene had given novels like *Brighton Rock*, *The Power and the Glory*, and *The End of the Affair* unforgiving endings, which were true to his view of the world, and the studios made them nicer, more comestible. Suicides became accidents; terrible cruelties were turned into something not so bad after all.

Greene solved his problem—stoop or not?—by claiming that his fiction fell into two categories. There were his "novels," his serious work, and then there were his "entertainments," as he called them—thrillers, comedies, forms he clearly esteemed less. These latter books, he implied, were things he did in his spare time: *The Quiet American* (1955), about the war in Vietnam; *Our Man in Havana* (1958), set in Cuba shortly before Castro's revolution. The fact that both of these were made into wonderful movies, with famous actors—Michael Redgrave in *The Quiet American*, Alec Guinness in *Our Man in Havana*—did not, in his mind, make them more legitimate. On the contrary. But that was his problem, not the reader's. There are duds among the serious "novels," while *Our Man in Havana*—a dazzling blend of menace, humor, and resignation—is one of the finest things he ever wrote.

His greatest achievement, *The Heart of the Matter*, is certainly, in his terms, a novel—indeed, a Novel. Published in 1948, between *The Power and the Glory* and *The End of the Affair*, it is, like them, tightly underpinned by Roman Catholicism, but it has none of the chest-banging or the tawdriness into which that subject sometimes led Greene. It is a chaste business. Henry Scobie, a dutiful, observant Catholic, works as a deputy police commissioner in a small, quiet, corrupt town in West Africa in the early years of the Second World War. Scobie has a wife, Louise, whom he can't stand and whom, at the same time, he feels sorry for. (They had a daughter, who died when she was nine.) And so, when Louise says that she can't stay in this stupid town one minute longer, he borrows money from a local diamond smuggler—he knows this is going to lead to trouble, but he does it anyway—to send her on vacation in South Africa. While she is away, a French ship is torpedoed off the coast, and Scobie has to go help minister to the survivors. Among them is a nineteen-year-old girl, Helen, newly married, whose husband was killed in the torpedo attack. Helen has no one, nothing. Her sole possession is an album—given to her by her father—containing her stamp collection. She clasps it to her chest. She will speak to no one, until finally she does speak, to Scobie.

Whereupon he falls in love with her, or seems to. In Greene's work, it is hard to tell, when two people go to bed together, whether it is love that took them there, or even desire. It could be pity. As Greene has already told us, that is Scobie's reigning emotion toward his wife, and other things as well. Looking at the sky one night while tending to the French refugees, he wonders, if one knew the facts, "would one have to feel pity even for the planets? If one reached what they called the heart of the matter?"

So he enters into an affair with Helen, but soon she is screaming at him that he doesn't love her and is going to leave her, whereupon, of course, Louise returns from her vacation, fully informed by the town gossips as to what Scobie has been up to in her absence. (It's like *Ethan Frome*. Trying to escape from one nagging wife, the hero ends up with two.) He seizes upon a desperate solution: he will fake a heart ailment and then take enough sedatives to kill himself. That way, each of his two women will be free to find a more satisfactory mate. As for him, he will be damned to hell for all eternity, but he's willing.

In the end, it doesn't quite turn out that way. It turns out worse, and that's Greene for you. But in the twentieth century pity was hard to write about. That this dark-hearted man managed to—even that he tried—is surely a jewel in his crown.

The Unquiet Englishman is what might be called a Monday-Tuesday biography. On one page, it tells you what Greene did on a certain day in, say, June 1942. On the next page, it tells you what he did the following day, or three days later. This method surely owes something to the fact that Richard Greene, a professor of English at the University of Toronto, edited a collection of Graham Greene's letters. In other words, he *knew* what Greene did every day, and thought that this was interesting material—as it could have been, had it contributed to a unified analysis of the man. Mostly, however, the book is just a collection of facts. Trips without itineraries, sex without love, jokes without punch lines—we look for the beach, but all we see are the pebbles. Neither are we given much in the way of literary commentary. That is not a capital offense. Many good literary biographers have excused themselves from the task of criticism. But, if we don't get the man or his novels, what do we get?

Graham Greene was an almost eerily disciplined writer. He could write in the middle of wars, the Mau Mau uprising, you name it. And he wrote, quite strictly, five hundred words per day, in a little notebook he kept in his breast pocket. He counted the words, and at five hundred he stopped, even, his biographer says, in the middle of a sentence. Then he started again the next morning. Richard Greene's book often feels as though it were composed on the same schedule. Many of his chapters are only two or three pages long. This engenders a kind of coldness.

To be fair, it should be said that many people found Graham Greene hard to know, and Richard Greene does make a contribution to our understanding of his subject. In place of earlier biographers' interest in Graham's sex life, he set out to cover the writer's life as a world traveler—specifically, a traveler in what was then known as the Third World, and therefore an observer of international politics. This biography, the jacket copy says, "reads like a primer on the twentieth century itself" and shows Graham Greene as an "unfailing advocate for human rights." I don't think that Richard Greene ever quite makes the case for Graham's status as a freedom fighter, but, despite what his publicists felt they had to say, he doesn't peddle this line too hard. Eventually, the book says, Graham settled into what might be loosely described as "a social democratic stance," and that sounds closer to the truth. In Panama, he hung around with a gunrunner named Chuchu. In El Salvador, he brokered the occasional ransom. He hated the United States, but outside the United States that is not a rare sentiment.

I think that Graham Greene's distinction as an observer of Africa, Asia, Latin America, and the Caribbean is less as a political thinker or activist and more just as an artist, a recorder of the way a taxi dancer in Saigon comports herself if she wants to snag an American husband; the way the Americans and English and French, the journalists and officers, sit around on hotel patios drinking pink gins and complaining about the bugs; the way a Syrian diamond smuggler handles an English policeman whom he is hoping to blackmail—and then what happens when the bombs start to go off. The same is true of the novels Greene set in less far-flung climes: the spiritual and political crises they tackle fade in the memory, and it is his effortless feel for the everyday that stays with us. That is the heart of Graham Greene's matter: not profundity—how hard he reached for it!—but an instinct for the way things actually look and what that means.

The New Yorker, 2021

Francis Bacon in his studio. London, 1963

ART MADE FLESH

Francis Bacon

"I have always been very moved by pictures about slaughterhouses and meat," the painter Francis Bacon told an interviewer in 1962. He regarded meat with fellow feeling. "If I go into a butcher's shop, I always think it's surprising that I wasn't there instead of the animal," he later said. Cloven carcasses—indeed, piles of miscellaneous innards—recur in his paintings. Basically, he liked whatever was inside, as opposed to outside, the skin.

His favorite body part was the mouth. Once, in a bookshop in Paris, he found an old medical treatise on diseases of the oral cavity. The book had beautiful hand-colored plates, showing what Bacon called the "glitter and color" of the inside of the mouth, the glistening membranes. He bought the book and cherished it all his life. He said that he always hoped he could paint the mouth as Monet had painted sunsets.

The moment that the mouth showed its insides most unashamedly, Bacon realized, was when it screamed. In his studio, he kept a still of the Odessa Steps massacre from Eisenstein's *Battleship Potemkin*: an old woman, gashed in the face by one of the imperial soldiers, screams violently, her shattered pince-nez hanging from her eyes and blood running down her cheek. When Bacon saw Old Master paintings of the Crucifixion—he especially loved Matthias Grünewald's *Isenheim Altarpiece*, with Jesus almost rotting on the cross—they lined up in his mind with the meat and the screams.

All of this went into his work. In his *Head I* (1947–48), now in the Metropolitan Museum, in New York, we see a head sliced off just below the nose. The mouth is open, screaming, and the teeth are a mess. Bacon included that picture in his first major one-man show, in 1949, in London. The critics had a field day at this exhibition. They told their readers that if they went, they would see "a tardily evolved creature which had slithered out from below a large stone that had been in a noisome cellar for a century or two." Wyndham Lewis described "shouting creatures in glass cases, . . . dissolving ganglia."

Yet the ganglia were interesting, Lewis added: "Bacon is one of the most powerful artists in Europe today." Likewise the critic of *The Sunday Times*. While "nothing would induce me to buy one of Bacon's paintings," he wrote, "a representative collection that did not contain one would lack one of the most definite and articulate statements made by contemporary art." In fact, curators and collectors were not initially eager to buy: How could you hang something so unpleasant on your wall? Bacon caught on in France faster than he did in England or the United States, but eventually he caught on everywhere. For the opening of a 1977 show in Paris, so many people showed up that the police had to close off the street. "You are the Marilyn Monroe of modern art," a French minister said to Bacon that night. During the few decades before his death, in 1992, his celebrity doubled and redoubled, and it has gone on growing since. In 2013, his triptych portrait of Lucian Freud set what was then a world record for an artwork sold at auction—more than $142 million.

Many books have been published on Bacon since his death, but now he has been accorded the Big Biography treatment, *Francis Bacon:*

Revelations, by the husband-and-wife team Mark Stevens and Annalyn Swan—he a former art critic for *New York*, she a former arts editor for *Newsweek*. The pair won a Pulitzer for their 2004 biography of Willem de Kooning, and the new book is a comparable achievement. It is enormously detailed; we get the details, and the details' details. When some friends come to visit Bacon in Monte Carlo and go off on a side trip without him, we hear about their side trip. When he pays for his brother-in-law's funeral, we learn what it cost. We're told about the business of art—prices, taxes, exhibitions, catalogs, catalog essays, shop talk that most art books are too high-minded to get into. Such exhaustiveness can be deadening, but here, for the most part, it isn't. Swan and Stevens are very good storytellers. Also, the book is warmed by the writers' clear affection for Bacon. They enjoy his boozy nights with him, they laugh at his jokes, and they admire his bloody-mindedness. They do not believe everything he said, and they let us know this, but they are always in his corner, and they stress virtues of his that many of us wouldn't have known to look for: his gregariousness, his love of fun, his erudition, his extreme generosity. However many people were at the table, he always picked up the tab.

Bacon was born in Dublin in 1909, into an English family that might have preferred a different sort of boy. His father, Eddy, had been an army man, serving in Burma and South Africa and retiring in 1903 with the honorary rank of major. By the time Francis arrived, Eddy was a gentleman horse trainer. He didn't earn any money, but that wasn't a problem. His wife, Winifred, from a Sheffield steel family, had come with a considerable dowry. Francis, shy, girly, and asthmatic, was a poor fit for Eddy's idea of what a son of his should be. Eddy tried to straighten him out. He got the grooms in his stables to thrash the boy regularly, but this didn't change him, or not in the direction that Eddy intended. If we are to believe what Francis later suggested, the stablemen, when they got tired of beating him, liked to sodomize him. If this is true, it presumably nurtured his lifelong association of sexual pleasure with physical punishment, and with men.

Homosexuality was hardly unknown in Francis's world—many of the young men of his class were probably bisexual, if only by virtue of having attended all-boys schools—but a firm intent, in an adult male, to confine his sexual relations to men was widely regarded as disgusting. Until 1967, homosexual acts were illegal in Britain and subject to harsh punishment. George V, upon being informed that someone he knew was homosexual, is reported to have said, "I thought men like that shot themselves." When Eddy happened upon the sixteen-year-old Francis dressed only in his mother's underwear, he threw him out, Bacon later said. The banishment was not entirely brutal. Winifred gave Francis an allowance of £3 a week, enough to live on in London, which is where he landed, taking odd jobs—cook, house cleaner, dress-shop assistant.

Soon afterward, Eddy, still hoping to make a man out of his son, suggested that Francis accompany a cousin of theirs, a certain Cecil Harcourt-Smith, ten years older than Francis—a fine young man, Eddy thought, from a fine family—on a trip to Berlin. Harcourt-Smith collected Francis, took him to Germany, and introduced him to all the raunchiest sex clubs of Weimar Berlin. And then? Bacon was never willing to say, on the record, but he seems to have confided in his friend John Richardson, the future Picasso biographer, who reported that Harcourt-Smith was an "ultra-sadistic sadist" and, according to Bacon, a man who "fucked absolutely anything." Whatever Francis might have learned from his father's grooms was enlarged by this postgraduate course. After a couple of months, Harcourt-Smith tired of Francis and took off with a woman.

Abandoned, Francis was somehow not discouraged. He knew little of the world. He had been to school for only a year and a half. (He kept running away from the place, until, he said, his parents finally gave up and let him stay home.) But he'd surely heard that Paris was the capital of the European avant-garde, and he headed there, learning the language, making friends, and seeing, for the first time, art shows, art books, and art magazines. He encountered Picasso's work and was stunned. "At that moment I thought, well I will try and paint too," he recalled. He went to a few group classes—the only art education he ever had.

At the end of 1928, Bacon returned to London, which remained his headquarters, more or less, for the rest of his life. For a while, he tried to start a career in furniture design. But slowly, fitfully, he inched his way toward painting.

Bacon as a young man had a face like an angel, together with beautiful manners and a ready wit. He had some bad habits, but they were of the regular, walk-on-the-wild-side variety. He enjoyed the company of sailors and petty thieves. When he was hard up, he didn't mind doing a bit of escort work. As an adult, he was drunk most nights, and in the course of his revels he offended a fair number of people. Come morning, however, they could expect to find on their doorstep a note of apology and a bunch of roses.

He was a kind, loyal, and generous friend. A good example of this was his treatment of his childhood nanny, Jessie Lightfoot. When he moved to London, he took Nanny Lightfoot with him. (What? You're British, and you move to London with no money, and you don't have your nanny with you? Suppose you're drunk and can't get upstairs?) When he was young and poor and scrounging for a living, she would shoplift groceries for them. She scanned the newspapers to find personals from wealthy older men seeking a young companion. "Well, Francis, look here," she would say, when she found a good prospect. Later, when he held illegal roulette parties in his apartment, it was she who collected the fees for use of the bathroom. By the time Nanny Lightfoot died, in 1951, she and

Francis had lived together for twenty-odd years. It broke his heart that her end came when he was out of town. Every week, for years afterward, he visited the friend of hers who had looked after her in her final days.

Bacon was included in a few group shows in London in the mid-thirties, but, insulted by the reviews, he destroyed most of what he had made. When the Second World War began, he was excused from military service on account of his asthma. (Reportedly, he rented a German shepherd to stay with him the night before the medical examination, to exacerbate his condition.) He then worked for the Red Cross and Air Raid Precautions, a program that helped protect Londoners during the Blitz, but the dust from the bombardments eventually irritated his lungs to the point where he had to leave the city.

Toward the end of the war, Bacon seems to have felt the forces in his life, as in the world, converge, and in 1944 he painted a triptych that he called *Three Studies for Figures at the Base of a Crucifixion*. The figures in question were not those one ordinarily saw in paintings of the Crucifixion. There was no Madonna in her blue cloak, no Magdalene in red, but, rather, three Furies from Aeschylus's *Oresteia*, gray-white creatures, monstrously truncated, looming against a livid orange background. In the left panel is a shrouded figure, its face ominously turned away. The creature in the middle panel is an ovoid shape, seemingly trapped in the corner of a room. Its long neck sticks out to the side, terminating not in a head, exactly, but just an open mouth, with two rows of menacing teeth, and a dripping bandage where its eyes might be. In the right-hand panel is the most horrible figure. Vaguely female, she rises from a patch of spiky grass, long neck thrust forward. Her mouth, too, is open—she is ready to eat us—but, apart from the one leg and also one ear, that is all Bacon gives us of her.

This piece may be the most disturbing painting produced in Britain in the twentieth century. Executed when Bacon was thirty-four, it was the first one, apparently, that truly satisfied him. In any case, he did not destroy it. Eric Hall, his respectable older-man boyfriend at the time, bought it before it could be exhibited. (Hall later donated it to the Tate, Britain's national showplace for modern painting, where it hangs today, doubtless scaring the pants off anyone who passes by.) With this picture, Bacon said, "I began." That is, he had found his artistic core—a reigning emotion of suffering and menace. The discovery was influential. "There was painting in England before the *Three Studies*, and painting in England after them," the critic John Russell later wrote. "No one can confuse the two." Damien Hirst, who often cites Bacon as a hero, has observed, of a different Bacon Crucifixion, "That splat over the head of the brush is definitely like brains."

Why, in a period when abstraction was the going thing in Western painting, did Bacon insist on doing figurative painting? It's worth remembering that British art, relative to its Continental neighbors, had long been conservative. Years after Picasso produced *Les Demoiselles d'Avignon*, Bloomsbury artists were still doing pictures of one another sitting in their tastefully furnished parlors. The Tate didn't acquire its first Picasso until 1933, and the piece was from 1901, a nice picture of a vase of flowers. When Bacon was coming up, probably the most respected painter in England was Graham Sutherland, who made his reputation with landscapes and portraits. Lucian Freud, Bacon's foremost competitor—and, for many years, his best friend—was a portraitist, too.

But national trends can't fully explain Bacon. For all his intelligence, he was an instinctual artist, and he couldn't really operate without the human figure. It was always before his eyes. If, when discussing his forebears, he wasn't talking about Velázquez, he was talking about Grünewald or Rembrandt or Degas. The human body—the face, the joints, the armpits—spoke to him, told him the story he wanted to hear, and make us hear. When describing to interviewers what he was aiming for, he often used the language of physiology. He said that he wanted his images to strike the viewer's "nervous system." (He had a diagram of the human nervous system pinned on his studio wall.) He wanted, he said, to "unlock the valves of feeling." Again and again, he used the word "poignant"—not, I think, in the sense of "sad" but in the archaic, concrete sense of "piercing," and thereby making one's opponent bleed. Bacon wanted to make us bleed, and in order to do so, he had to show us the thing that bleeds, the body.

Some of his early viewers, pledged to abstraction, saw him as a purely figurative painter and therefore old-fashioned. Indeed, because his work was so often gruesome, he was not just figurative but Grand Guignol, they said: a shock jock. Others grouped him with German Post-Expressionists of the New Objectivity school, such as Otto Dix and Christian Schad, an association Bacon indignantly rejected. Nothing was further from his intentions than the objective representation of reality, which he called "illustration," or, God forbid, "narrative," the mobilization of such representation for a story.

Certain critics, sensing this, took the position that Bacon was *both* figurative and abstract, and that the power of his art derived from the tension between the two trends. Bacon sometimes gave a tentative nod to that position, but he was insistent that, however distorted his figures, he was not an abstractionist. (Most artists believe that they are sui generis and, above all, that they are not part of the big new craze. In the fifties, when Bacon came to prominence, the American abstractionists were the new craze. Bacon said that Jackson Pollock's drip paintings looked to him like "old lace.") Bacon wanted his work to convey human emotions, but not unambiguously. He said, "I would like my pictures to look as if a human being had passed between them, like a snail, leaving a trail of the human presence and memory trace of past events as the snail leaves its slime." This is oblique, but it is not a bad description.

Bacon spoke about his paintings with honesty and intelligence. There is a book, *Interviews with Francis Bacon*, of conversations he had between 1962 and 1968 with the art critic David Sylvester, who was a friend of his. Sylvester asks the most important questions: Why did Bacon so often destroy his early paintings? Why, a firm atheist, did he paint the Crucifixion again and again? Why did he obsessively paint meat? What was it with him and meat?

Almost better than reading these exchanges is looking at them, which you can do on YouTube. Sylvester asks his questions, and Bacon, looking him straight in the eye, answers him directly. Yes, he says. No, he says. Well, he says, what interested me about meat was . . . Artists don't owe us explanations of their art, and many aren't able to provide them, but it's nice to hear someone, now and then, who actually tries.

Bacon went on to paint many more triptychs, including a lot of Crucifixions. Beginning in the 1950s, he also produced many paintings inspired by Velázquez's famous *Portrait of Pope Innocent X*, but with the pontiff's commanding face often contorted in a scream. In the sixties, Bacon concentrated on portraits. But almost all of these pictures partake, in some measure, of the same wrenching emotion as the *Three Studies*. It had been with Bacon for a long time.

He came from a rough world, however moneyed. Being beaten and possibly raped by his father's grooms as a boy is shocking enough, but casual violence seems to have been taken for granted in the family. Bacon's father was given to terrible rages, and his grandmother was married to a man who, on the morning of a hunt—that is, several times a week—would catch cats, cut off their claws, and throw them to his hounds, to pique the dogs' taste for blood. When he was drunk, he also liked to lynch cats, hanging them from the branches of a tree in the garden. Then, too, the family lived among Irish Catholics who hated Anglo-Irish people like them. They always feared a knock on the door from the IRA. Bacon's mother refused to sit with her back to a window at night.

Stevens and Swan view the violence of Bacon's painting as a direct result of his childhood: "Some volatile sexual compound—father, groom, animal, discipline—gave Francis a physical jolt that helped make him into the painter Francis Bacon." That seems to me too direct, too sure, and too sexual. Still, the world of Francis's childhood was a dangerous one, and the authors are probably right to take its influence on Bacon's iconography seriously. As Bacon said, "Time doesn't heal," and his preoccupation with violence was unquestionably deep. Once, when he was sick, a neighbor, checking in on him, went into his bedroom, ordinarily off limits. On the wall opposite the door was a large mural of a crucified arm, she recalled: "Just a hint of torso and an enormous arm with nails in it."

The lacerating intensity of the emotions in Bacon's work can be felt in his destruction of his paintings. By the time he was nearing forty, *Time* reported that he had slashed apart some seven hundred canvases. It was when a painting came close to completion, he said, that the trouble started. Sometimes he was elated by what he saw on his easel and wanted to push it further, whereupon he ended up spoiling the piece. At other times, he would let the painting get as far as the gallery; then he would call and ask for it back, and mess it up. His main handler at the gallery, a shrewd and kind woman named Valerie Beston, became adept at sensing when he was finished with a piece. No sooner had the two of them got off the phone than she would appear at his front door in a gallery van and proceed to distract Bacon with tea and gossip while the driver quietly took the painting away.

Many of Bacon's early commentators were shocked not just by the gruesomeness of his work but also by its seeming lack of moral purpose. He himself disavowed any such purpose. A number of writers felt that he was actually mocking their postwar gloom. The influential critic John Berger wrote that although Bacon was a remarkable painter, he was not, finally, "important," because he was too egocentric to address the moral problems of the postwar world: "If Bacon's paintings began to deal with any of the real tragedy of our time, they would shriek less, they would be less jealous of their horror, and they would never hypnotize us, because we, with all conscience stirred, would be too much involved to afford that luxury."

Remarks like Berger's were probably a response to Bacon's life as well as to his art. He was not a discreet man, bless him, and his daily routine was widely known. He woke up at dawn and was at the easel by about 6:00 a.m. If things went well, or fairly well, he painted until midday. Then he put on his makeup (he wore lipstick and pancake makeup and touched up his hair, including his carefully positioned spit curl, with shoe polish) and went out and had a big lunch at one of the Soho bars that served him not just as drinking establishments but also, with their louche clientele—drunks, slackers, hoodlums, gay people—as social clubs. Then he was back at the bar, where he drank pretty much until he dropped. (When he was young and short of funds, the proprietress of his favorite bar, the Colony Room, gave him £10 a week and free drinks to bring his friends in, which he did.) Sometimes, before resuming drinking, he had sex. For that, he liked the afternoon best.

Whom did he have sex with? In his early years, there were relationships with older men who loved him for his charm and his talent, and didn't mind supporting him, but that phase ended eventually. Around 1952, he met the person who was probably the love of his life, Peter Lacy. Lacy was a handsome and dashing man from a prosperous family with Irish connections, like Bacon's. He had been in the RAF, but only as a test pilot; he was a pianist, though only in piano bars. Like Bacon, he was a far-gone alcoholic, but further gone. And he was a mean drunk. He frightened people. Bacon said that at gatherings other guests would ask him, "'Who is that awful man you're with?' and of course I had to say, 'Well, I don't really know.'" Lacy frightened Bacon as well. As Swan and Stevens tell it, Bacon would provoke Lacy until Lacy turned on him, beat him up, and then took him by force. At one point, he threw Bacon out of a high window, an experience that the artist, relaxed by drink, somehow survived. When doing his makeup, Bacon made no effort to hide the bruises that Lacy had left on his face.

There is a painting by Bacon, *Two Figures*, from 1953, soon after he met Lacy, that shows two men in a desperate-looking embrace, one on top of the other. Although the work drew on an Eadweard Muybridge photograph of two wrestlers, it is widely said to be a portrait of Bacon and Lacy in bed. (Lucian Freud bought the painting shortly after it was finished, hung it above his own bed for decades, and resolutely refused to let it out on loan for shows of Bacon's work.) It has been described as tender; no one seems to mention the sharp teeth displayed by the man underneath. For much of the 1950s, Bacon and Lacy tried to be together. Then they tried to be apart. Lacy's alcoholism got worse. Bacon began taking amphetamines. Lacy, who had inherited money from his father, moved to Tangier. Bacon followed him, even renting his own place there. Eventually, though, the two men gave up and stopped seeing each other.

In 1962, Bacon had a retrospective at the Tate, the most important show of his life thus far, which would confirm him as one of England's foremost painters—perhaps even *the* foremost. The day it opened, Bacon sent Peter Lacy a telegram about the show's success. The telegram that came back said that Lacy had died the day before. In Tangier, he had finally drunk more than a person can drink and stay alive. As Bacon later put it, his pancreas had exploded.

The following year, it is said, Bacon one day heard a terrible crash in his studio. A burglar had fallen through the skylight, and the painter, discovering the young intruder, ordered him into the bedroom. The two men were together for the next eight years. The story became famous—it appears at the start of the 1998 biopic *Love Is the Devil*—though it was widely contested by people close to Bacon, who said, sorry, the two men just met in a bar, like everybody else. The new man, George Dyer, really was a burglar, though, and, like Lacy, a sort of dropout. Unlike Lacy, however, Dyer did not have much in common with Bacon. More than twenty years younger, he was an East Ender with a thick Cockney accent, and he was not the only criminal in his family. According to a friend of Bacon's, he wasn't even primarily homosexual. He just knew how to be accommodating; he had learned that in prison.

In the beginning, Bacon loved just to look at George, with his wonderfully muscled forearms and his commanding nose. If you saw that nose in a Bacon painting, you knew you were looking at George. Indeed, it is said that the artist's turn to portraiture in the 1960s was due, in large measure, to his having George to paint. (He did more than twenty portraits of the man.) Bacon also appreciated Dyer's ability to sit in a chair in his underpants for hours on end and just pose, without fidgeting or distracting Bacon with conversation.

That was, in part, because George had no conversation. He was innocent. It was something of a tradition, in London's gay pickup world, that in the morning the younger man stole the older man's watch, the heavier and more expensive the better. Dyer, after he and Bacon first slept together, instead *left* him the gold watch he had stolen from the man with whom he had spent the preceding night. Such things touched Bacon's heart. He liked to spoil Dyer. He paid him a salary, £60 a month, for posing and doing handyman work. He also gave him money to buy expensive Edwardian-style clothes, which George was very proud of.

And then Bacon tired of him. If Bacon was drunk every night, George was drunk every day and every night, which gradually made him impotent and prone to wet his pants on people's couches. Bacon began to wish he could unload him, a fact that did not fail to register with George. In response, George threw Bacon's furniture down the front stairs. Later, he ripped up a number of Bacon's paintings and set fire to his studio. He planted drugs in the studio and called the police. The court case dragged on for months.

In 1971, Bacon had a retrospective at the Grand Palais, in Paris. Nothing could have been more important for his reputation. The day before the opening, Bacon came back from a lunch and found George, who had accompanied him to Paris, drunk and incoherent, in bed with a rent boy. He eventually went downstairs, to the room occupied by the gallery's driver, and slept in the spare bed there. In the morning, he asked the driver to look in on George. On the way upstairs, the driver ran into Valerie Beston, Bacon's heroic handler. The two of them found George on the toilet, leaning forward, apparently dead.

So, in a sort of appalling rhyme with Lacy's death, Bacon received similar news on the cusp of another great triumph. If I read Stevens and Swan correctly, Bacon was both stolid (he might even have been relieved) and devastated. The hotel manager was summoned, and the situation was explained to him. Would it be possible to defer the news of George's death until the next morning? he was asked. Otherwise, his death would overshadow the opening. The manager, evidently the soul of discretion, agreed and locked the room with dead George inside, still on the toilet. Bacon got through the festivities—the private view, the official opening, the honor guard—with aplomb. Then the authorities came and took George's body away, and the newspapers published the story. Bacon flew back to London, but he was never the same. The French coroners put down the cause of death as a heart attack, but people who knew George—including, eventually, Bacon—assumed that he had died, accidentally or deliberately, of an overdose of alcohol and pills. He had made previous suicide attempts.

In the next two years, Bacon painted four triptychs that dealt with George's death. The first three show George in various guises. The last— *Triptych, May–June 1973*—is more confessional and more sensational. Here we are shown the actual death. In the left panel, we see George naked, on the toilet, leaning forward, almost to the floor. On the right, we see him vomiting into the sink. And in the central panel, where the Christ would go if this were a Crucifixion (which, in a way, it is), we get just George's face, bloated and bloodshot, presumably dead. In all the postmortem-George triptychs, Bacon uses looming shadows. We seem to watch George spilling over, leaking his life onto the floor. But, in the central panel of this last triptych, there is something yet more horrible. A shadow comes to greet George that is like nothing we have seen before: huge, black, like an enormous bird.

Many people would nominate *Triptych, May–June 1973*, with its narration of George's death, as Bacon's most formidable painting, because it is so bluntly what his work is said to be: horrific. But I would pick one of the series of canvases—there are something like fifty of them—that he based on Velázquez's *Portrait of Pope Innocent X*. In them, the Holy Father is shown in full papal regalia: cape, cap, lace-trimmed cassock. (In some versions, you can even see the throne.) And then, in place of the calm, even crafty face that Velázquez gave the seventeenth-century pontiff, we see a screaming mouth, with a full set of sharp, vicious teeth. This is Bacon's familiar marriage of menace and suffering, expanded now by a mixture of shock and formality. You can see this mixture in the George Dyer triptychs, too, but there it is more studied; Bacon is working something out, getting George's death out of his system, as he himself acknowledged. In the popes, on the other hand, the terrible thing seems to come from nowhere, both controlled and spontaneous, ineluctable. You could be the pope and not be able to stop it.

When Bacon was about forty, his doctor told him that if he had one more drink, he would die. In fact, he lived another forty years, drinking just as much as before, and therefore was around long enough to have a "late period." It is sometimes painful to watch. He still painted, but he had to have oxygen canisters near him at all times in case he had an asthma attack. His fame was assured. Honors rained down on him, but now he often refused them. French intellectuals—Michel Leiris, Gilles Deleuze—had written books about him and he was proud of this, but now he shooed book writers away. He also stubbornly delayed the production of a catalogue raisonné. Many of his old friends died. Many others he avoided, including Lucian Freud. (In the words of a friend of Freud's, "Lucian took the view that Francis's late paintings were frightfully bad. Bacon was saying the same thing about Lucian. 'Such a pity he doesn't go on doing his little things.'") Old pleasures, too, were lost. He had a boyfriend, but the boyfriend too had a boyfriend.

The spark that had always been in him still flared up sporadically. He himself spoke of the "exhilarated despair" that underlay his paintings, accurate words to describe the sheer vigor—you could even call it delight—with which he produced his grim visions. The pope might be screaming, but, oh, that purple and gold, and even the wit, or at least surprise, of the painting. You're not the only one screaming about life; so is the pope.

In 1991, during a trip to Madrid, Bacon decided that he had to see the collection of Velázquez paintings at the Prado, and to do so alone. He telephoned Manuela Mena, a senior conservator at the museum, and asked if he might come on a day when the museum was closed. This was hard to arrange—the guards were on strike at the time—but Mena worked it out, and told him to knock on a little-used side door, next to the botanical gardens, at the appointed hour. She later recalled, "We opened that door for him at midday, and in with the sun came Francis Bacon."

He was back in Madrid the following year. Eighty-two and frail, he nevertheless had a nice Spanish companion, and in the last photograph of him that Swan and Stevens offer us, we see him at his favorite bar, sitting there with what looks like a quart-size martini in front of him. He looks hearty; he wasn't. Within a few days, his friend had to check him into a hospital. The supervising nurse said that he was starting to suffer from "slow suffocation." Soon his breathing stopped, and then his heart. He was meat at last.

The New Yorker, 2021

ACKNOWLEDGMENTS

My great thanks to Jonathan Galassi, for wanting to publish this book and for helping me get it into shape. I am indebted, as well, to Farrar, Straus and Giroux's assistant editor Katharine Liptak and to my valiant assistant, Alessandra Larson. Standing behind the front lines are those who midwived the essays' original publication: David Remnick, Henry Finder, Virginia Cannon, Michael Agger, and my irreplaceable editor, Leo Carey, at *The New Yorker*; Robert Silvers at *The New York Review of Books*; and my longtime friend and agent, Robert Cornfield. Bless them all, together with Noël Carroll, always my first reader.

INDEX

Page numbers in *italics* refer to illustrations.